GW01162563

GO TO IT, OLD BOY!

A family memoir of early pioneer days
on the prairies of Alberta, Canada

by

Ruth Beard

AuthorHouse™
1663 Liberty Drive, Suite 200
Bloomington, IN 47403
www.authorhouse.com
Phone: 1-800-839-8640

© 2007 Ruth Beard. All rights reserved.

No part of this book may be reproduced, stored in a retrieval system, or transmitted by any means without the written permission of the author.

First published by AuthorHouse   12/14/2007

ISBN: 978-1-4343-2544-0 (sc)
ISBN: 978-1-4343-2543-3 (hc)

Printed in the United States of America
Bloomington, Indiana

This book is printed on acid-free paper.

ACKNOWLEDGEMENTS

I have long thought of writing about our farm life in Alberta, Canada in the early 1900s, and now due to my advancing age and the unfortunate death of all but one of my siblings my procrastination must stop and action must begin. I also hear my youngest grandnephew, Ben Detrick, asking me about the farm life of his beloved Grandma, my sister Elizabeth, and his voice provides an additional push for me to quit dawdling.

Even with all the home moves I made, I have saved practically every letter from every sibling as well as from Mama. Unfortunately there is none from Daddy, as he died before I had left the home area.

I've sorted all these letters and will use them to remind me of activities and especially the many changes in our beliefs or feelings since childhood. Most of these early years' activities that we all experienced – farm life, teachings, schools and church activities – are described in Section One. "Coming of Age" covers high schools, career decisions, and leaving home. It is difficult to separate the second age level from the adult level, and to make it even more difficult to separate time-wise, I have asked my nieces and nephews to contribute their memories of their parents' life. Their memories will come from a different perspective than mine. Of course, Robert is stating his directly; also I've expanded a bit on Edward, who died in 1986.

When I write of my siblings' lives in "Coming of Age" and "Adulthood," I'll begin with the eldest and go down the line, leaving my autobiographical memories for last.

Portions of old letters from my deceased siblings and our mother may be included; they most certainly have renewed my memories. My special thanks go to my younger brother, Robert, now my only living sibling. He has provided farm identification, location, and many informative and interesting anecdotes not mentioned by anyone else. He lived on the home place and subsequently on the adjacent farm long after the rest of us had left. I am also including stories written by various other relatives and friends in years past, and if known, will identify the writer and the date composed.

The brief genealogy of Mama's family is given in Appendix A. The Genealogy of the Beard Family, 1786-2006, is included as Appendix B. This massive document from 1786 to 1959 was first produced by our Aunt Cora (see Genealogy, 4th generation). Later Cousin Paul William (5th generation) updated this to the present. The entire Beard clan appreciates this tremendous undertaking by both these relatives. We join Cousin Paul in trusting that some family member will continue to keep this record current in future years, just as he fulfilled Aunt Cora's wishes.

Now years later, I'm ready to write about my family. Events and stories from any of us may have different interpretations, memories and opinions; though I take responsibility for stating or interpreting these, I ask for understanding from all relatives if their interpretations and memories differ from mine.

Thanks to my editor and friend, Andrew Reed, for his skills, interest, and advice in recording these pioneer days of the early 1900s in our great land up north, in Alberta, Canada. Appreciation also is given to Gerald McNabb, who most willingly gave technical and hands-on help with computer problems, especially pertaining to photo work and saving various files. Both these friends gave me great encouragement to pursue this project, which would have been far more difficult to achieve had they not done so.

INTRODUCTION

It has occurred to me that all aspects of these early years might enlighten present youth and future generations about hardships and conditions that existed in pioneer days, helping them understand the reactions, despair, and also successes of past generations, and especially of their own grandparents. Such insight might even make them more aware of situations that might occur in their own lives. Thus I will be accomplishing multiple objectives in recording the early history of the David Beard family in the prairies of Alberta, Canada, beginning almost 100 years ago.

Since my parents' background, the reason for their move to Alberta, and the actual location and agreement to purchase property from the Canadian Pacific Railway Company play an important part in understanding the situation, I have given explanations in various places. For a more detailed report of indentures, see Appendix C; for Church history, see Appendix D.

Additional information about later years and especially about my life will be included. My college years enforced earlier parental teachings with regard to critical analysis, weighing all sides of arguments, and developing or discovering personal beliefs, and these approaches should be evident throughout this book. Perhaps this will be most evident in the abstracts from my college paper revealing my opinion of myself, and in the selection, "This I believe," both found in Appendix E.

Some of my poems, stories, and abstracts or notes are from my college papers as well as more recent writings. I readily confess the ineptitude and shortcomings of this non-poetical writer. The well-known phrase "Frailty, thy name is woman," comes readily to mind when I closely examine my poetry. But this phrase also expresses possible shortcomings of all of us, male or female, young or old! Writings and memories from my mother, siblings, relatives, and friends add to this history.

The terms "Mama" and "Daddy" were generally used in these early years. Later society accepted "Mother" and "Dad." Cousin Paul will be identified as "cousin;" otherwise references to "Paul" indicate my brother Paul. My married surname was "Shatto," and our children carried that surname.

Ruth Beard
Spring, 2007

DEDICATION TO MY PARENTS

It is with great appreciation for my parents' teachings and encouragement that I dedicate this book to both my parents. Mama endured many days of my childhood complaints, "I wish you'd never had me," or "I wish I'd never been born," or even, "I wish I were a boy." She supported me in every way possible, and as I matured through time and college education, her responses changed from "What would you do if you couldn't say 'Mama?'" to "Ruth, if you don't do it, who will?" Her method of giving advice often was expressed by posing non-personal questions or facts, with the decision to be mine and mine alone. I cannot say how much these questions contributed to my examining my religious beliefs, or her confidence that I was capable of accomplishing what others would not even undertake. In addition to the above statements of encouragement were her words, "Live your life so that the world is a better place for your having lived in it." That is a most wonderful guide for each and every one of us.

Mama, I am certain that all of your children appreciated your positive characteristics, perhaps especially your patience and perseverance. Your parenting and teaching skills gave all of us strength in our own future accomplishments. Thank you, dear Mama.

The "good" features of Daddy's parenting offset the "bad" ones and undoubtedly helped us all, even though this was extremely difficult to admit or to recognize. I believe his physical disability – having to wear a heavy artificial wooden leg—caused him to think that we children who were "normal" could do tasks much better and faster than he could. His disciplinary methods were less harsh with us girls than with his boys. Society, too, expected better behavior from us as minister's children as compared to other boys and girls. In time, as our poverty lessened and we all matured, Daddy became less demanding and more understanding of our questions and our behavior. Perhaps it was my college psychology courses that caused me to analyze his characteristics and also accept his weaknesses.

As a younger member of the family, I found his teachings truly gave me high moral standards. He stressed the need to examine all sides of every issue and even to argue with one's own self. This certainly gave me strength to evaluate and establish my beliefs whether in religion, politics, or moral issues. This was, and is, a far better learning technique than any parent or adult declaring solely one's own belief.

For me his encouraging words of "Go to it, old boy," and his urging of "Try, try again," were most beneficial in building my accomplishments and in forming my beliefs. Stressing the Golden Rule became the ultimate goal for all of us. So thank you, dear Daddy, I can accept the "good" and both understand and forgive the "bad."

TABLE OF CONTENTS

BACKGROUND and BEGINNINGS

1. The Beginnings 1
2. Our Parents 7
3. Fifth Generation 31
4. Our Alberta Prairie Home 41
5. Farm Life 59
6. Our Kitchen 77
7. Christmas in Our Childhood Days 87
8. My Most Memorable Christmas 91
9. Maryland Relatives Visit Us 97
10. Our Church 105
11. Alberta Schools and Canada's Educational System 117
12. Grade Schools 123
    - Herbert Spencer Public School 123
    - Hawthorn Public School 127
    - Recreation And Games 133
13. Childhood Lessons 137
    - Dreams 137
    - Treats 139
    - Tricks 142
    - Tragedies 147
14. Teachings 153

COMING OF AGE

15 Kathyrn High School 161
16 Career Decisions 167

ADULTHOOD

17 Parents and My Siblings 179
18 Author's Journey 205
19 Our Children 223
      Carol – Our First Adopted Child 223
      Nelson – Our Second Adopted Child 227
20 Transitions 237
21 Conclusion 247

APPENDICES and WRITINGS

A Christophel/Wenger Genealogy 257
B The Beard Genealogy, 1786-2006 261
C Indenture 275
D History of the Church and the CPR Settlements, Notes From Paul's Letter, and Interview With Esther Crawford 279
E Writings By: 291
      Ruth Beard 291
      Nelson Shatto 308
      Richard Bickford 312
      Elizabeth Detrick 321
F Career History 325

BACKGROUND and BEGINNINGS

"Land of our Birth, we pledge to thee
Our love and toil in the years to be."
(Rudyard Kipling, <u>The Children's Song.</u>)

CHAPTER 1

THE BEGINNINGS

It was almost four o'clock and the folks weren't yet home from Calgary, where they had gone to take our five-gallon can of cream to sell at the Farmer's Market. Calgary was almost thirty-five miles away, at least eleven of them along narrow dirt roads. My parents were in their old Model T Ford, and Daddy was the only one who could drive.

I was anxious for them to get back home. Mama usually brought me a treat from the market – that is, if she didn't eat them all herself. Who today would think that dry tasteless crackers could be a treat? They were for me!

When Mama and Daddy went to Calgary, I had to prepare the noon meal for my four brothers; sometimes for only three if one had gone to Calgary with them. My two older sisters, Barbara and Elizabeth, had been sent that year to high school in Calgary, so I had to cook when Mama was gone. This usually meant that Paul was helping me in the kitchen, if only to wash the dishes. Paul was eleven; I was ten years old.

Our family consisted of seven children, but with my sisters gone, I was the main helper for Mama. Whether I knew it or not (if I even thought about it), it was quite a responsibility for a ten-year old. Paul was just eleven months older than I, so naturally we argued all the time.

Unfortunately, he was usually right, and that not only hurt me but made me stubborn, too. He wasn't a kind gentle brother like Raymond, who was almost three years older than I and with a personality very different from either Paul's or mine. Raymond was often the one to go to Calgary with our folks. If not, he would be out helping Edward with farm chores, and our youngest brother, Robert, would be feeding the chickens or gathering the eggs.

How did we land up here in the Alberta prairies when Daddy grew up near Westminster, Maryland and Mama in Wakarusa, Indiana? What motivated our parents to leave their homeland and come to this barren prairie? Where did the temptation come from and when?

Sometime around 1910, probably during the 1910 Annual Conference of the Church of the Brethren, an announcement from an agent of the Canadian Pacific Railway Company circulated among the congregation and the general public. The announcement described the numerous benefits of this as yet unsettled country to the north, and urged Americans to move there and obtain farmland from the CPR at a very reasonable price. It was still the era of pioneering across the American continent, of moving westward to "unsettled" lands, which included much of northwestern Canada. The westward movement was not confined within national borders. Eventually so many residents of the prairies around Calgary were from the United States that our entire home community came to be known as Yankee Valley.

In the following chapters, some* of these family names may be mentioned, so let me indicate here where some of our neighbors came from and the year they moved to this general area. Information is taken from "KIK Country," published by K.I.K. Historical Committee, Keoma, Alberta, ca1974. KIK stands for Kathyrn-Irricana-Keoma communities. (Note that "Kath*yr*n" is the correct spelling; it is not "Kath*ry*n.")

FAMILY	FROM	YEAR to ALBERTA
Axel Anderson	Sweden; Hawley, Minnesota	1909
Oscar Anderson*	Sweden; Hawley, Minnesota	1909
Einar Anderson	Sweden; Minneapolis	1920
David Beard*	Maryland; Idaho	1910, 1917
Edward Blocker	Pymont, Indiana	1918
Clarence Bond	Prince Edward Island	1916
Roy Brant	Laffette, Indiana	1919
William Burns	Flora, Indiana	1917
Alex Calder	Toronto, Ontario	1920
Ernest Cawley*	Roanoke, Illinois	1911, 1917
John Clark*	Cando, N. Dakota	1909, 1914
Bert Caldwell	Gainford, Alberta	1926
John Culp	Waldo, Ohio; Bowbells, North Dakota	1909
William Culp*	Indiana; N. Dakota	1909
Charles Deeter	?	1912
John Drake	Prince Edward Island	1918
Lewis & Ruth Durie*	Avon, Illinois	1913
Aaron Gault	Bowbells, North Dakota	1910
Henry Haag*	Plymouth, Indiana	1917
William Heinz*	Illinois	1917
Wilfred Longson*	Gleichen, Alberta	1929
Thomas Loney*	Ireland; Grand Forks, Dakota	1909
Ed Nerland	Norway; Minnesota	1909, 1930
Andrew Swenson	Lime Springs, Iowa	1907
Ellis Wagoner	Indiana	ca1917
Leonard Workman*	St. Anthony, Idaho	1910
Houston Wray*	Bowbells, North Dakota	1909, 1910
Joshua Henry Yates*	Oregon	ca 1922

It is difficult now, early in the 21st Century, to truly picture the pioneer situation in the early 1900s, and the strong drive that would cause a person to leave the eastern United States and go to an uninhabited new area. To understand the westward movement and the pioneering challenge, one might read some of the many works written about the growth of the western provinces, including histories of the two major railway systems, the Canadian Pacific Railway (CPR), and the Canadian National Railway (CNR).

In our case, two influential institutions combined to entice my parents and many other American families to move both west and north to Canada. These institutions were the CPR, offering fairly cheap land, and the Church of the Brethren, one of the three "peace" denominations that thrived in the late 19th and early 20th Centuries in Alberta.

"Two roads diverged in a wood, and I —
I took the one less traveled by,
And that has made all the difference."
(Robert Frost, <u>The Road Not Taken.</u>)

CHAPTER 2

OUR PARENTS: MARTHA CHRISTOPHEL And DAVID RAY BEARD

(Much of the genealogical information in this chapter will be of interest only to Beard family members and genealogists or historians. Other readers may wish to skim lightly over this material.)

The ancestors of my parents will be mentioned first, accompanied with a brief history of my aunts and uncles. Since information on the Christophel line is limited, I will include brief information from Grandma Christophel's obituary and the death of Grandfather Christophel. The only source for my mama's background comes from a brief Christophel/Wenger volume, which states that Christian Wenger and his wife, Eve Grabiel, arrived in Philadelphia, Sept. 30, 1727, from Europe, presumably a northwestern province of France, now Bavaria, Germany. He bought land in the Earl Township of Lancaster, County, PA, May 19, 1759. (The genealogical charts of both my parents, as complete as presently available, are in Appendices A and B.) Mama's parents, Isaiah Christophel and Barbara Wenger, married on January 6, 1878. They had four daughters, the latter two being twins. Both families were Mennonites. Different sources give various spellings of the town "Nappanee" or "Napanee," Indiana.

CHILDREN OF ISAIAH CHRISTOPHEL AND BARBARA WENGER

Susie	b. Jan. 2, 1879	d. Feb. 1964
Martha	b. Dec. 15, 1883	d. Feb. 20, 1963 (my mother)
Emma	b. Aug. 27, 1886	d. Oct. 3, 1894 (twin of Anna)
Anna	b. Aug. 27, 1886,	d. sometime in the 1940s of severe burns.

BARBARA WENGER CHRISTOPHEL

Her obituary reads: "daughter of Christian and Elizabeth (Good) Wenger, was born in Wayne Co., Ohio, March 16, 1855; died at her home in Napanee, Indiana May 7, 1931. She married Isaiah Christophel, January 6, 1878, and they lived on a farm 5 miles north of Napanee until his death in 1912, then in 1913 she moved back to Nippon. One brother, Zimmerman Wenger, survives her.

"She gave her heart to Christ early in life and united with the Mennonite Church. As a mama she was very kind and loving, willing to sacrifice anything for her children. Funeral services were held in Nippon on Sunday afternoon, May 10. A short service was conducted at the home by Bro. J.S. Hartzler and at the North Main St. Church of the Brethren by H.F. North and D.A. Yoder. Burial in the Yellow Creek Cemetery."

ISAIAH CHRISTOPHEL

The only information I recall is my Mama telling us that her father died in 1912 from being struck by lightning when out in the farm field, which I think was their home property.

We have little information as to the original country of our grandparents' forefathers, who arrived in Philadelphia in 1727. Since

Mama had such pitch black and lustrous hair and sparkling dark eyes, we always claimed that her forefathers must have come from Ireland.

MARTHA CHRISTOPHEL

Mama was born in Wakarusa, Indiana, December 15, 1883, to Barbara Wenger and Isaiah Christophel, the second of four daughters. The eldest was Susan, whom we always called "Susie;" she married Sylvester Miller and they adopted a girl, Ruth, when she was four years old. The younger sister, Anna, was married much later in life to a widower, whose name I cannot recall. Anna had a twin sister, Emma, whose death occurred at an early age. These four girls are listed on the ROLL OF HONOR, School District No. 3, Elkhart County, Indiana, September 18, 1893. This form shows that Isaac Christophel was the Director, but the relationship, if any, between him and Isaiah, the girls' father, is unknown.

The Christophel family was Mennonite, one of the three Peace denominations; the other two are the Church of the Brethren and the Society of Friends, or Quakers.

Mama attended Goshen College at Goshen, Indiana, as did her younger sister Anna. A brief history of this religious college was obtained from its publication *The Reflector*, 1904 and 1906. The old Elkhart Institute housed this new educational facility, which advanced through five steps between 1895 and 1903 to become Goshen College. In 1905 the expansion led to a four-year Biblical College Course leading to the Ph.B.degree. The 1904 *Reflector* tells of very strict dormitory rules for female students, such as "every maiden shall be in her own room from the eighth to the tenth hour…wherein thou shalt abide until the morning hour. Neither shall there be light any more until the morning hour."

Such tight control is indicative of the discipline inflicted especially upon women, and perhaps is the reason why our Mama endured such a controlled married life in later years.

The college's Vesperian Society states its motto as "Excelsior," and Mama is listed on its Roll of Honor and as Historian in 1905 and as one of the Society's presidents in 1906. With the 1905 photo, her nickname is given as "Sis;" her familiar saying "O, You!" and her aim in life as "Forget Trouble." Her younger sister, our Aunt Anna, is also listed during these years. Later, Mama attended the Bible Training School at Bethany, where she met and married our daddy in 1914.

Christophel Sisters, ca 1905, Martha (Mama) standing, Seated L–R Anna, Susie.

ROLL OF HONOR.

SCHOOL DISTRICT NO. 3.

Elkhart County, - INDIANA - Union Township.

Opened Sept. 18, '93. Closed May 7, '94.

ELI ROOSE, Teacher.

Martha Christophel Pupil.

"One rule to guide us in our life,
Is always good and True:
'Tis do to others as you would
That they should do to you."

NAMES OF PUPILS.

NO.		AGE.	NO.		
1.	Frank E. Palmar,	19	27.	Kitie Wambaugh,	13
2.	Louisa Palmer,	17	28.	Louis Wise,	10
3.	John Skinner,	17	29.	Salina Lehman,	8
4.	Ella Skinner,	15	30.	Philip Kilmer,	8
5.	Thomas Wise,	15	31.	Maggie Kohli,	10
6.	Effie Truex,	16	32.	Morse Blosser,	8
7.	Frank Pitman,	17	33.	Warren Blosser,	10
8.	Susan Christophel,	15	34.	Frank Earnest,	9
9.	Abraham Lehman,	15	35.	Edward Brennaman,	10
10.	William Wambaugh,	12	36.	Ellen Brennaman,	8
11.	Martha Ernest,	12	37.	Julia Miller,	9
12.	Charles Lehman,	13	38.	Noah Martin,	8
13.	Irvin Miller,	14	39.	Emma Christophel,	7
14.	Vernon Miller,	12	40.	Anna Christophel,	7
15.	Hettie Miller,	16	41.	William Davidhiser,	8
16.	Harvey Blosser,	14	42.	Marion Shank,	17
17.	Martha Christophel,	10	43.	Irvin Wise,	9
18.	Mary Kilmer,	10	44.	Clara Blosser,	7
19.	Martha Lehman,	11	45.	Fannie Ernest,	8
20.	Katie Martin,	12	46.	Freddie Davidhiser,	6
21.	John Davidhiser,	10	47.	Lawrence Blosser,	6
22.	Weaver Martin,	10	48.	Nellie Lop,	7
23.	Eli Lehman, (died Jan.'28.)	9	49.	Lulu German,	6
24.	Irwin Culp,	10	50.	Minnie Wise,	6
25.	Noah Bechtel.	10	51.	Henry Umbaugh,	6
26.	Ira Christophel,	12	52.	Timothy Kohli,	6

Henry Wysong, Tp. Trustee.   Isaac Christophel, Director.
GEO. W. ELLIS, Co. Superintendent.

Roll of Honor, listing Christophel Sisters

When her mother died, in 1931, Mama took Robert and me to Indiana. I remember hearing Mama and her sisters talk about finding someone to take care of Robert, as they felt he was too young to attend the funeral service. I do not remember the service, but I do remember going up to the coffin and seeing my grandma lying there. It was the first time I had ever seen a dead person. Later Mama said I was to have her mother's Thomas Gilbert "Grandma's" shelf clock. (I enjoyed it for many years and have just this year passed it on to my great-nephew, Alex Detrick.)

JOHN BEARD (2nd) (Beard Genealogy) was our Daddy's grandpa, the author's great grandpa. The following report, typed by Aunt Ida Belle, was sent to me many years ago but without the original source mentioned.

"John Beard, a well-known mill-wright of this county, died at his residence near Uniontown on Tuesday afternoon, aged 67 years, 10 months and 25 days. Mr. Beard was paralyzed about three years ago, and has been comparatively helpless since that time. He was a man of remarkable strength and size, measuring six feet, four inches in his stocking feet, and weighing, at the time of his death, nearly four hundred pounds. He was a prominent member of Salem Lodge of Odd Fellows, which organization had charge of his funeral that took place at Krider's Church of Friday morning. The religious services were in charge of Rev. H.W. Kuhns. Mr. Beard's remarkable strength won for him the reputation of being the strongest man in Western Maryland and probably in the State of Maryland. He could lift a 56 weight with as much ease as men of ordinary strength could lift a small package, and in performing the duties of mill-wright, could easily lift that which taxed the combined strength of three or four men. The heaviest weight ever lifted by Mr. Beard was a casting weighing 1600 pounds, which he raised by means of a rope thrown over his shoulder.

Mr. Beard has a brother residing in Chili (sic), South America, who is a man of considerable wealth and standing in his adopted home."

(Note: Lewis Beard, 2nd generation, was the brother in Chile. See genealogy for Carmen Paulina Beard, the 5th generation. She and her family are pictured in the family reunion at Cousin Paul's home, June 23, 2000, Westminster, Maryland. Names in bold are the relatives from Chile.)

Reunion with Chile relatives, held at Cousin Paul's home in Westminster, MD; 2000

L to R. 1st Row: Seated: Miriam, **Carmen Fuertes**, LaVaughn, Bernice, Paul William.

2nd Row: Al Guyer, Hazel, Elsie, Thelma, Ruth, **Paulina Paz, Sergio Fuentes,** Clarence, Baby, behind baby in all rows are Earl's children, Edward, Bette at end in blue slacks & their children in-between their parents.

3rd Row: (behind Al) Christine, Harold, Joe, Jeff, Earl, Nancy, SaraBeth, Joyce, Ralph.

Behind Carmen Fuertes is daughter Paulina, next is father, Sergio, and son **Cristian Sergio Fuentes,** is in center behind Paulina and Sergio.

Edward Beard and Ida Caylor, my grandparents

Edward Henry Beard Family, 1904
L - R, Back: Harvey, Matie, Anna, Cora, David (my daddy)
Front: Edith, Edward Henry (grandfather), John, Ida Caylor (grandmother), Ida Belle

DAVID RAY BEARD

Daddy was born March 9, 1881 in Uniontown, Maryland, second son and third child of Ida Caylor and Edward Henry Beard, and is listed under the 4th generation in the Genealogy chart. Daddy had six sisters and two brothers.

Daddy's family lived near Westminster, Maryland. Daddy and his older brother, Harvey, became farmers like their forebears. The youngest son, John Paul, started his married life as a farmer, but entered the business world with Farmer's Fertilizer & Feed Co. and became president of that company. He then served on the Board of Union National Bank in Westminster, MD. All three boys and two of the girls, Anna and Ida Belle, married. Matie, Cora, and Edith never married, and the other sister, Mary Alice, died in 1892 when only three days old.

Daddy taught grade school in 1905 in Uniontown, Maryland, a few years before enrolling in Bethany College in Chicago, Illinois. According to an alumni directory published by Bethany Theological Seminary in 1990, Daddy graduated from Bible Training School in 1914 with the degree of B.T.T. (Bible Teacher Training). He is listed in the Brethren Encyclopedia as an ordained minister, no date given. His marriage to Mama occurred on September 2, 1914. M.C. Lehman, Minister of the Gospel, Goshen, Indiana, officiated.

Daddy in his ministerial robe

His oldest sister, my Aunt Matie, continued to live at her parents' subsequent home at 90 Liberty Street in Westminster, Maryland. It was there that she quilted more than five hundred quilts, not an unusual skill in those days, but certainly an overwhelming quantity. (Now it is done as a craft.) Every one of my aunt's relatives was given one of her quilts, and somehow or other I became the proud owner of half a dozen or more. Some of those I inherited might have come from Mama's family, but I cannot determine which ones were from her family, rather than from Aunt Matie.

Aunt Matie, our quilter!

A fine article, with pictures of Aunt Matie and her quilts, was published in the popular Baltimore weekly newspaper in the late 1950s or early 1960s, with a story by Muriel Dobbin and photos by Richard Stacks, and the heading, "400,000 Yards of Thread Have Kept Her in

Stitches." "That is about the amount Miss Matie Beard has put into quilts since she began sewing, in childhood." It further states that Aunt Matie began sewing when she was six years old, and had quilted over four hundred quilts by the time she was eighty. She continued until her death in 1965 at age eighty-eight.

Aunt Matie's quilts are now registered with the North Carolina Quilt Project, a 1988 undertaking at the North Carolina Museum of History and the North Carolina Quilt Symposium. I was a new resident of the Tar Heel state when this project began seeking out all quilts made before 1976 and currently or originally located in this state. Her most unique and beautiful quilt was coded as F105 but the registrar could not give it a pattern name. However, Claire, the six-year-old granddaughter of my niece, Gael, called it "the crow on the post." Later, Daddy's youngest sister, my Aunt Ida Belle, quilted a large quilt and crocheted a beautiful off-white bedspread, both especially for the antique walnut bed that I also inherited.

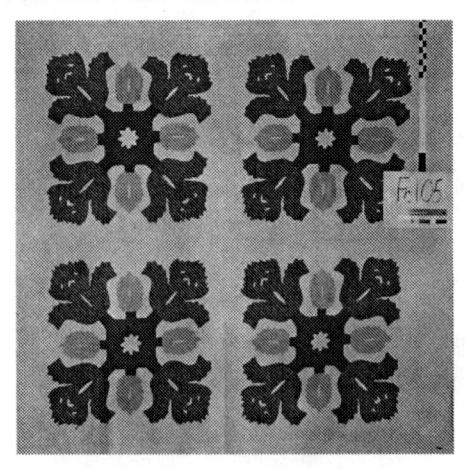

Aunt Matie's Quilt FC105, "Crow on the Post"

Daddy's second sister, Aunt Cora, was born in Jasontown near New Windsor, on July 14, 1883, her father's thirty-fourth birthday. She attended Springdale School, taught by their cousin Charles Otto. The family moved near Uniontown in March 1893, and she and Aunt Anna attended the Morelock School, taught by Jesse Billmyer. Later they went to Uniontown, a two-room school, taught by Norman Eckard. In 1898, she entered Maryland Collegiate Institute (later named Blue Ridge College) and became valedictorian of her class. For two years she taught school at Springdale, Maryland, and then worked for Babylon & Lippy, a Westminster store. In 1909, she began working for the Printing and Engraving Department, and during World War I was employed by the War Risk Insurance Division, from which she retired in 1946.

Daddy's youngest sister, Ida Belle, submitted this information about herself several years before her death in 1993. She lived to one hundred years old, requesting special medicine to keep her alive until she saw her soon-to-be born first grandchild. She writes:

> "I was born February 6, 1893, in a small village known as Jasontown, near New Windsor, Maryland, being the fifth daughter of Edward and Ida C. Beard. I had two older brothers and one four years younger than I, John P.W. Beard, who is still living. We were a well-organized happy family.
>
> When six weeks old, so I am told, we moved to a larger farm near Uniontown. At age six I walked a mile to school in that quaint village and made two years perfect attendance. When Sunday came, it was understood that we all go to Sunday School and Church at Pipe Creek, including my Grandmother, of whom I have fond memories.
>
> In September 1909, I enrolled as a day student in Blue Ridge College, which was then located in Union Bridge, Maryland. Those were horse and buggy days, so I drove three miles each way in all kinds of weather, quite often through the snow in a sleigh.

I came to Baltimore in 1912 and lived with my sister Anna and husband, J. Arthur Smith for fourteen years. During that time I worked as a typist for an insurance company, known then as Riggs, Rossman, and Hunter, beginning with the huge salary of $7.00 a week. It was there I met George B. Hunter and married him in 1927. We were married by the Rev. Jacob A. Hollinger at his home in Washington, D.C.

I always attended Sunday School and church but did not become a member until 1915, when Billy Sunday held meetings here in the city. Rev. F.D. Anthony baptized me in the pool by the side of Woodbury Church. I took part in all activities, sang in the Choir and sometimes played the piano.

In 1940, we moved to my present location and then became a member of First Church. Rev. I.S. Long was then the pastor. I became active in the Ladies Bible Class and was treasurer of the Women's Fellowship for fifteen years.

My hobbies are memorizing poetry, reading, making quilts and afghans, and I keep a diary."

While two of Daddy's siblings died fairly young, as did he, others lived from eighty-five to one hundred years. Daddy suffered cerebral hemorrhage and died at age sixty-one. He was in Calgary Hospital when Pearl Harbor was attacked in 1941, and family visits to him found that this event was on his mind more than any other issue. In 1936 he had registered us all as American citizens, and there was always more talk at home about the politics and history of the United States than about the Canadian government. I suspect that at least for these first several generations of pioneer families, those living in Canada knew far more about United States society and government than the southern ones knew about Canada. The technological advances of radio, television and computer have all had even more effect than newspapers and family correspondence in sharing information about each country.

Daddy taught grade school in Uniontown, Maryland, and Cousin Paul found the following information: "The Maryland Collegiate Institute was started in Union Bridge in 1898 on the second floor of a bank building. The first year there were about fifty students. It was charted to meet the academic requirements at that time. Since it was very successful it was decided to build buildings on a nine-acre lot on the south side of Union Bridge. Four buildings were built although not all at the same time but as money became available, prior to 1910."

The Graduating Classes of Maryland Collegiate Institute request the honor of your presence at their Commencement Exercises May twenty-seventh and twenty-eighth nineteen hundred and eight Auditorium, Union Bridge, Md.

Class Roll
Literary and Art Department
Motto—Ad Majorem Dei Gloriam
Colors—Old Rose and Canary
Flower—Sweet Pea

Latin Scientific
H. Harper R. Brechbill   Ada B. Hershberger   Ruthelia Myers
      Alvin J. Miller   Chas. B. Resser

English Scientific
Etta R. Smith   Gwendolyn Estella Buckey

Music
Norma Leola Flemming   Charles Luther Rowland

Bible
David Ray Beard   Bruce C. Whitmore   Barry Theo Fox

Commercial Department
Motto—Not Finished but Begun
Colors—Orange and Blue
Flower—Pink Rose

Book-keeping
Roscoe Ellsworth Etzler   Norman Robert Baumgardner
    David Earl Neikirk   Harry Lee Roy Bowers

Stenographic
N. Browning Norris   Elza O. Biser   Mabelle A. Kauffman
       E. Blanche Ward   Mary Lee Clarke
              Harry Lee Roy Bowers

Maryland Collegiate Institute

Daddy attended Maryland Collegiate Institute at Union Bridge, Maryland, and graduated in 1908. (This Institute later became the building that housed the International Gift Shop at New Windsor, Maryland. I have long had a glass paperweight showing this collegiate building.) When Daddy attended Bethany, there were three levels of ministry: first and second degrees, and a third one of eldership, which Daddy achieved in 1936 while living in Irricana, Alberta. I was thirteen years old, and I remember him standing at the front of the church with two other ministers anointing or blessing him.

It was probably during the foregoing college years that our Daddy lost his leg. He had to take a year off before he got his prosthesis, according to Cousin Hazel, who relates that during that time he sold books from door to door, and once a dog bit into his wooden leg – quite a surprise for both of them.

It was still the custom at that time that the father of the bride – or the mother if the father was not living – was asked and had to give permission for their daughter to marry. Of course there were some instances when a marriage occurred regardless of any parental consent. Mama's father had died by 1914, but here is the consent given by her mother. A handwritten note, dated May 30, from Grandmother Christophel reads:

"Mr. D. R. Beard

Kind friend.

In answer to your letter, I must say that I have given the matter over to the lord. If it is his will So I will be satisfied. Hope you will be good and kind to her as long as life lasts.

From mother, Barbara Christophel."

**Our parents' wedding picture,
Martha Christophel and David Beard, 1914**

The State license is signed by Milo H. Cripe, Clerk of the Elkhart Circuit Court. It is also noted that "This document was filed at the American Consulate, Calgary, Alberta, December 20, 1932, by David Ray Beard in connection with an application for registration as an American citizen," signed by Charles W. Allen, American Vice Consul.

Because both our parents were members of Peace denominations, conscientious objection to war was the ethic instilled in us. While writing this on July 10, 2006, I watched as the public TV station aired historic news and showed a "Certificate of Conscientious Objector" established at the beginning of World War II.

What brought these two American citizens to Alberta and away from their own families and to a very bare flat land with extreme hardships? Did they ever regret doing so? Let us look at some of the situations that existed in Alberta in those days.

The town of Calgary is seen in Alberta on Section 15 in 1883-84. By 1905, its population was approximately 10,000, about 20% were children, and Chinese were the largest non-Anglo-Saxon group. Calgary was early known as the "cattle town." The city's first stampede took place in 1912, and the name has lasted, even though the economic picture has greatly changed. A headline in the USA TODAY issue of November 10, 2004 reads "Calgary leaves cow town image in the dust." Many other sources are available on this subject, but here are some interesting facts about Canada printed in the Medicine Hat News, Medicine Hat, Alberta, Canada, July 1, 2006:

> "Canada has more than half of the world's lakes within its border. (A question on *JEPARDY* recently, and all 3 contestants missed it.)[1]
>
> Niagara Falls is the largest waterfall in the world by volume.
>
> Canada's oldest rock is probably Acasta gneiss, found east of Great Bear Lake, and is 3.96 billion years old.
>
> World's richest area of dinosaur fossils is in Dinosaur Provincial Park, Alberta.[2]
>
> Canada is the world's second largest country after Russia."

From 1901 to 1911, Alberta's population grew from 72,000 to 375,000. In 1944 when I left Calgary, the city's population was 42,000, and when I went back to visit in 2002, it was nearly one million. A friend visiting Calgary on July 25, 2006, learned that the population reached one million that very day when the first July 25th baby was born; ten more babies were born later that same day.

We had always been told that Daddy wanted to be a missionary but due to his health conditions, and perhaps unknown reasons, he did not follow through on the additional step needed. But thoughts of pioneering were high on his mind back in 1910, and he yielded to that temptation rather than seeking further ministerial studies, or even remaining closer to his or Mama's home land. Whether the nature

---

[1]The Alberta newspaper spelt it 'JEPARDY.' R.B.
[2]Not far from my home, but established long after I left in 1944 R.B.

of his temptation was to seek adventure, or to prove himself, or to distance himself from his family, or just plain foolishness, it certainly was a hardship for my parents and all of us. (Doesn't everyone wonder sometimes if and how life would have changed if even a minor incident or decision had been different?)

Two stories circulate about the timing and cause of the amputation of one of Daddy's legs. Some say that in the last years of high school, he had a knee injury from baseball and had to have his leg amputated. Others believe that when he was teaching grade school he had tuberculosis and this sickness ended in one leg being amputated above the knee. I could not remember which leg it was but Robert assured me it was his right leg. I do remember that Daddy had to have a checkup for tuberculosis, so it seems logical that this was the reason for the amputation. When Daddy was tested, we children were required to undergo testing too. I was about five years old.

Because Daddy's leg was not cut off high enough, every artificial leg he eventually owned was too long, so he always had to swing it sideways rather than in the usual forward motion. He tired easily, especially when wearing a heavy wooden leg and not the aluminum one, which was not available until about 1935 or later. All his children came to believe he should never have been a farmer and should never have sought a pioneer life. Nor would we have approved of his being a missionary, which we understand was his initial wish.

Daddy and Henry Harvey, prior to 1911

Daddy's pioneer experience began in 1910, when he and Henry Milton Harvey signed an agreement with the Canadian Pacific Railway Company, (CPR). (See Appendix C for details of this information.) The land was noted as "160 acres between Irricana and Airdrie." Daddy was the cook for Harvey's farm crew, and this would have given him first chance to take over the CPR agreement from Harvey. Since Daddy's amputated leg gave him no strength for heavy farming chores, he stayed by the tent and did the cooking, and probably other necessary chores also. We have no indication of any dairy cattle or poultry at that time, but we do have a photo of the large tent and shed that were their accommodations. They must have obtained horses and primitive farm machinery to begin their farming experience. (We didn't even get a tractor until I was about seven years old, and I remember that only because Edward was capable of taking care of the mechanical work when he was not yet fifteen! Maybe that's when I started snooping under the auto hood when he was working on it.)

Daddy's tent, near our later farm home

Daddy used to entertain and thrill us with his story of the time he heard a thunderous noise outside the tent. Coming across the wide bare prairies were many wild cattle, or longhorns as they were officially called, storming towards him. Fearing damage, or even death, he was desperate. He grabbed a heavy metal ladle – no plastic in those days – and a metal dishpan, ran outside, and began beating the pan as hard as he could. As the cattle got closer, they became scared and split apart running in all different directions. So lives were saved, as were their tent and shed.

Following my parents' marriage in 1914, their first son, Edward, was born in Indiana, in June 5; they then moved to Nampa, Idaho, where my sister Barbara was born in October 1916. Events of this ministry are given in Appendix D.

Sometime between Barbara's birth in 1916 and that of my sister, Elizabeth, in early 1918, the folks moved back to Irricana, Alberta. Daddy still had that "pioneer" or "missionary" spirit and so returned to the prairies of Alberta. Our land was approximately thirty-five miles northeast of Calgary.

Robert also believes Daddy got the one-quarter section northeast of the church about 1937, when our neighbors, the Heinzes moved away. A Mr. Gardiner of the CPR advised Daddy to buy it, which he did. In 1944, Mama bought the farmhouse and land to the east of us from the Fergusons, which had been owned by the Henry Haag family, also originally from the States. Eventually, our original farmhouse was torn down, and Mama and Robert, the only child still at home, moved into the Ferguson place. At that point, the Beards owned about eight hundred acres.

As for the rest of the pioneer Beard Family, here's the brief genealogy of my parents and their children.

Descendants of David Ray Beard.

4 David Ray Beard   b. 09 Mar 1881 d. 06 Jan 1942

+Martha Christophel   b. 15 Dec 1883   d. 20 Feb. 1963   m. 02 Sep 1914

__ 5 John Edward Beard	b. 17 Jun 1915	d. 23 Mar 1986
__ 5 Barbara Catherine Beard	b. 14 Oct 1916	d. 21 Sep 2001
__ 5 Anna Elizabeth Beard	b. 09 Jan 1918	d. 06 Jan 2002
__ 5 Margaret Irene Beard	b. 17 Mar 1919	d. 23 Mar 1920
__ 5 David Raymond Beard	b. 26 Nov 1920	d. 23 May 1984
__ 5 Paul Webster Beard	b. 27 Apr 1922	d. 21 Mar 2005
__ 5 Ruth Caroline Beard	b. 23 Mar 1923	
__ 5 Robert Kipling Beard	b. 09 Sep 1924	

Let me start with my own birth, in 1923.

"All the brothers were valiant, and all the sisters virtuous."
(Anonymous)

CHAPTER 3

THE FIFTH GENERATION: CHILDREN OF DAVID AND MARTHA BEARD

"Barbara, come see your new baby sister." Mrs. Randall, the midwife, called softly to Barbara who was waiting expectantly in the living room. Barbara came swiftly but quietly, and saw her new sister for the first time. She took a quick glance at the baby and then at Mama, who looked miserable. Mama had come down with pneumonia, which was probably the reason for giving birth at eight months instead of the usual nine. From the first photo of this newborn, the baby looked miserable too. In fact, in hindsight, I looked rather moronic at this early birthing. (Fortunately, I did appear more normal in later years!)

"Now, Barbara, I want you to take your baby sister to her bed. We showed you the baby's bed yesterday. So hold out your arms and carry her carefully like we practiced with your big doll. When you put her down, pull the covers up gently just to her chin. See that her arms are covered. Her name is Ruth, but you may call her 'Honey' if you wish."

And so Barbara, who was only six years and five months old, carried me to the special crib that was converted from an old apple crate. It was now padded with blankets and heated bricks all around the four edges, and placed on top of a bigger crate so that no one had to bend too far down to place me or get me back out. Since Mama's bedroom was cold, my crib was in the adjoining room and placed at the specially cut wall opening between my parent's bedroom and the round coal stove that heated this living room area.

It was many years later, in the mid-1980s, that Barbara told me about this experience, and I wondered why I had not heard of this before. Was it really true? By this time I knew from experience that this dear sister had a good imagination and could exaggerate, whether intentionally or not. Perhaps Mrs. Randall carried me to the crib but invited Barbara to come along and help tuck me in. I'll never know. But Mrs. Randall's help was needed. Mama, who had already had six children within eight years, had now, despite pneumonia, just given birth to a premature baby on March 23, 1923, three years to the day after the death of her third daughter, Margaret. Thus I was the seventh birth but the sixth living child. In 1955, Mama, in her birthday greetings to me, said I was born about 11:00AM Mountain Standard Time, and was tiny at only five pounds.

Mama had earlier told me that Daddy wanted to name me "Martha," but she did not agree, and I am thankful that she won that issue, although I wonder how she managed to do so. Most of my siblings' names were either biblical ones or in the family line. So I found it surprising that "Webster" and "Kipling" were the chosen second names for Paul and Robert.

Before I describe all my brothers and sisters, let me list some interesting facts during the year of my birth, 1923. Just look at price increases!

Gas prices take front-page news today in 2007, and here in Asheville, North Carolina, in May 2007, a gallon costs from $2.69 to $3.07 and rises daily!

Item	1923	2007
President:	Warren Harding	George W. Bush
Vice President	Calvin Coolidge	Dick Cheney
Invention	self-winding watch	cell phones
Life Expectancy:	54 years	M 75 F 78
Average Income	M $2,126	Varies greatly by gender/position ($12,000 to $12,000,000)
House	$7,400	$150K–$250K–$350K
New Car	$295	$25,000
Loaf of Bread	.09c	$1.98–$2.99–$3.19
Gallon of Gas	12c	$2.99 and rising
Gallon of Milk	.56c	$2.50

The year 1923 was a boom year in Canada, and I think also in the United States. It was also the only year that the Church of the Brethren Annual Conference was held in Calgary or anywhere else in Canada.

While I cannot describe the births of any of my siblings, I am confident that most if not all of us were born at home, probably with a midwife present, as was typical in those days. Also, we lived over thirty miles from Calgary Hospital, which we could not have reached in good time; the nearest doctor was eleven miles away, and we had no phone to call him. If a midwife had not been available, neighbor women would have helped.

Grandma Christophel, Paul, Ruth, Raymond, 1923

Photographs of all the Beard children appear on the following pages. Where is the usual delightful sweet new baby smile in the first photo? Our Grandma Christophel came from Indiana shortly after my birth to help take care of her six grandchildren. Since we have just one photo of her, I've included it. She is holding me with smiling Paul and attractive Raymond while I appear rather pathetic. About three months later, a photo of me shows that I'm delightfully dressed, smiling and lying in the family's favorite rocking chair. (We had this rocking chair even long after I left home for college in 1944. Now my nephew, Joe Detrick, tells me that his older brother, Ralph, has it and that it still has a distinct squeak. Joe remembers his mother, Elizabeth, rocking him and singing to him.)

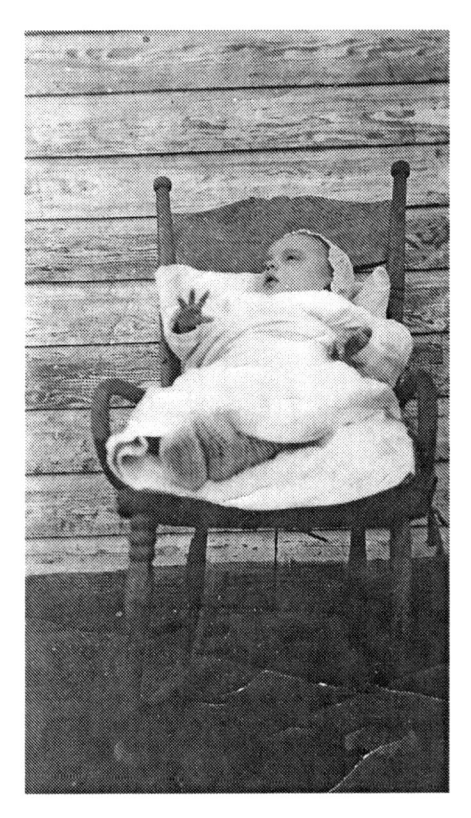

Baby Ruth in family rocker, 1923

But take a look at my brother Paul in the former photo. Within a few years, his joy of birthdays disappeared when he realized I would catch up with him for a full month every year, for which he would be teased. Of course he silently questioned why or how I could catch up when none of the other siblings did, nor did any of his friends have to experience this jesting. It took many years before he understood the situation or enjoyed – and joined in – the teasing.

In addition to the three of us, Mama endured five other pregnancies, making eight live single births within nine-and-a-half years. The first and second children, Edward and Barbara, and the fifth, Raymond, were born in the States, and the other four, Elizabeth, Paul, Ruth (that's me) and Robert were born in Canada. I find it interesting to note that

that the three born in the United States stayed in Canada, and three of those born in Canada eventually moved to the States; only Robert, the youngest, born in Canada, remains there today.

Edward was born in June 1915 in Indiana, Mama's home state. Within a year Daddy completed his first two steps of ministerial studies in the Church of the Brethren Training School in Chicago, and our parents moved to Idaho, where he held a position with the Fruitland congregation. Barbara was born in Nampa, Idaho in October 1916.

Edward and Barbara, Nampa, Idaho, 1917

Financial problems existed with most of the area churches, and Daddy's agreement with the Nampa congregation ended after a brief ministry. Since Daddy still had his 1910-1911 experience in Alberta in the back of his mind, with the desire always to return to these prairies, he brought his family back to the same general area later in 1917.

Elizabeth, born in January 1918, was the first Beard baby born in Canada. Here is one of the earliest photos I have of her. She is the only one Daddy called by a nickname.

Betsy, 1919

The third daughter, Margaret, was born in March 1919, but died of pneumonia just a year later on March 23, 1920, three years to the day before my birth. Some obituary notices list her death as March 25 or 26, but Aunt Cora, who constructed our first genealogical chart, placed this baby's death at March 23, and I'll accept her date. What a reminder of Margaret's death my premature birth must have been for Mama. (Note the use of "its" in the obituary to refer to an infant.)

"Margaret Irene, youngest daughter of David R. and Martha C. Beard of Irricana, Alberta, Canada, died March 26, 1920, from bronchial pneumonia. Age 1 year.

Granddaughter of Edw. H. and Ida C. Beard, of Liberty St. Westminster, Md. Its little hands are folded On its gentle breast, Safe in the arms of Jesus, Gone to that happy land of rest. By its grandparents, Edw. H. and Ida C. Beard."

Eight months after Margaret's death, Mama went to Indiana for the birth of their second son, Raymond, born November 1920. We can only assume she went back to her Indiana home for the care she needed after the recent death of Margaret.

But the last three children: Paul, April 1922; Ruth, March 1923; and Robert, September 1924, as well as Elizabeth, were born near or at the home place we later got to know and had Canadian birth certificates, while Raymond, Barbara, and Edward had American ones. But in 1936 Daddy had us all registered as American citizens, a process he started in 1932.

The Five Oldest: Edward, Barbara, Elizabeth, Raymond, Paul

Robert and Ruth, the two youngest but taken years later

Of course there was no such thing as contraceptives in those days – at least none known in "nice" society – and Roe vs. Wade freedom was fifty years away. Many years later, when we learned about abortions, some of us wondered whether Mama might have had one or two abortions after Robert's birth. She was very ill at times. We questioned the rather weird appearance and activities of a woman in our church congregation who might have had methods to induce an abortion hidden in her big black bag and might have shared these with Mama. The eight births that Mama endured in less than ten years was quite enough! Well, more than enough.

With Robert's birth in 1924, our family comprised two adults and seven children. For many years, our pioneer childhood consisted of severe hardship, extremely cold winters, poverty, and year-round lonesomeness. Little would have been different had we grown up in Idaho rather than Alberta; the western States were not yet fully developed either, and without a doubt many pioneering conditions existed there and elsewhere in the west almost until World War II.

"When it's springtime in the Rockies,
I am coming back to you.
Little Sweetheart of the mountains
With your bonnie eyes of blue."
(Mary Hale Woolsey & Milt Taggart,
<u>When It's Springtime In the Rockies.</u>)

CHAPTER 4

OUR ALBERTA PRAIRIE HOME

Whenever springtime is mentioned, especially in Alberta, this song moves gently through my heart and soul. It even makes this Beard gal wish she had blue eyes! The song may not have been written about the Canadian Rockies, but it did become our favorite to describe our area. Elizabeth often played it on our reed organ and later on the piano when we had one.

I guess we all know that prairies are generally flat, and our area was no exception. But flatness does not always mean treeless. Nor does it mean that we could not see the beautiful Rocky Mountains seventy-five miles to the west! And they were snow-topped every day of every year. So the mountains of North Carolina are just "hills" to me.

Certainly the "flat and treeless" description was true of our immediate area. Way back in those pioneer days, there were virtually no trees except for the caraganas that ran along the fence between our garden and the adjacent church grounds. In fact, when a mirage existed, as it sometimes did during winter months, we could see the CPR train travelling either north or south approximately nine miles away on the Irricana tracks.

We were always told that Daddy gave the five acres at the northeastern edge of our property to the Church of the Brethren. From reading the Indentures, and the manner in which the church site was chosen, the first church had already been built at this corner by 1917; in fact about seven years earlier, but this information may contradict other records. (More on how the church site was chosen appears in Chapter 10 "Our Church.") Perhaps the location was adjusted a bit so that it would coincide with an intersection of the two main roads. It was the practice, where possible, that roads east and west were parallel every mile, and intersected every two miles with the main road then running north and south. So it would seem that Daddy donated this property to them after he signed for this acreage rather than charging them or asking them to relocate.

The new church building was dedicated in 1919 and the old one was moved approximately one-quarter mile south to become our home. By 1919, there were four Beard children to be housed with their parents in this small building. The main floor had a partition that divided our parents' bedroom from the living room. The three doors in the hallway opened to our future basement, future kitchen, and upstairs to the classroom that would now become a girl's bedroom. The sloping roof extended beyond the full length of the building and provided storage space. It is possible that all four siblings slept downstairs for a while. Later Barbara and Elizabeth moved to their new upstairs bedroom, and the boys had beds under the northern slope until the main addition was built.

This two-story addition to the old church was built some years later. The first level of the addition became our pantry and family area. The upstairs addition became the boys' bedroom, and was divided into one large and one small bedroom. The boys slept in the large room and any hired man had the smaller room. Later Edward moved to the small room when hired help was there only during harvesting.

Our House, south view. Far right section was old church.

The home was never finished as planned. Mama wanted a porch and an outside swing for her children, and of course both parents expected the outside walls to be tight and windows properly installed with screens. Insulation was not common in those days, but certainly was expected inside the walls. Instead, there were frosty nails coming through the exterior, and openings for flies and other insects.

I remember sleeping on a cot in the living room when I was young, and a curtain was hung to separate my bed from the rest of the room. I also remember crying from fear and Mama came to find out what was the matter. I said there were ghosts coming and going and I was scared. Mama showed me how the curtain was being moved by the cool air from the open window, and there were no ghosts! What a relief – but I was still half scared.

I recall the icy nails in wintertime, but not the newspapers lining the walls that some siblings remember. Later my cot was moved upstairs when the boys got to move to their new rooms. And when I was ten, Barbara and Elizabeth went to Calgary for high school, so I got their room – my first bedroom all for myself!

Here the windows dropped down between the walls, so obviously there was no insulation there. Maybe these windows were planned by

Daddy or were part of the church construction; at least the larger one does not appear in the photo of the old church. Why can't I remember whether we propped them up by a latch, a stick, or as I've read in letters, that we used large nails to hold them? There were gaps and openings at both windows through which dirt, wind, and flies entered and hairpins disappeared. Not having any screens on any of the windows was a delight for bees and insects but a headache for us humans. Of course there were no storm windows, and the panes were single glass, not double – and not Plexiglas, as the latter invention was decades later.

In winter we placed heated bricks in bed, but their heat lasted only a couple of hours, and we also used hot water bottles. I recall the time I accidentally pushed the bottle out of bed during the night, and when I found it in the morning, it had turned to ice chips – the air was that cold even inside the house!

At the turn of the stairway, Daddy placed a window that faced west to provide light for nighttime climbing of steps. Summer daylight in northwestern Canada is evident before 5:00AM, and twilight does not come until about 9:00PM or later; night descends about 10:00PM or even later. So we children went to bed by twilight, and even our tired parents retired early!

The basement was cool enough to store our vegetables all winter or our cream for weeks before being taken to Calgary for sale. It was a dug-out area that also had an opening for unloading truckloads of soft, flaky, and very messy Alberta coal. There were no railings along the wooden steps to the cellar. I can recall carrying coal up to the kitchen stove when I was the only girl at home, though Paul and Robert performed this duty too.

Our heating, such as it was, was primitive. At one time the wood and coal stove was in the kitchen area, and later it was moved to the narrower rectangular area we referred to as our pantry. There were cupboards and shelving along the walls as well as at the far end. Besides the entrance to the kitchen, which was just inside the back door, there was another opening at the far end leading to the northern end of the dining or family area. Just a foot into the family area, to the left, was the doorway to the northern section of the house, which gave entry to our living room, parents' bedroom, and also upstairs. I never remember our using the term "dining room," just "kitchen" and "pantry."

Two incidents in later years will impress upon you the reason for describing these areas as I have.

In the living room, which was formerly the church sanctuary, we had a small round heating stove. Daddy cut a hole in the ceiling above the stove so that the stovepipe led up through our girls' bedroom. Thus we had a minimum degree of warmth. We girls would stand as close to this pipe as possible for dressing but remained watchful in case our brothers were down below looking up, as there was a gap of several inches around the pipe. We learned that the hard way!

The boys' bedroom had no stove. The kitchen pipe ran across the kitchen ceiling and into the brick chimney. The chimney led upstairs against the partitioned wall of the boys' bedroom and then out to the roof. This offered even less heat to the boys than the girls. It is my understanding that the soft coal available in our area burned faster and supplied heat more quickly than hard coal.

Robert gives the size of our barn as "18'Wx24'L," but the photo might make it look longer, as there were lean-tos at both ends. The southern lean-to was for pigs and calves, the northern one for butchering. I do not believe I have heard the term "lean-to" since those country days. A "lean-to" is an overhang beginning a few feet down from the roof on the side of the building, with the back (and sometimes the end) boarded up, providing an extra semi-covered area.

The hayloft was not fully closed on the front, so straw or hay could be pitched up from wagons. There were also floor openings above each manger through which hay could be forked down as needed to individual stalls. For those who have never forked up to a hayloft, be assured that forking down was much easier.

I remember, too, the years when a granary shed was placed adjacent to our back door. Our milk separator was placed inside then and not out in the open. A separator is the unit that separates the cream from the fresh milk as someone turns the handle. It had a big metal bowl on top of the hand-operated engine to hold the fresh milk. Two spouts led to two different containers: the large bucket or pail held the "skimmed" milk while the smaller one held the cream. This type machine never obtained 100% separation.

About a quarter of a mile down a slight slope at the back of the barn a shallow pond would appear from time to time, especially in the winter, and it was the first and only place I've ever seen rubber ice. I wonder how many folks have slipped or skimmed on such surface, or even are aware of such a surface as rubber ice. It forms only on very shallow water, is never as thick as regular ice, and bends to heavy weight placed upon it without breaking as regular ice would. Rubber ice also has its own unique color: it reminds me of yellow vinegar or olive oil.

Our first well, hand-dug of course, is described by Robert as follows: "It was approximately 20-25' deep. I don't recall putting ice in the well, but maybe so. I was told a horse fell in the well. When? Which horse? Later a second well was drilled about 12-15' away and was approximately 65' deep, and may have been dug deeper later. The first one was used for cold storage. Both of these wells were hand-pumped for many years. Eventually, about 1938, we got a Fairbanks Morse motor. The spark plugs had to be cleaned quite often but the weather and dirt had nothing to do with that – it was the worn out engine."

Carrying heavy buckets of water some tenth of a mile from well to house was no easy matter. Our water was soft, not hard, and when freshly drawn up would be very cold. I dislike warm water even today, and hard water for drinking brings forth an absolute "No, thanks," from me. However, many women at our church declared that soft water did not make good coffee, so they supplied their hard water for church events.

Our neighbors, the Hutchings, lived across our field to the southwest, about one mile away, and were the closest family with a phone. They did not attend our church, and we really did not know them well, although later their one son was a fellow student at our Hawthorn public school. However, in emergencies, we would go to their home to use their phone. It was a wall phone; desk phones did not become available until decades later and then it was many more years before phone extension cords could be used. Initially, an operator would take your call and dial the number you wanted. On several occasions, Mr. Hutchings would make a special trip to bring a message to us. Generally, it was a case of someone being in need of a ride home, such as when Daddy returned early from a cancelled trip to the States. In the other direction, we would have had to go about three to four miles for phone contacts. Robert, who later owned our prairie home, tells me he finally got a phone line installed in 1961!

The only hospital was in Calgary, some thirty miles away, and the closest doctor, Dr. Edwards, lived in Airdrie, eleven miles straight west of our home. Can you imagine travelling 11 miles on dirt roads in a horse and buggy, to take your youngster with a broken or injured shoulder to the doctor? Mama could not drive an auto, and those who could were out in the fields, so that is exactly what she had to do on one occasion.

Spring was April and May, Summer was June, July and August, Fall was September and October (sometimes late August to early November) and Winter – well, November, December, January, February and March! And maybe April going into May! Winters often had temperatures of 30F and 40F below zero, even lower sometimes. In a letter May 9, 1952, Mama writes that the temperature was 40 degrees below zero, so clearly seasons were not restricted by their usual schedule.

Ready to slide down icy plank

Not very many places experience Chinooks. They are the most welcome change in weather one can imagine. They originate in the west or northwest as a mild wind of much higher temperature. The temperature can be twenty-five or more below zero all week, and then here comes a chinook: in a couple of hours the warmth has begun defrosting everything, even people. "We are so relieved to have the icy winds gone and warm air hits our soul" that we praised the Lord readily! It is such a blessing I wish the entire world could be blessed with them.

When a Chinook came on a school day, imagine the change: we walked to school wrapped in wool scarves, two pairs of gloves or mittens, and heavy boots, and after the Chinook rolled in, we walked home in spring-like comfort – no scarves or mitts, just the boots!

Spring was most welcome, and usually farming activities could be underway by May, with gardens planted by mid-to-late May. The plowing and grain planting were the two major reasons that hired help was needed until harvesting days in late September and into October and early November.

Summers were not hot, although we may have thought so since we were used to nine months of weather that ranged from cool to icy cold. There usually were one or two rains, quite limited, and occasionally a hailstorm. (In 1960 while visiting his northern homeland, Paul took a photo of hailstones mixed with eggs, and it is very difficult to tell which is which.) Dust storms were far more common.

Finally farmers learned to alternate lots from plowed to unplowed fields, and to alternate from horizontal to vertical plowed lots. This was a great help in reducing the effect of dust storms.

It was not unusual to have our first frost by September 1, when school started. I think even the coyotes were aware of this special date, as I remember their howling in celebration of this event. Was it my imagination that they were quiet all summer, even on August 31, but on September 1, they had become vocal? Harvesting occurred in late September and October, and boys especially would miss school to help in the fields. Older girls were needed at home to help with cooking for threshers.

These descriptions of housing and conditions were fairly typical for many of our neighbors, although some may have had better housing with insulation, and also fewer children. We were the family who lived farthest from the grade schools, but closest to our church. (Elizabeth's description of our kitchen, in Chapter 6, is not limited to that one room as her title suggests.)

I remember our Model T auto, then a Model A, and then a Studebaker. Daddy, with only one leg, could drive any manual car – the only type there were in those days – by having a gas lever attached to the steering wheel.

Barbara, Ruth and Elizabeth, about 1931

Edward was especially good at mechanical subjects, and he was always the one to check the spark plugs and carburetor before trips to Kathyrn or Calgary. I, who constantly said, "I wish I were a boy," was often there with him, with both our heads under the open hood, but only Edward knew what he was doing. I realized later how kind and patient he was with my interest in his doings when I was totally ignorant of these operations. Feeding the pigs or milking the cows was of no interest to me, but I always wanted to be with Edward when he worked on our automobile. Partly this was due to his kindness; but I also appreciated the fact that the car never swished its tail, like the cows, nor grunted like a pig! I suspect he was the one who taught me how to drive, and I drove several weeks to high school while Paul and

Raymond were out of school to harvest crops. Way out in the country, we did not need a driver's license to operate vehicles.

Ruth – Go to it, old boy!

I do not recall if we children also used Daddy's gas lever, or used our feet like other people. I do remember driving the Studebaker to high school, and once backing into another student's car. (His girlfriend was mad, but he did not say anything to me.) Also one time I went over the edge of the entrance to our own driveway and Edward had to come maneuver the car back onto the drive. I wonder yet if anyone else in the family knew about that.

Every time we went to Calgary, we had to stop to mend a flat tire or perhaps do some other repair. There was an inner tube within the tire, and that is usually where the puncture was, thus causing complicated and time-consuming labor. Not only did we have to have rubber patching and glues, but an air pump to re-inflate the tire. So an extra hour or two was allowed for this 30-mile trip. I remember also hunting for haywire or wire of some sort from the adjacent fences, but I do not recall what kind of problem needed wire for repair.

A lifetime later, in 1984, when I was driving from York, Pennsylvania down to my new job at Warren Wilson College in Swannanoa, North Carolina, I had an auto breakdown. I was not familiar with this US 19/23 route but had taken it this time instead of getting off Interstate 81, then following I-77 South and I-40 West to Asheville.

This 19/23 was a two-lane, mountainous road, with few exits and heavily traveled by commercial trucks. All of a sudden my Ford Falcon did not respond to any pressure on the gas pedal! I could hear trucks behind me, though I could see no lights even though it was after 9:00PM. I was frantic. No gas pedal working! What could I do? There was only tall grass on either side, no pull-offs. I thought "I'll just have to jump out when the car stops or when a truck gets too close and dash to the side, hoping that there isn't a deep ditch there. Maybe, just maybe, the car will make it to the top of this hill and at least can be seen by the truck behind me." Believe it or not, I made it to the top, and got about two feet to the right off the highway! There was a grocery store in front of me, and on the other side there was a gas station. "Oh, happy day." Or so I thought. The store was closed, as was the station. And worse too, there was no outside phone!

I could hear dogs barking, probably about a quarter mile away. And this was North Carolina, Jesse Helms' Bible Belt, where one typically saw trucks with guns across their cab windows, and I had heard about attitudes of southerners towards us Yankees. What should I do? Try to find a way to where the dogs were barking and hope the owner would be home but not greet me with a gun? Or stop a car or truck and hope for help rather than attack? Or hide in the car until morning when the store might open?

For the next half hour, I ducked down whenever any auto was coming. Then I thought, "Ruth, this is getting worse. You're getting more scared, the danger is worse the later it gets. You've got to get help. Either go to the nearest farm where you hear the dogs barking, or stop an oncoming car." So I decided to flag down the next truck coming my way by flicking my headlights. Fifteen minutes later, a light delivery truck stopped and parked on the far-left side. I pulled my driver's side window down about five inches, and a teenage boy stopped at his side of the street when he saw my reaction. And I thought, "Oh thank you, dear mother, you've taught him right."

I called to him asking that he call the police because I was having car trouble. He answered in a broad Southern accent, "Ma'am, there ain't no police around here. I'll call —-," well, some southern named mechanic. And I said, "Please have him come in his marked mechanic's car." The boy said he lived just fifteen minutes from there and he'd get me help.

While I waited, I again ducked every time any car or truck came from either direction. Exactly half an hour later, a station wagon pulled off and parked just ahead of my Falcon. I was not relieved. There was no sign that this was the mechanic. But just then the helpful boy arrived and pulled over on the other side of the roadway, and I thought, "Well, Ruth, now you've got two of them, for better or for worse."

The mechanic said who he was and asked me what the trouble was, and then told me to get out of the car. I did so, and he tested the pedal. "Yup, you've lost the connection." Or words to that effect. And he turned to the boy and said, "I don't have my tool kit in my station wagon, do you have a flashlight?" And I answered, "I have a flashlight. I always carry a flashlight." And I retrieved it from my car trunk for him.

He opened the car hood, and found the problem, and said to the kid, "Do you have a pair of pliers?" And I, not the kid, answered, " I have pliers. I always carry pliers." So I retrieved them. And in a few seconds, he said that he did not have the necessary equipment to make a connection, and asked the boy, "Do you have any wire?" And again I answered, "I have wire. I always carry wire." And I retrieved a coat hanger from my emergency homemade tool kit.

None of those items he needed were unknown to the Beards. We needed them practically every trip to Calgary, and sometimes even to

Kathyrn or Airdrie, so we always had them in any car we ever had. And yes, I always carry them myself, even today.

The mechanic accepted my AAA insurance but the boy declined the $10 I wanted to give him. I got to my Asheville mountain apartment about 2:30AM. The next afternoon I took the car to Firestone repair shop on Tunnel Road for proper repairs. The mechanic there said, "Ma'am, I wouldn't change a thing. This wire connection is much better than the original." Tell that to General Ford Motors!

Thank goodness for childhood experiences!

One more major item about our childhood farm! How could I forget describing bathrooms! Bathrooms? Or restrooms? What are the latter? That's a modern name for inside outhouses, or toilets. Our outhouse was to the west of the house, just beyond the chicken house, and could be seen from the west window in our pantry. It was a two-holer, I think! Well, it served the purpose whether one or two holes! Now what do you think we used for toilet paper in those days? I can assure you there was no tissue, soft or otherwise, out there in the country. What other families used I can only guess, but we Beards used the catalogs of Sears & Roebuck, Montgomery Wards, and even the weekly newspaper, *Prairie Home Farmer*. Only the stiff colored pages of the catalogs were not used!

Did we have to go outside to the outhouse during the night, or during the winter? And how about Daddy? Where did he go? He could not put on his artificial leg to get out at nighttime. Nor did we kids go outside at night except the boys when they slept in the haymow at times. What did we use? Slop pails or slop buckets: noisy, low, white enamel buckets, maybe with a lid or maybe an old magazine if the lid was gone! So we had at least three buckets at all times, one for parents, one for girls, and one for boys. I think the hired men used the boys' bucket, or when they slept in the haymow, they would use good old mother earth. We called these slop jars our "friends." When Robert was home by himself, some neighbors who visited infrequently had dropped in, and he was reading off the list of errands left for him to do. He innocently read "take the friends out." I don't know how he cleared the air with them!

Bathing? Washtubs, of course, or sometimes a basin. Saturday evening was bath time and at least in the winter, this activity took place around the space stove in the living room. We girls got to bathe first in the tub, then perhaps more hot water was added and the boys got their turn. Actually the washtub held only one person at a time if the bather wanted to sit down in it, only possible when one was fairly young. This was also before deodorants and long before any sanitary napkins!

We learned that at least one of our neighbors had to share toothbrushes. I'm sure we Beard children did not share, but then I can't remember any toothbrushes at all, although I do recall we had dry grainy salt-like cleanser, with a Listerine taste, for rinsing our mouth. We did all drink out of the same water dipper, and of course it was returned to the pail after each drink. Who would approve of that today? No one drank eight glasses of water per day; in summer those working outside might drink some at each meal, and possibly a little between meals, perhaps totaling one glass per day. I certainly drank very little water, just good old whole milk strengthened with pure cream! (Taking certain medicines today requires a glass of water and that may be the total amount taken all day, yet I am in very good health. Must be something else than water that is important, methinks!)

We had no inside running water, no electricity, nor gas stoves – just tough endurance!

Elizabeth recorded on tape her memory of Mama being sick and two of the children being "farmed out," but she doesn't know which ones. I would assume it would be the two youngest, Robert and me. I do remember that once a number of us stayed overnight with neighbors: the girls slept on the floor with a curtain dividing the area, and the boys slept on the other side. I think it was the Brant family. Elizabeth also said that some family wanted to adopt her and Raymond though she does not know who the prospective parents were. I'm guessing who it might have been, but I'll not mention it here. Mama said she would not give up her children.

It is no surprise to me that Elizabeth and Raymond would be the two chosen for adoption. They were the sweet and obedient ones, and probably of the best ages, and were neither argumentative like Barbara, nor constantly musing to themselves over ugly stones or bugs, like Paul.

> "Use it up, wear it out,
> Make it do, or do without."
> (New England maxim)

CHAPTER 5

FARM LIFE

How do parents assign tasks for their children today? Do the children have certain duties they must do before catching the bus for grade school? Do they ride a bus or are they taken by car by their parents or neighbors?

Undoubtedly, farm children still have jobs to do in the morning, but these must be very limited in comparison to the chores we faced. Modern elementary schools commence at 8:00AM, high schools at 8:30AM, and the bus may pick them up at 7:30AM or even earlier. Here in Asheville, North Carolina, elementary schools are dismissed at 2:30PM and the high schools at 3:00PM, from mid-August to late May.

Our Alberta school day began at 9:00AM and ended at 3:30PM. The school year ran from September 1 until June 30. There were no snow days – we'd have been home from school for months if that had been the policy!

I do not remember what time our alarm clock was set but I do recall hearing a parent calling up the stairs for the older boys to get up. They had many cows to milk by hand, once in the morning before leaving for school and then again either before or just after supper. They also pitched hay down to refill the mangers, especially if a cow had just given birth or if for some reason that cow was not heading out to the pasture. This too was done morning and evening. And Edward, as the oldest, was expected to see that all such chores were done before leaving for school. What happened if he did not? He would get punished by Daddy when he got back home. It's little wonder his life turned out as it did. Whipping any child, and especially boys, with straps or sticks in those days was not unusual. Fortunately society has restricted any such punishment whether at home or in school, in both Canada and the States (though North Carolina leaves it to individual counties to allow or ban paddling).

Barbara was responsible for operating the separator that divided the milk from the cream. She then usually washed the separator before leaving for school, as Mama would have plenty of other work to do, including washing our breakfast dishes. I would often help wash each separator disk, but I couldn't handle the big heavy metal bowl at the top, so Barbara did that as well as put the milk and cream away. Before we got the separator, the cream would have been dipped off the top where it naturally rose when left standing for a good while. All the manual work we did took the place of the health clubs that are so popular today.

I never understood how running milk through numerous disks would send the milk to one spout and the cream to another. Of course, a quantity of milk was maintained morning and evening for our own consumption, but Mama would often first skim off some of the cream for sale if the supply had stood long enough to begin to separate naturally. After Barbara finished, the cream was moved to a cold area – either our basement or stored where the first well had been dug. These cream cans held five gallons and when they were filled, we took them to either Calgary or to Kathyrn. If the latter, it was usually done weekly, and then the local store would ship them to Calgary.

I doubt if Mama ever knew that when she was not around, I would drink half of the whole milk and then fill the cup up with cream! Today we're told that even whole milk is harmful and will eventually clog one's arteries. Out of my eighty-four years, for about half of those I drank whole milk, and during the first fifteen or so I added the additional cream. I'm still waiting to hear whether I have clogged arteries or any other condition from all that cream! For the last ten years or more, I've used two percent only. Now one can even get soymilk – chocolate as well as regular!

Sometimes when the folks took the cream to the Farmers' Market in Calgary, Robert and I, being too young to stay at home alone, would go too, as would some of the older children. I remember twice that when we got to the market Daddy took Robert and me to a nearby home, knocked on the door, and asked a perfect stranger if he could leave us with her until he came back after marketing was done. I can recall the surprised look on the women's faces, but both times they accepted. I know Robert and I were quiet and well-behaved. Today, would a homeowner not immediately call the police because of fear that an estranged husband had grabbed his children, or might not return to pick them up? I doubt if any money or lunch provisions were given her, but possibly Daddy bought soup from the market to give to our "caretaker." Or perhaps we took peanut butter sandwiches and milk from home for our own lunch.

The booth workers at the Farmers' Market were mainly Chinese, and they may even have been the owners. There were no Negroes – as they were politely called – or Mexicans.

Many years later, a neighbor boy, Everett Culp, started a delivery business: he would pick up these saleable goods from neighbors and take them to Calgary, and on the same trip would get groceries for us. Selling cream frequently was the source of much needed income, since grain sales were often delayed and much less frequent, depending upon the market.

For breakfast, we had oatmeal or wheat cereal and sometimes cream of wheat. This last one was the best of the three options, in my opinion. That I avoid any such porridge today should tell the readers how distasteful this "absolutely essential" and 365-days-a-year breakfast was, at least to me. I do not remember if we ground our own wheat in order to have cream of wheat, but we did grind the coarse wheat for some purpose.

Elizabeth prepared our school lunches that consisted of peanut butter, sometimes with a thin spread of jam added. That was a real treat—to have a bit of jam on top of the peanut butter. Our school lunch also included milk, which made our bags heavier to carry when we had to walk. Today students can get a lunch at school in the dining room or from the coin slots. We had our own schoolbooks to carry, too. The government did not provide any textbooks.

As I got older, I would help Elizabeth in the kitchen by setting the table, getting wood for the stove, and of course cleaning up after a meal. Small tasks to help either of my sisters or Mama were often given me. Sometimes these tasks would come across as a direct order, and other times as a request or suggestion. I'm sure I responded more favorably to the latter and Elizabeth especially would put such requests in question form. I must mention that Mama was very patient, kind, and not abusive in the least. Occasionally she might crack her knuckles on a child's head as punishment but never anything harsh or brutal. Undoubtedly, we had to sit in a corner sometimes, but that was better than being spanked or whipped.

Robert remembers that at five years old he would help Barbara with feeding the chickens and gathering eggs. The chickens were fed twice daily, and this included carrying water to their small troughs too. Sometimes baby chicks were brought into the house where it was warm, as were newly born calves in very cold weather.

Barbara's job to feed chickens. Family quilts on line

Elizabeth and her pet calf, taking it to school fair

The chicken house was about midway between the barn and the house. By the time Robert was six years old, and in grade one, he had to milk one cow every night, and eventually more each year. I recall at least eight cows and very likely many more. However, I did not have milking duty.

Whenever a cow or pig was slaughtered, we younger children were kept at a distance so that we could not see what was going on. We knew what was happening out there by the pump, but we were discreetly kept busy somewhere else. Adult male neighbors, hired help, or a veterinarian came to help with the slaughtering. As the butchering progressed, the freshly cut tongue, heart, and liver pieces were brought to the kitchen so Mama could start canning them. The odor was horrendous; and what do you think cooked canned meat tastes like? I was so thankful Mama never made me eat those pieces. With no refrigeration, much of the balance of the animal was also canned, but enough for several meals was stored in the old well for a short time.

Only once did I see Mama wring the neck of a chicken. The head was then cut off and the body was dipped into boiling water so that the feathers could easily be removed. Well, we children would pull the feathers off, and it wasn't always that easy: sometimes it was necessary to dip it back into the hot water again. It's a mystery why we children did not become vegetarians.

Of course we all pitched in to help others if we had finished our own chores, unless the task was too hard for us younger ones. Carrying just one bucket of water from the pump to the house was hard not only on us children but on our parents too. With his heavy wooden leg that he had to swing sideways, even Daddy could carry only one bucket at a time—and thus not even out the load by carrying two smaller ones. The pump was much closer to the barn, almost adjacent, because the trough was attached for watering farm animals.

We had pigs, horses, and cows, as did our neighbors, but no goats in the prairies during my youth. We also had many chickens. Much later, shortly before I left the farm, we got some turkeys. It is one thing to hear a rooster crow in the early morning, it is quite another to hear the gobbling of turkeys! I'll stick with roosters, thank you.

Most or all these morning chores were repeated in the evening. A few, like feeding the chickens and gathering the eggs, could be done before supper, and in the winter the milking and separator work was done while we still had daylight. In the house we had kerosene lamps. The kerosene lantern for the barn was inadequate for all the milking and other farm chores, but we had only one barn lantern and had to make that do.

I do not recall us selling many eggs, but it is possible we occasionally did when we attended the farmers' markets in Calgary. Nor do I remember the average daily count of eggs—probably a dozen or so. When hens are sitting on eggs to hatch them, they are not producing new ones. We used so many eggs because everything was cooked from scratch; nothing was boxed or in mixes as we have today. Daddy taught us how to shell hard-boiled eggs in the quickest time, and today I still feel ashamed that I criticized my mother-in-law for the way she peeled them. She would crack the egg shell all around and then begin pulling at one piece, which might pull several adjacent ones off at the same time. I was taught to crack the shell only at the top and the bottom. Then start pulling off at one end and the inner skin would remove a much larger area than my mother-in-law's method. Why do it Daddy's way? Well, it saved maybe a whole second of time, maybe a second and a half. Sixty seconds saved is a minute gained to apply elsewhere. And one of Daddy's constant lectures was "if it takes five minutes to do the job today, try to do it in four minutes tomorrow, and three minutes the next day, until you've done it the quickest way possible."

(Perhaps my mother-in-law never knew that I learned from her a good way to clean the knife after spreading jam or peanut butter on toast: insert the knife through the edge of the toast. Had I told her, I could have lowered the frustration she felt about her egg peeling.)

In the summer, the cows were often herded out on the public roadway. We younger ones would head them out and then stall them where there was grass for them to eat, often as far as four miles away. We may have taken a ball along to play catch and more than likely I, at least, would take a book to read. From mid-morning to mid-afternoon was a long time to be out herding cows far from home.

Recently I heard a television announcer ask if animals could tell time. Well, of course they can, and it's been no secret these many years, at least not to farmers. None of us had watches to tell us when to start back home with the cows. The animals told us. The herd automatically began turning around in late afternoon and headed back home. Roosters crow when sunrise begins whether the sun can be seen through clouds or not. Coyotes would howl when school started on the first Monday of September.

Those days of cattle herding were among the few times I milked a cow. There was no need to empty the entire udder but only squirt out enough milk to provide a drink with lunch, which was usually a sandwich, either dry or mushy. Can you imagine drinking warm unstrained milk?

At home we had fly stickers hanging from the ceiling and we covered the water bucket with a tea towel, which initially had been a seed bag. When it came time to use the towel to dry the dishes, we first had to shake the insects and dust off the towels first. What a good way for humans to gradually build up resistance to diseases or infections! Surely not the way we would prefer, but I do believe this gradual and constant facing of germs, colds, etc. is what made many of us very strong and resistant to greater illnesses. Today there are sprays and wipes to use on grocery carts. Does it not make you wonder if being too careful has its own drawbacks?[3]

Most families, like ours, held the oldest child responsible for seeing that all the chores were done before heading off to school

---

[3] An e-mail I received on January 11, 2005 titled "Those were the days" lists many abominable situations and I'll mention just a few here. "Mom used to cut chicken, chop eggs and spread mayo on the same cutting board with the same knife and no bleach, but we didn't get food poisoning. My Mom used to defrost hamburger on the counter and I used to eat a bit raw sometimes. Our school sandwiches were wrapped in wax paper, in a brown paper bag, or in a metal lunch box. There were no such items as icepack coolers or back bags as we have today. I can't remember anybody getting e.coli. Oh yeah, and where was the Benadryl and sterilization kit when I got that bee sting? I could have been killed."

or church or play. If Edward left before these tasks were finished, Daddy would punish him when he got home from school. But Mr. Ruskin, our teacher at Herbert Spencer School, also held the eldest one responsible for getting his siblings, as well as himself, to school on time. If not, Mr. Ruskin would order that child to the barn and whip him with a leather strap. I think there were not many days when Edward was not punished either by Mr. Ruskin or by Daddy. Fortunately Mr. Ruskin was employed there only from 1929-31, so my older siblings had just two years to endure his cruelty, which was far too much in any event.

I'm not sure just when the task of washing supper dishes fell to Paul and me. Certainly we assumed this chore when Barbara and Elizabeth were in their tenth grade in Calgary High School and thus away from home, and we would have been ten and eleven years old. Paul always washed and I dried, sometimes getting them put away at the same time. Paul would daydream or work out a mental problem while I stood waiting for him to hurry up with his portion of the work.

Once, during an argument, he broke a plate over my head. I do not know whether Daddy ever knew about this, or even if Mama knew how this plate got broken, but I don't remember Paul being punished. Why Paul always argued with me, I'll never know. If I said something was red, he would disagree and say it was maroon; and if he said it was 10:05, I'd say, "No, it isn't, it's five minutes after ten," or whatever. He was smarter than I was, and I did not like him for that. As we both matured, we grew to appreciate each other's talents, personality, and individuality, and in some ways we were closer with each other than were any of our other siblings. Some of that closeness might be due to the fact that he and I were students at LaVerne College at the same time, knew many of the same students, and eventually one of my friends became Paul's wife.

Seasonal Work *"Bringing in the sheaves, Bringing in the sheaves.*
We shall come rejoicing, Bringing in the sheaves."
(Traditional)

It wasn't only sheaves that farm children handled. In early summer before school ended June 30, we would plan to rush early on a Saturday morning to pick the wild saskatoon berries that grew only in the coulee area. It's been so long since I've seen or tasted them that I can't say what they tasted like. Unfortunately, almost every year we missed gathering them when they were truly ripe. On our way home from school on Friday, we saw the berries were there for us to pick on Saturday morning. But on Saturday they were practically all gone – at least those that were perfectly ripe for picking. A distant colony of Doukabours[4] would beat us to it. Some of the members could come either late at night or very early in the morning, as they were not bound by provincial school schedules, while the Beard and Culp children would be asleep or doing their morning chores.

The foregoing description of our chores was basically the five-days-a-week schedule during the school year. However, other special tasks were necessary during plowing and planting in the spring and harvesting in autumn. In the spring we children helped plant potatoes. Daddy usually cut the potatoes, making sure that at least one eye of the potato was in each portion. Then as he dropped the portion into the previously plowed row, one child would follow and scoop soil over that "spud" to cover it completely. This required the older children to be absent from school for several weeks to help in the fields and in the kitchen. A hired man might be present year round, but extra help

---

[4] The Doukabours and the Hutterites established colonies both in Canada and in the States. Histories of these groups are generally found in descriptions of the western areas. The National Geographic, June 2006, has an interesting article on a Hutterite group.

was hired during harvesting season. A full threshing crew with their machines was needed each fall. Because harvesting was more time-consuming than spring work, all male students missed many weeks of school every fall.

Hired crew threshing our wheat crop

My brothers stacking hay

How did we find these hired men? As I recall, they walked from farm to farm until someone hired them, which was not unlikely except during the winter. Our hired men ate meals with us, so we had ten people sitting at the long kitchen table. They slept in the haymow during spring and fall, as we had no room in the house. I am quite sure Daddy would hire only non-smokers (though probably none of them could afford tobacco, nor had access to buy any when out in the country.) Some hired help were congenial and polite, and some were more distant and rough. At a much later age, I got the feeling that it was the first type that our parents had to watch, since my older sisters were either "daring" or "sweet." Later I heard that at least two different hired men wanted my sisters to go with them when the seasonal work ended.

Sometimes, even when school ended on June 30, there would still be planting to do, and certainly there was weeding. Above-ground vegetables were ready to eat, cook, or can by July or August. Sneaking young peas to eat was tempting, but an older sibling would tattle on us younger ones. It was always a treat to have young white potatoes, but usually most of this crop was not dug until late September.

A memorable photo was taken of our first pumpkin crop and our first corn. It is dated 1933, when I was ten. Growing seasons were too short for sweet corn, so our Maryland relatives sent us field corn – still a pleasure to us who had never had any home-grown corn! Probably they sent pumpkin seeds too, and I know that after we had our first pumpkin crop, pumpkin pie was eagerly awaited in the fall.

Our first crop of pumpkins & corn, 1933

Saturdays were more hectic, and Sundays were our one "rest day;" interpret "rest" as you wish. On Sunday mornings, Daddy peeled the potatoes for Sunday dinner and shined our Sunday shoes. Mama and we girls prepared breakfast and the rest of the noon meal. Sunday evenings I think we often had bread and milk, or something light, maybe homemade potato soup. Far better than today's canned potato soup, of any brand, I assure you!

Of course we churned our own butter. When whole milk stands a good while, the cream rises to the top, so before we got the separator, Mama would dip the cream off the top and place it in a large container to save for churning later, once or even twice a month. The wooden churn was turned by hand, never a motor. Usually Paul, Robert, and I shared this job as it took so long that one child would get tired even when changing from right to left hands. Mama would promise a nickel or maybe even a dime to the child who finished the churning; thus no one wanted to start it but we were always ready to take over when it seemed close to completing this separation of cream to soft butter. The remaining liquid was buttermilk. We children did not like buttermilk, but we were encouraged to try it. Undoubtedly here in our country no one ever gets butter this way today. If any farm child still churns, I wonder what they get paid today.

These wooden churns have long since become antiques. I'd take one today just for memory's sake and as a great conversation piece!

A dime or even a nickel was a real treat in those days. Robert tells me that he and Paul would crawl under the church steps several times a year hoping to find money. Sometimes they might find a penny, even a nickel, but hardly ever a dime. They felt "rich" when they found anything. In 1939 or 1940, Robert took several horses to Irricana to sell to a Mr. Eliott, and he asked Daddy for twenty-five cents. Evidently he had hoped to buy his supper on this approximately sixteen mile round-trip, but Daddy told him to ride faster and get home to eat.

Another way the boys earned a few cents in winter was to catch weasels, skin them and sell the hides to some company. The skinning took place in the kitchen! Maybe the smell wasn't as bad as that from skunks, but within that confined space with its hot stove, it was still horrible. Usually, this chore was done in the evening while some of us were sitting at the table doing our homework. It's a wonder we ever finished any homework!

We all trapped and caught gophers; but they were not skinned, nor worth even a few cents. Often we poured water down the gopher holes to drown them, but it was not always possible to know if the pest was in the hole at that time, so we also set traps. These animals were all destructive to our gardens. I remember pouring water down the holes; but my brothers did the follow-up of killing the gophers by clubbing them. That is something I could not do. (It was not until 2003 that Paul told me that the animals we called "gophers" were really Richardson's Ground Squirrels.)

Coyotes were destructive to calves and young animals, maybe even to our poultry. Edward had a twenty-two-gauge rifle and would try to shoot them. I think we did have several traps set for them, but these traps were not the small type suitable for the gophers and weasels. None of us girls handled the rifle, nor did my other brothers at that time, though they might have later.

At a later time, I got a dog that I claimed as my pet, but he was queer looking. One morning I found him dead beneath the granary shed beside the house. Much later I heard that the older Haag boys shot him because he looked like a cross between a dog and a coyote. I really did not have him long enough to know how he would have developed.

I remember that Edward, in grade nine or ten, made our first crystal radio that required ear phones, and Mama would let me listen to a program while the others were lining up for supper. Usually, though, we all hit the supper table at the same time. Imagine not being able to listen to the radio without wearing earphones.

I can remember wearing warm lined winter pants to school and removing them before school began. Girls did not wear slacks in class until much later. In 1944, when I flew to California for college, Mama was firm that I must wear a hat and gloves – like a lady! Nor did we have Kotex or any type of sanitary napkins until about 1935, at least not in our family, and Tampax was even later. Barbara and Elizabeth were in high school in Calgary, and I remember Mama asked Elizabeth to explain the "monthly curse" to me, which my body was about to start. (We never used the proper term of menstruation. In the pantry cupboard, many years earlier, I found a book entitled <u>What every young girl ought to know</u>, but I hadn't the foggiest notion what it meant.) At a later trip home, Elizabeth suggested to Mama that she provide me with the store-bought disposable type of napkins rather than old sheets cut up – tough old sheets that had to be washed and re-used! And how bulky! Ugh! At least by this time, I knew I would never be a boy, and had stopped expressing such dreams to Mama.

Once, and once only, did I see Daddy put his arm around Mama and kiss her on the cheek. She was embarrassed. Elizabeth mentions the one time she saw this behavior – I can't truthfully term it "affection." When I slept in the living room, I would hear Mama begging Daddy to stop but again I hadn't any idea what was going on.

Monday was wash day. Initially Mama had the old wash boards but later acquired a gas-operated Maytag washing machine. Electricity was not yet available in our area. Edward helped keep this Maytag running. (I have the little tin oil can which held the quarter cup of oil needed for the Maytag. I use it as a toothpick holder and it always starts a conversation with guests.)

Several long clotheslines ran to the west of the house near the hen house. So what does one pray for when you've got these long lines pinned fully with clothes from a nine-member family, and a tenth if it included a hired man's washing? We did not have to pray that it would not rain because only a couple of rains came during the entire year. No, we just hoped that there would be no dust storms, which came on quickly and with virtually little warning. Paul took a picture once of our clothesline after we had brought in all the wash, but as usual, the clothespins were left on the lines. These pins show in his photo and the naive person is asked to guess what they are. I haven't found a person yet who guesses correctly.

Yes, it's a dust storm, but what are the images on the line?

Clothing that was not yet dry had to be hung over chairs or wherever we could find a suitable place, including right on the oven door! That door was also used to keep newborn piggies and chickies warm and alive until they could survive in our minus forty degree weather!

When a dust storm was close, we would get a warning from cattle rushing for cover. We would rush out with brooms to gather the poultry and direct them to shelter. I can remember a number of times when Barbara and I hurried to round up chickens and turkeys and get them inside the hen house before the dust storm hit. Turkeys, the dumbest of all poultry, were the slowest to respond.

Elizabeth tells about her duties of laundering, combined with many other interesting memories, in "Our Kitchen." Her youngest son, Joe, has shared these recordings with me. Elizabeth was Mama's main helper in the house, and often had to take her place when Mama was sick, and of course when Mama went back to Indiana in 1931. So her story is a first-hand description.

However, she forgot to mention how we got our beautiful reed organ that was mainly for her. Our neighbor, William Culp, either had one that he was willing to sell or knew where he could get one for us. What it cost was a bushel of good potatoes! Robert remembers going with our older brothers in the wagon to haul it across the coulee to our home. Then it had to be raised up the two steps to the living room. Not an easy job.

Mrs. Haag taught Elizabeth how to read music and how to pump the organ, not easy when one's legs don't yet reach the pedals. Elizabeth soon was playing the church organ for our services. It was not until much later that we got a piano, and I was given lessons by another neighbor.

"The home we first knew on this beautiful earth,
The friends of our childhood, the place of our birth.
In the heart's inner chamber sung always will be,
As the shell ever sings of its home on the sea!"
(Frances Dana Gage, <u>Home.</u>)

CHAPTER 6

OUR KITCHEN

By Anna Elizabeth Beard Detrick
January 1982

  The kitchen in my home in Alberta, Canada, as a child from 1922-1937 was large. There were three small windows, one facing south and two facing east. The south door led out to the yard south to the pump and barn and West around the corner to the chicken house, and the privy. (The privy changed locations several times.) On the west wall were two windows. The one at the north end of the kitchen opened west into the pantry where there were cupboards and shelves.

  The doorway at the south end of the kitchen led west into the wash room. In here were two orange crates with a board across, and two basins and a water bucket. Towels and wash cloths hung above. The wash cloths were salt sacks. Also in here were boots, coats, mittens, two big buckets for dish water and scrap slop, which went to the pigs. One time I made a mistake and asked the hired man to please empty the slop jars. I meant slop buckets. The slop jars were our inside privies!

  Let's go back to the main kitchen although the whole area – wash room and pantry – was part of the kitchen. Between these two archways toward the south was an iron MAJESTIC STOVE with two warming ovens at the top. It was in here we laid sick chickens wrapped in soft cloths. One day I was standing in front of the stove stirring food. Suddenly to my horror the chicken became revived, crept out of the cloth and landed on the stove. My first thought was that the chicken would get hurt by burning. I picked it up, screamed, and flung it clear across the room. The others in the room looked to see what had happened. My sister, Barbara, picked it up. The poor thing was dead. I do not know why I threw it.

The stove had no water tank as many stoves did. It was made of heavy iron and the oven door was so strong that my dad could sit on it. I often warmed my back sitting on it. Many an evening after supper and the work done all of us children gathered up our chairs and sat around the stove with our feet in the open oven. Certainly in winter our feet were always cold.

It was by this stove that we took our weekly bath in a round tub, all using the same water with more being added as the older ones got in. We didn't wash our hair very often during the winter. Bricks were heated on this stove for our beds at night.

In this kitchen we made snow cream. We'd beat up some eggs, add a little sugar and vanilla, cream, or milk and cream, and pure white snow. The air wasn't polluted like it is today. This was made in a very large kettle or dishpan.

There was a very dilapidated couch along the north wall. Here is where a sick child would lay. After I was married in the U.S. and went back to visit I changed our boys' diapers on this same couch. That was 1941, 1944, 1945. Tramps often came to our door. Summer times they slept in the haymow, winter times they slept on this couch. One time during summer one came and fell off the straight-up ladder to the haymow and spent at least a week on this couch as he had broken a rib. A salesman of pots and pans came one day, and my folks bought some

'Wear Ever' products and they did last. I still now in 1982 have the water dipper we all used hanging it in the water pail.

There were no curtains in our kitchen as there wasn't any money. Later we made some from feed bags. Feed bags were also used for tea towels and sacks for dish cloths. The walls of the kitchen were never finished yet when I left home to come to the U.S. in 1937. The two-by-fours were there with the outside boards. I do not know if there was any tarpaper and another layer before the very outside boards. I do know that in winter snow came in cracks and in summer dust from dust storms filtered in.

One of the most repulsive conditions in the summer in the kitchen were droves of flies not only on walls and ceiling but they got in the food – many were taken out of milk or food before eating. It's a wonder we didn't all get something terrible. We got the usual communicable diseases. For the flies we put up stickers and fly paper but they still came in. Often our screen doors had holes and no money for new ones. To rid the kitchen of flies a bunch of us children got used tea towels and started at the north end and drove the flies to the south where one of us opened the door. We did this several times. They never did get all out.

We had fun in this kitchen especially in the winter. It was the only warm room. The stove in the living room was small and held the fire poorly. For fun we children lined up the chairs (there were ten of us counting the hired man) around the wall. We'd put papa's chair at the north end as it was shaped different and had arm rests. His chair was the train engine. The other chairs were the coaches and we'd go on many an imaginary train ride. Little did I know then that in 1937 when I left home that I'd take a real train ride to U.S. and a few years later my brother Edward and I took a train ride to Nippon, Indiana to visit aunts, uncles and cousins. Another game we played was musical chairs.

It was in the kitchen that my dad brought in the harness (horse) to mend in wintertime. Our shoes were mended here. He had a real cobbler's outfit, including several different size stands to take care of different size shoes.

When I was twelve or thirteen my mother was not well. There was one baby right after another and miscarriages. The folks slept in a room north end of the house. Sometimes some of us children slept in the living room. My mother, we called her "Mama" would call to me in the middle of the night. I would go to her bedside. She asked me to fix her some warm milk as her stomach was empty (we hadn't much to eat) and she couldn't sleep. So I went to the kitchen. There wasn't time to build a fire in the coal and wood stove. She (mom) told me to light the lamp, pour some milk in a pan and hold it up over the flame. This I did many times during several years. My dad did not do this as he had an artificial leg and it would have been quite a chore getting it on and the harness on.

There was a brown cupboard in the kitchen. I was around three or five years old and decided to hide so crawled in the cupboard and pulled the doors shut from the inside. It was not airtight. Soon Mama missed me as did the others, they called and called but I did not answer. When I heard how really worried they were sounding I came out. I do not know why I hid. I do not remember being spanked. I remember Mama talking to me about it and not to do that again.

Behind the stove in the spring especially often were boxes of chicks – sick and blinded from the dust storms. I ran out when I saw a storm coming to save as many chicks as possible and tried to wipe caked dust from their eyes and put them behind the stove. In the winter many a half-frozen piggy lay in a box behind the stove. Our winter boots and wet pants or socks or overalls were hung or placed behind the stove that was the wash room that I mentioned earlier. Half-frozen calves were taken down stairs to thaw out. The cellar had a dirt floor. Horse bits hung in the wash room in the winter so they would not hurt the horses' mouths (by) pulling their skin on cold bits. Some farmers did not do this. Many a horse's mouth bled as the ice cold bridle bit was forced in its mouth as the skin pulled off.

I got really scared one night when I was up to fix milk for my Mama when I opened the kitchen door I saw what seemed a man sitting in a chair at the south end of the kitchen. His hat was pulled over his eyes. My heart leaped. The figure did not move. Shaking I got the lamp lit then saw it was papa's overcoat with his cap on top. Often in winter our dog, Carlo, (black and a little white) slept on an old rug in the kitchen.

One spring when I was thirteen, my mother and two of the children, Ruth and Robert, went to the U.S. to see her relatives. I stayed home from school one day a week to do the washing. We used to have a cradle type washer and tubs and board, then got a hand wringer but by the time I was thirteen the folks got a Maytag gas washing machine. It took many months to pay for it. So it was with the gas Maytag I tried to do the washing. One time the engine stopped on me. My dad and hired man were way out in the field, my older sister and older brother and my younger sister and three brothers were in school. It ended that I did the wash by hand. Oh what a mess! We wore the same clothes all week and had a clean set for Sunday, so we girls usually had two or three dresses each for school plus a nicer one for Sunday.

It was in this kitchen I learned to make bread and did so. Mrs. Haag, our neighbor, baked bread for us while Mama was gone. The long kitchen table was a significant piece of furniture. It stretched north to south. Papa sat in his armchair with a cushion on at the north end. The hired man (we always had a hired man because of papa's wooden leg) sat at the south end. My four brothers sat behind the table along the east wall and Mama and us three girls on the west side. I often sat at the end near where the hired man sat. One hired man tried to put his hand over mine when he thought no one was looking.

For table grace we usually sang. The only two songs that I can remember were "Holy, Holy, Holy, Lord God Almighty" sung at breakfast and "Where is My Wandering Boy Tonight?" Papa had us sing "Where is my wandering girl tonight" since there were three of us girls. I often wondered if any of us would really get lost.

Of course the kitchen table is where we did homework. Papa helped us. It was hard. Many a session ended in tears. Dishes were washed on this table. Often there was no rinse water. Our pump was at the barn, which was a long way from the house, and we pumped a long time before the water got to the top of the pipe to come out. Of course all dishwater was saved for slop for the hogs.

It was hard to see to cook or sew or do homework with lamplight. It sure was a dirty job cleaning the lamp and lantern chimneys.

Since papa had only one good leg and not too good an artificial one, he often peeled the potatoes. We ate sixty-five bushels a year if we could raise that much. I was sent down stairs often after them and hated that job, as it was dark. The floor and walls were dirt. The spuds were in a hole hollowed out of the floor dirt. Even though I took a lamp or went down by guessing my way feeling it was scary as often the potatoes were rotting or there were slimy salamanders among them. One time when Daddy carried a half frozen calf down, I lit a lamp to go see how it was doing. One of my sisters came with me. We got to the landing and the light shone and reflected in the calf's eyes only we didn't know our light caused these two big eyes to glare at us. We got so frightened we almost dropped the lamp as we went upstairs as fast as we could. We were sure there was a monster down there. Our brothers tried to tell us it was the calf.

We had no other room for eating like a dining room so all Sunday company, all evangelists, all our friends, whoever – ate in the kitchen. One time my Sunday School class came to dinner. We had pumpkin pudding for dessert and I had forgotten to put any sugar in it. Most of the time we didn't have desserts as there wasn't any money for sugar.

It often was cold in all other rooms in the house. We ran fast after something and hurried back. One time my fingers got caught in the door. My how that hurt.

Mending and sewing of clothes was done in the kitchen. Neighbors came in the kitchen door. The linoleum on the floor soon got worn, then looked black and ugly as did the white table oilcloth. It was always a great day when we could afford a new tablecloth and new linoleum.

In the pantry off the kitchen was a big cupboard. Seemed awfly high to me. One time I hid a deck of real playing cards up on the top shelf using a chair to reach it. Now we were forbidden to play or touch cards, even Rook. We played Rook in school at recess time but never told the folks. I got these real sin cards out of an old suitcase one of our hired men left. After a few days my conscience bothered me so I put these sin cards in the stove.

I still dream of building fire in the stove as I often did, of making all those school lunches (6), I figured my older sister could make her own. They were peanut butter and honey on homemade bread nearly all the time. My older brother preferred peanut butter. It was in the kitchen we ate shredded wheat on Sunday morning, got an orange for Christmas, opened relief boxes of second-hand clothes including shoes from uncles and aunts in the States.

It was in the kitchen that anyone who needed it got a hair cut. We never liked Daddy to cut us girls' hair so we did each others.

Butter churning was done in the kitchen. Not the stomp type but the barrel type. At times Mama let us have a plate of thick cream when it got to that stage. Some times we sprinkled a little sugar on it. Of course we ate the cream or bits of butter that splashed outside the lid. We also had a drink of buttermilk once it was done.

One time Mama was talking to me and I started singing. She then said it isn't polite to start singing or talking when someone is talking to you. I did not do it on purpose but often broke out in songs. Later many years after I'd come to the U.S., was married, and visited her, my dad had died and Mama lived in Calgary, I asked her what she remembered about me. She said I brought happiness to them with my spontaneous singing.

I left home in 1933 to go to Calgary for the rest of high school. Grade nine was taken nine miles away in Kathyrn, a small cow town. I was born 1918 in a shack on someone else's farm. Later Dad bought a farm where the old church house was and moved it down to become our first home. The kitchen including pantry and wash room and upstairs bedroom over the kitchen was started soon after and was never all finished when the farm got paid off twenty years later. I was gone by then.

Eventually both parents died. My younger brother bought the farm, now being married. They moved to another farm south – the old Haag place – when they bought that farm also. Eventually my (old) home became a storage place for grain and some years after that it was all torn down including all the farm buildings. But the memories of activities in the kitchen are very vivid, as are memories of the whole place – the school – the church – the community...

"Put on your old gray bonnet,
With the blue ribbons on it,
And I'll hitch old dobbin to the shay.
Through the fields of clover
We will ride through the dover
On our golden wedding day."
(Murphy and Wenrich, Traditional)

CHAPTER 7

CHRISTMAS IN OUR CHILDHOOD DAYS

Can grandparents remember how long a school holiday their grandchild had at Christmas and New Years? I'm guessing we had two weeks. Every school held a Christmas program prior to the closing, and all the children participated. Sometimes it would be group singing, recitations, plays, or other acts. Families tried to attend the programs at all the neighborhood schools.

Ever hear of the song "Put On Your Old Gray Bonnet?" This one particular event still sticks with me. I was in the eighth grade when the teacher had the sixth grade boy, Kenneth Yates, join me in acting out, in simple motions, and singing this song at our school Christmas program. Thank goodness we had no tape recording in those days, because I don't want to know what my singing sounded like.

Our schoolteacher always gave each child a small present at our Christmas programs. Santa presented them at the end of the evening program. I cannot remember any particular gift I received at school – probably a book or crayons. At one time I did have a small celluloid doll and a big cloth doll with porcelain face. I believe the big one came from Maryland relatives and the little one from Santa. I hardly ever played with either one.

Of course we all got a small paper bag of candy from the church as well as from the school. Each bag had a few nuts, mostly peanuts, though I do remember later on we used a nutcracker, so there must have been some other kind, probably walnuts. And every bag had one apple and one orange – making two of each – the only time of the year that I recall that we got fruit! To my knowledge, we never got bananas.

And what gifts did we get at home? Neither Robert nor I can recall any Christmas gift received as a child. I remember a gift from Daddy, but I believe it was for my sixteenth birthday, rather than Christmas. It was a set of glass salt and pepper shakers on a metal stand. How proud I am to still have the shakers today. (I am stymied and sad over the loss of the stand. I know I had it for many years, and think it must have been lost in one of my last moves, probably from Cumberland, Maryland to York, Pennsylvania in 1974.) It was daddy's way of saying, "I know you're going to have your own home some day, so here's a gift for your future."

It is quite possible that the Maryland folks sent us children small gifts. They often sent used clothing and even shoes, and I would guess this was usually done at Christmas time. Perhaps they sent some boys stuff too. While we girls appreciated the dresses our aunts sent us, the styles were for much older women. We had to hide our embarrassment, although some of the neighbor children were in the same fix as we were. Once a neighbor girl looked scathingly at me in a dress I had never worn before and said to her mother, "Isn't that my old dress you threw out?" I would guess her mother was even more embarrassed than Mama or I.

One of the coats that Elizabeth got was a black and white checked pattern of three-quarter length. It eventually became my coat. It would have been fine for an adult woman, but not for us just entering our teens. My very first new winter coat was the one I bought after I had my first job in 1943. It was a beautiful teal blue with a lovely fur collar, and fit me to a tee!

It is the gifts my brothers, Raymond and Paul, received when I was five or six years old that I clearly remember. That summer Mama had given me a length of white elastic with blue flowers on it and said I could have it for doll clothes. That Christmas, she asked me if I still had the elastic and if so could she have it back. I hadn't made any use of it for my dolls so I willingly gave it back to her.

Christmas day I found out what she had done with it. My brother Paul got new white and blue figured elastic armbands! That's all he got. But I felt so sorry for my brother, Raymond, a year older than Paul, who got a dime. Not something to play with and you couldn't get anything at the local country store nine miles away until your folks went, which wasn't very often. I have no idea what the other siblings or I received. I've always declared that I was born old; not the happy child some youngsters are. I do remember playing house up in our attic, and maybe I set up the dolls there. The steps to the attic were between the two-by-fours so the climb was one hundred percent vertical. Fortunately I never fell.

For Christmas dinner we ate chicken, mashed potatoes, and stuffing and maybe some pie – a real treat. Eventually we also had Copes Dried Sweet Corn casserole, using corn sent to us by our Maryland relatives. Dried sweet corn is generally unknown outside of Pennsylvania, where the Copes factory is, but today I often place a direct order to Copes and make this dish for church or group dinners.

"O Christmas tree, O Christmas tree,
How lovely are thy branches."
(Traditional)

CHAPTER 8

MY MOST MEMORABLE CHRISTMAS

In a faraway place way up north in Alberta where it was very cold, and hardly any trees to shield one from the cold winds, there where the snow drifts often three to four feet high, a little boy, Robert, and his older sister, Ruth, along with their brothers and sisters lived with their parents on a farm near Calgary, Alberta.

They lived in an old farmhouse where they could see for miles and miles because the land was very flat with very few trees. In fact, when there was a mirage, they could see the train going through the wheat fields some eleven miles away, and the one-room schoolhouse looked close though it was four miles away. The children often walked to school, but sometimes they rode in a cart and some of them rode a horse.

Now in those long-ago days, there was no janitor for the one-room schoolhouse, so the teacher would hire an older student to sweep the floor, empty the wastebasket, and wipe the blackboards. And when any older students got to school before the teacher, they would go to the basement and stoke the furnace.

In 1935, when Ruth was twelve in the seventh grade, she was the oldest student in her school, Hawthorn, and the teacher hired her at ten cents a week to do the janitorial work each day after school.

Ruth would give her little brother, Robert, who was ten, a few pennies each week to empty the waste cans and clean the blackboards and the brushes. Ruth swept the floor and the two outhouses.

In those days every school put on a Christmas concert and children and parents from other school districts attended each other's concerts. So Ruth and Robert also had to clean the schoolroom after the Christmas school party, and this is what happened when she was twelve years old and Robert was ten.

"Hurry up, Robert, get Madge hitched to the cart so we can get off to school as soon as I get these sandwiches made for our lunch," Ruth called to him just as soon as he had finished breakfast. She reminded him that "The school might still be a little warm and it's going to take us five or six hours before we get back home, and we're not to add any coal to the furnace."

"What do you think Miss Anderson is going to give us for doing all this work by ourselves?" Robert asked as they jogged along in the old cart.

"She didn't say," answered Ruth, "but you know how nice she's always been to us and last week she brought me two books from the city library instead of just one." And then she added, "Besides, we'd just have to work at home today if we weren't helping the teacher."

The children decided to warm up a bit first by sweeping the desk area; then they would take the ornaments off the tree. If the school was fortunate to have electricity, the Christmas tree would have tree lights, which always made the children happy, but Hawthorn didn't have electricity yet so there were no light strings to remove.

"Boy, I wish we had decorations like this," Robert said, "but we don't even have a tree. We've never had a tree like some of my friends have!"

All of a sudden Ruth's eyes widened and she almost scared Robert by exclaiming, "Why don't we take this tree? We don't have to let it die outside here! We can take it home and use it for ourselves."

"But we don't have any decorations," Robert answered, though his eyes were saying, "That's a great idea, what does it matter, we'd at least have a tree!"

"We can leave all the tinsel on. Miss Anderson told me not to worry about removing that. And I heard her tell the superintendent that these real old scratched balls had to be replaced before next year. Can't we take at least a few of them?"

So the children carefully chose a few of the old decorations and found a paper bag to hold them.

"You know we're going to have to drag the tree behind the cart and the icicles will blow away or at least get all tangled. Shouldn't we take them off and put them in later?" That was Robert's idea.

The children chatted excitedly, while picking off the streamers, and wondered how they could get the tree home without being seen – and could they hide it somewhere until Christmas Day? Surprising the family was the best part of all. They decided they should get back home when it was getting dark and could more easily hide the tree somewhere. While they pondered this problem, they kept on working and stopped to eat lunch. Then they realized that the work was going to take them longer than either they or their parents expected, so they wouldn't have to lie about any cause for being late getting home. What a relief – because fibbing was a real no-no.

When Robert came back from feeding Madge, he was all smiles. "I think we can push the tree trunk far enough under the cart seat from the back and let the tree hang out so it doesn't drag on the ground."

Ruth was glad for this idea. She was already frowning over all the problems that their surprise would raise if someone found out about it ahead of time. At least they would have a tree this year just as many of their friends did.

Well, the tree was carefully hauled home and hidden safely on the far side of the closest haystack, with some straw thrown over it so that the green branches and glistening icicles wouldn't show. And during those next few days, Robert and Ruth cut out pretty colored pictures from the old Sears catalog and put strings on them so they could be hung from the tree. And Ruth made a sign that read "HOME SWEET HOME" from colored letters from the catalog.

On Christmas Eve, Robert really hurried with his outside chores, so that when it was just dark and the other boys were ready to leave the barn and go into the house, he ran to the haystack and dragged the tree up to the shed by the house. Ruth got all the decorations from their hiding place and hid them downstairs, way back in the kitchen cupboard so they would be handy just a short time later.

When farm folks go to bed, they are really tired, so while the rest of the family went to sleep, Ruth and Robert sneaked the tree into the kitchen and decorated it there in the pale lamp light.

What a surprise when their older brothers and sisters and parents opened the kitchen door in the morning! Their shouting wakened both Robert and Ruth. And not only was the tree a great surprise but to think that the two youngest children thought of this and carried it out successfully!

Everyone pulled up their chairs and ate their oatmeal around the tree. Then the older boys carried the tree into the living room. Everyone gathered around the tree and sang Christmas carols while Elizabeth played the old reed organ. Robert and Ruth sang the loudest of all because they were so happy with their surprise gift to their family!

"A family tree is like riding in a train backwards:
it shows you were you came from,
but not where you are going."
(Evan Esars, <u>20,000 Quips & Quotes.</u>)

CHAPTER 9

MARYLAND RELATIVES VISIT US

Some of the details of our life are vague after eighty-four years, but it's interesting to read an outsider's memory of her visit in 1933. My cousin, Hazel Beard, wrote this account of her family's visit to see us, and it echoes my own memories very clearly and strongly.

CANADIAN TRIP 1933
By our Maryland cousin, Hazel Beard

In the spring of 1933, at the height of the Great Depression, my father had lost money in the stock market. However, he still had three hundred dollars in the bank. He was determined to use that money to take a trip by car to Alberta, Canada where his older brother, David Beard, had homesteaded some years earlier.

From time to time, Uncle David or Aunt Martha, his wife, would write long letters about their life in Canada. When a letter came, we would go to Grandmother Beard's on a Sunday afternoon, Aunt Cora who lived in Washington D.C. might be there and she would read the letter aloud. Life in Canada was not an easy one and I recall that my aunts would prepare a box of blankets and perhaps some clothing to send to Canada.

The car we traveled in was a 1928 Buick with a luggage carrier on the back, no trunk. My sister, Elsie, then three years old was to stay with our mother's sister and husband, Aunt Nellie and Uncle Charles Hull, on their farm near New Windsor, MD. My brother Harold (11 years old), my brother Paul, (7) and I (13) and our parents started out the latter part of May. We children would miss the final two weeks of school but our teachers said that we would learn more on this trip than during those last two weeks in classes. I did miss my 7th grade graduation, not a big event in my life.

Mother packed dishes and pans that we would use for cooking in the cabins where we would have to stay overnight and could do our own cooking. There were times when we stayed in "tourist homes." Also the necessary clothes and all were carefully placed on the luggage carrier. Daddy placed water bags on the fenders in case, for when the motor got too hot in going up mountains. I recall the first mountain to climb was the Tuscarora in Pennsylvania.

The roads through Pennsylvania were hilly and twisting in many places. It took us quite a long time to get through Pittsburgh. Our route took us through West Virginia, then Ohio, and the farmland of Indiana and Illinois. We skirted Chicago and headed north through Wisconsin. In the Chicago area, as we traveled, the traffic kept getting heavier and heavier and Daddy was getting quite frustrated. I looked up and saw a sign that said "Cermak Road." At that time, the mayor of Chicago was named Cermak and when I called attention to what I saw, my father realized that he was driving into the city instead of around it. To say that he was annoyed with the situation is putting it mildly.

After leaving the Chicago area, none of the roads was paved. Riding on them was like traveling on a washboard. In addition, there were holes where prairie dogs, or gophers lived and we would see them popping their heads up to look around. In the evening, after stopping for the night, Mother would get the box of pans and dishes and prepare the evening meal. Before any preparation began, the dishes had to be washed and after the meal, they were washed again and repacked.

We stopped at a place called Wisconsin Dells where we were attacked by the largest mosquitoes we ever saw. For years after, when we saw a particularly large one, we would say that it must have come from the Wisconsin Dells.

It was a long trek from Chicago to Alberta, going through Saskatchewan and on to Uncle David's. My father would get quite tired, especially his eyes. I recall that on occasion, he had me sit on his lap to steer while he would rest his eyes. The land was very flat and the roads relatively straight. I felt very grown-up when I steered.

Sometimes, at noon, we would eat in a restaurant. One particular day, we had spare ribs and sauerkraut. My father thought the meal was wonderful and I believe left a tip. He had bones with a lot of meat on them but the rest of us had "bones." My mother always said that the waitress was very smart to give my father the best portion of meat.

Uncle David and Aunt Martha had homesteaded about thirty miles west of Calgary. There were seven children in the family: Edward, Barbara, Elizabeth, Raymond, Paul, Ruth and Robert. The house was a frame house, two stories, the upper one being papered with newspaper. My first impression was of the distinct odor as we went in through the kitchen. I learned later that it was from the cream separator that was right inside the kitchen door. In order to accommodate everyone for sleeping, the boys slept in the haymow and the rest of us slept upstairs in the house.

The relatively large kitchen had a cookstove and a table with a long bench against the wall. It was quite a feat to feed fourteen people each meal. In the "front room" there was a piano, which Elizabeth played. She explained to me in a confident manner the materials and method used by her teacher.

At about 9:30PM, while the sun was still shining, Aunt Martha said that it was time to go to bed. I was quite surprised that we would go to bed while the sun was still very visible. It took me awhile to understand that being that far north, the sun doesn't set in the summer until much later than in Maryland.

The Canadian children were still in school and Edward, the oldest, drove an open touring-like car, being concerned about whether the car would make it up the "hill" that had to be negotiated. I was still looking for the hill when we got to the school. From my perspective, it was what we might call a "rise" in the road. The car "made it." He also pointed out some aspects of the land and where the water flowed.

When we got to the school, we were introduced to the teacher. My father had come to the school also and I remember being concerned because the teacher said that my father looked like King George. I thought she was making a pass at him. How naïve I was to mistake a compliment for a pass.

The school was a one-room building and was so different from what we had in Maryland. I was impressed with the structured curriculum and the way that the different grades were accommodated. I seem to remember a pot-bellied stove in the middle of the schoolroom.

One of the things that I remember so distinctly is that, while Uncle David and family were not rich in material possessions and equipment, they showed us the various aspects of their life with pride in their voices and countenance. I had the impression that they were all, especially Uncle David, trying to prove the value of having homesteaded.

One day during our visit, we all went to Calgary to see a rodeo. We must have taken two cars and congregated together on the sidewalk near the rodeo grounds. I recall a very distinctive looking man with a cane and wanting to walk through where we were standing. In a very dignified way, he simply took his cane and moved it back and forth to clear the path for him to walk. I can still picture that scene in my mind.

I didn't enjoy the rodeo because it seemed such a cruel way to treat the animals. At another time, Uncle David offered to show me how to catch a gopher, also known as a prairie dog who burrowed to his underground home. We were in the front yard and Uncle David placed a loop over the gopher hole. When the gopher poked his head up through the hole, I was to pull the string around its neck. I followed directions and did catch one unlucky creature. However, I was more scared than the gopher and ran through the yard with gopher in tow, screaming at the top of my voice. Poor gopher!!

One evening, at mealtime, Aunt Martha made the observation that three cars had gone past their place that day. She said that maybe they would have to move farther back from the road because traffic was getting too heavy.

We went to church on Sunday morning, the very small Irricana Church of the Brethren, I think it was called. Uncle David was the pastor. I still have the picture in my mind of when he walked up the steps to the pulpit. As I recall he had trouble negotiating the steps because of being physically impaired.

It is my understanding that he lost a leg because of having had tuberculosis in it when he was a young man. He walked with the aid of a wooden leg, which made him limp somewhat as he walked.

Many of the church members had also homesteaded in the area and there seemed to be quite a friendly feeling among them. They welcomed us warmly and I have a happy recollection of being at the church.

Dad wanted us to go to Lake Louise, 80 miles to the west. My mother felt that she needed to rest from riding and so we didn't take that trip. I was sure that my life would never be complete because of not getting to Lake Louise. I am happy to say that I have been there twice since then and feel fulfilled. The same could be said about visiting a petrified forest. My father didn't want to stop there. Gratefully, I have since seen a petrified forest more than once.

    We have a number of pictures taken during our visit to Uncle David and his family. As I look at them now, I am aware of how many are no longer living. Life does move on with us and then without us. After leaving Canada, we headed to Glacier National Park where my father was eager to drive up Logan's Pass to the Continental Divide.

"Holy, holy, holy
Lord God Almighty
Early in the morning
Our song shall rise to thee."
(Reginald Heber, <u>Holy, Holy, Holy.</u>)

CHAPTER 10

OUR CHURCH: FIRST IRRICANA CHURCH OF THE BRETHREN

My knowledge of the history of the Church of the Brethren does not come from childhood memories, and I'm indebted to others who have properly researched it, or recorded information that will give the reader useful and, I hope, interesting background information. Some comes from Albert Hollinger's thesis in partial requirement for the Degree of Bachelor of Divinity, May 1943, and some descriptions are included from Mrs. Mae Gump and Mary Culp who submitted articles to "KIK Country."

Hollinger, in his paper, writes, "The earliest Brethren pioneer to establish a home in the Irricana district church was Charles C. Gump, formerly of Dayton, Ohio…in March of 1909." And Charles Gump writes, "As we look back over the early days it seems that each day brought new experiences, new joys as well as sorrows. As we were the first family of the church to settle in this district it was quite a joy to learn that several Brethren families were planning on moving to this locality in the Fall of 1909. Elder J.A. Weaver and wife, and brother J.S. Culp and family arrived in November 1909. Others followed in the spring of 1910."

Gladys Muir, a La Verne College professor and author of <u>Settlement of the Brethren on the Pacific Slope</u>, writes that a Brethren Church

Council, in 1914, appointed a committee to work with the Canadian Pacific Railway Company. The Railway Company was asked to make offers to immigrants to locate in the area where Brethren churches were already organized. This was close to where Daddy had been with Henry Harvey in 1910. Daddy and other families, mainly ministers, did move there and worked to build a new church in 1918.

Gump also tells of the first service in 1910: "Elder J.A. Weaver and wife, and J.S. Culp and family left their homes on a Sunday morning late in April or early in May of 1910 driving in a Northeast direction. The Victor Barnharts and our family went in a Southeast direction. We met near the present site of the church. A tent was pitched and Sunday School service held. The Miller family was also present and Brother H. Miller on that day donated the land where the church now stands. Plans were also made for the hauling of lumber and by the following Sunday services were held in the newly constructed building."

Miller states the cost of lumber was $125, a definite hardship in those days. On June 25 they organized, and Daddy was named superintendent of the Sunday School. Within seven years, the membership had grown to eighty-three, and on July 6, 1918, the decision was made to build a new church the next summer.

We know that Daddy had returned to the States in 1911 and then back to Canada in late 1917. It seems evident that while Daddy did not give them this property, he did not make them move. Perhaps he got the old church building free since it was hauled down to become our first home. This new church building was dedicated October 19, 1919, and membership was 110. Along with many others, Daddy was mentioned as serving in this free ministry. It was not until many years later that paid ministry was possible. Daddy's obituary states that he served twenty-two years as church clerk at the First Irricana church.

First Irricana Church of the Brethren, front entrance

North side, showing coal chute, rear entrance.
Cemetery, unseen, to the right

The coal chute can be seen in this second picture, but not the front steps leading to the main room, nor can you see the roof spacing where we would stand and yell across the open fields. The back door led to the steps down to the basement as well as to the front of the sanctuary.

Photographs of the interior are not available. The pulpit area, located at the southwest corner, was raised and spread across this area, thus permitting better viewing from all sides of the main room as well as from the adjacent classrooms. Daddy said he helped design the church, and it was he who suggested the side classrooms be on an angle and have folding doors facing the main room so that large audiences could be accommodated. Unseen in these photos but further west was the graveyard, and adjacent to the cemetery were the two outhouses.[5]

During my trip to Calgary in 2002, my niece Gael took me to our childhood farm area and I went inside the church. Of course it appeared to me to be very small compared to my memories as a youngster. There were about five rows of seats on both sides of the center aisle. I could not envision it even accommodating a hundred and ten people.[6]

---

[5] I've been told that just recently inside restrooms have been added, but I do not know where they were placed, nor do I know where or when running water was made available. Electricity and phone lines have also been added.

[6] About ten years ago when I was watching a TV program when the announcer was describing the movie "In Cold Blood," and suddenly there appeared my childhood church on the screen. To say I was startled is far too mild a statement. I literally jumped and stood with mouth and eyes wide open. Then I wondered if our 1918 leaders had gone to Kansas to get plans for our church, or if the movie folks had come up to Irricana. The latter was true.

An article in the Crossfield/Irricana isssue of the Rocky View Weekly, June 18, 1996, described the need to find a stand-in church during the remaking of this film. So it was only during this revision period that our church was used. The film company erected a cross on the outside upper story and another inside to the right of the pulpit, both left as donations after filming. By this time the church was no longer a Church of the Brethren congregation but had been turned over to the United Church of Canada. I think it was in 1969 that it was named a historic site. While others may appreciate the addition of the crosses, I dislike it, as it destroyed my childhood memories of my church.

The original plans had a baptismal pit accessible by removing floor panels from the pulpit area, but this turned out to be seldom used. A nearby stream was easier to use, and evangelistic services were held in warm weather so stream baptism was possible. The west and south windows were brown stained glass so that the bright sun did not cause problems.

A full basement, with a small coal bin, had concrete walls at a later date but not while I lived at home. The northern view of the church shows the coal chute where kids often slid down into the basement for fun instead of using ordinary entrances, which in those days were never locked, as they were in 2002.

One flight of stairs was immediately inside the front door to the right along the northern wall beneath the stairs leading to the second floor. Another flight was at the front of the sanctuary to the far right of the pulpit area and led down to the kitchen area. This meant the young people could go up to the balcony without ever coming into the sanctuary, and thus the adults down below may not know which youngsters were present.

A dumbwaiter in the classroom closest to the back stairs could be drawn down to the basement kitchen. Perhaps this chute was used during love feast services for the utensils needed, and supply of fruit juice, but it was not used on any regular basis.

By the time Edward was a teenager, a tennis court and baseball diamond were available, both close to our property line. Caragana bushes were on our side of the dividing fence. (This type bush was native to China but now were beginning to spread to other areas with similar climates.)

When Robert and I were young, we sat in the front pew with Daddy who was the song leader. When the organist was not present, he would use his tuning fork. Of course the organ was a reed organ, and many years later a piano was also available. Daddy had a good strong voice and none of the song leaders used any hand directing motions. Daddy could read shape notes, the usual formatting in those days. He would fill the pulpit at times but never as a hired minister, or full-time.

Young children sat with their parents and were kept quiet, usually by coloring or perhaps reading a book they had brought with them. We children had own Sunday School classes, but everyone gathered in the sanctuary for the main service. It was during these early years of having to sit through adult services that I got in the habit of daydreaming during the minister's talk, as did many other youngsters. (This is a habit that is hard to break, and believe it or not, it is very difficult today to keep my mind and attention on the sermon – a different atmosphere from a political speech or a civic meeting. Even today at my own Unitarian Universalist church I reason that children should have their own services and not be required to attend adult services even for fifteen minutes, although an occasional special program or holiday might be quite appropriate.)

At my home church, we were often short of teachers, and when I was in grade eight, I was asked to teach the grade one Sunday School class. My students were the twin Longson boys. No reflection on these delightful twins, but I did not enjoy this task. There were no other children my age, and thus no class for my age group. I was at the in-between age and not yet ready to join the high school class. Each summer we had a week of Vacation Bible School.

I have never heard of any other denomination or church playing Bible Baseball. (Perhaps Daddy was not the one who thought it up, but it would not surprise me if he were.) In Bible Baseball, the participants comprised two teams, and four bases were set up within the main room rather than the basement in order that the audience could be comfortably seated. As a question was answered correctly, the participant would walk to the next base. What originality was needed to plan a system for the traditional three outs! I doubt anyone remembers the reward or recognition given to the winning team.

During the year, there were dinners held at church, and picnics during summer, and some occasional special programs also. The one of most interest and importance to me was a recitation contest offered when I was about nine or ten years old. There were five contestants, including Paul and myself. Because we two Beards were participants, Daddy was not one of the judges, though he sat at the back of the room near the chosen judges. As I was called to go to the front, Daddy smiled broadly at me and said with the most encouraging attitude, "Go to it, old boy." Yes, I was Daddy's boy! And his expression of confidence "Go to it, old boy" gave me the needed push especially when I was competing against Paul. Mama constantly heard my complaint of "I wish I were a boy," or "I wish you'd never had me."

Well, now I had Daddy's encouragement with "Go to it, old boy," and when the judges went forward to announce the winner, we five contestants held our breath. I won, and Daddy proudly proclaimed, "You did it, old boy, you did it!" This is the one compliment in my youth that I remember from him, although I know he encouraged me in many ways. And of course winning over Paul really added to my pleasure.

Daddy had worked with both Paul and me on our recitations; he always stressed good elocution and public speaking. Even today, it comes to my mind most Sundays when the speaker is not using an amplifier, that Daddy could teach that person how to project his or her voice to be heard from the front to the back of the auditorium. He would not be satisfied until success had been reached, although he might have to allow for aged voices. Here's the poem I recited, author unknown. This poem reflects much of the Church's philosophy; do read it with that in mind.

PEACE ON EARTH

The men of the earth said "We must war
As the men of the earth have warred;
'Tis ours to wield on the battlefield
The unrelenting sword.
But they who had seen the valiant die,
The fathers of men, they answered 'why?'

The men of the earth said: "We must arm
For so we would reveal
The nobler part of the human heart
The love of the nations weal."
But they who had sung their lullaby,
The mothers of men, they answered 'why?'

The men of the earth said: "We must fight
For so the fit survive,
By the jungle law of fang and claw
The strong are kept alive."
But a crippled, cankered progeny,
The son of the fighters, they answered 'why?'

The men of the earth said: "We must fall,
And falling build the road
O'er which the race with quickening pace
Can find its way to God."
But down from a cross uplifted high,
The Savior of men, He answered 'Why?'

I do not recall the church ever holding another contest during later years.

Edward and Barbara had already joined the church when Elizabeth joined at age nine. Even then she felt called to the ministry but due to circumstances at home, she stifled this call; it remained unknown to most of us for many years.

It was the custom in many steps of life, to go in sequence of age, so I felt it only proper that summer day to wait until my older brother Paul had joined. The evangelist Paul Weaver, up from the States, had entitled his sermon "What Would Jesus Do?" At twelve years old, I told myself, "Well, Jesus would go forward and join." But I had to wait for Paul. And when he did, I thought, "I'm going to wait until we get to the chorus." When the audience began the second time to sing, "Going home, I am going home," I went up to the front row to indicate I was ready to join.

Baptism came soon thereafter, and took place in the creek close by. As one kneels in the water, the minister or evangelist dunks the head of the kneeling applicant forward, three times, "In the name of the Father," "the Son," and "the Holy Ghost." That was enough "water in the face" when one did not know how to swim!

Once a year, probably after the baptismal services, but at least in good weather, a Love Feast was held. This Feast was a simple church supper. Red grape juice was served, not wine. Prior to the supper was a short religious talk and of course the washing of feet. The men sat on one side of the aisle and women on the other. The person knelt to carry out the ritual of washing the feet of the person sitting next to them. "Washing" of course just meant dipping each bare foot into the basin and then drying it. After a female joined the church, she was obliged to wear a prayer covering, not only at Love Feasts and Sunday services, but whenever grace or a prayer was said. Mama was not strict on this at home, but my mother-in-law was very consistent. I must have worn one at our Love Feasts but not at any other time, either at home or in my mother-in-law's home.

Two of my siblings were eventually buried in the church cemetery, Margaret in 1923, and Raymond in 1984. Of these two, only Raymond's grave has a marker. There were a few other unmarked graves that also remain unknown, at least to non-family members.

Raymond's grave stone, 1984

There was no Church of the Brethren in Calgary, so when I was in business school, I went to the same church as Barbara did, at least while I stayed that first year with them. I think it was a Presbyterian Church. Barbara and her husband, Edward, both sang in the choir, so Barbara insisted I sit with Gael and take care of her rather than sitting with the young people. When I got my first job and moved to an apartment, I went to another church. I can remember Mama's disappointment when I told her I was now going to a Baptist church, but it was only for being with young people I knew, not because I had accepted any of their beliefs. This now makes me wonder if Mama's beliefs hadn't already become more liberal.

"School days, school days
Good old golden rule days
Readin' and 'riting and 'rithmetic
Talk to the tune of the hickory stick."
(Will Cobb, <u>School Days</u>.)

CHAPTER 11

ALBERTA SCHOOLS and CANADA'S EDUCATIONAL SYSTEM

How many children were punished with a harness strap out in the barn? And not only the hickory stick, but the leather horse straps! The hickory stick was really a ruler or a yardstick. I got one ruler punishment in the first grade and I never experienced standing in the corner as some students did.

The school year began the Monday after Labor Day, and ended June 30. Unlike the nine months or so here in the States, we attended ten full months with no snow days. All farm children in those days did so many chores at home that school did not start until 9:00AM and ended at 3:30PM, although for high schools the closing time was extended to 4:00PM. Lunch time was an hour. Fifteen-minute breaks in the morning and afternoon took care of one's "excuse me" needs.

Schools were closed for two weeks at Christmas. All grade schools had Christmas programs, and families attended as many as possible. It was one of the few "nights out" that any family had during the winter.

The inclusion of kindergarten came long after my time. A first grader was to be six years old by the beginning of the school year in September. Very likely the cut-off date extended to several months beyond that, as it would have caused a public outcry if a child turned six by November and had to wait another ten months before entering grade one. I turned six years old towards the end of March, so I was almost six-and-a-half when I started first grade.

The provincial ruling was that schools would be located so that no child would have more than four miles to travel those first eight years. High schools were approximately twice that distance apart. We lived right in the four-mile corner in one school district, which meant that we were also within four miles of the next public school.

Not all schools were exactly alike, but generally there were separate entrances for boys and girls, and this first area also provided the cloakrooms. Inside restrooms? Not on your life! And the outdoor ones were usually a good one hundred to two hundred yards from the school building entrances.

Each school had an outside water pump. The one at our Hawthorn school was next to the boys' entrance, and less than a quarter of a mile further were the barn and barnyard.

The girls' school entrance was on the north near the teacherage, a small cottage to house any non-residential teacher ten months a year, at least five days a week. The outhouses at Hawthorn were in a crisscross direction from the entrances: boys' entrance on the south towards the barn, with their outhouse to the north; the girls' outhouse was to the south. Why the outhouses were placed in just the opposite direction of the assigned entrances, I often wondered but never knew. It meant the trails from the entrances to the outhouses crossed paths. This could be embarrassing if any young boy and girl met at the same time at the crossing, though today our society has changed and most children, at least the older ones, would not be fazed at all. But today you would also have to look in the most remote areas to find these primitive bathrooms called outhouses!

Of course we had to raise a hand and ask permission from the teacher in order to leave the classroom during the school hours. I have no memory of any bathroom tissue at school, and am sure we had none. Had there been, no doubt we would have snitched some to take and use at home. Most likely we used newspaper or catalog pages as we did at home.

Schools were heated by wood and coal furnaces situated in a basement, with a register in the center of the room. While the teacher might start the furnace on a Sunday evening, often the first student who arrived each morning was expected to check and refuel the furnace as needed. As we all arrived in the cold morning, we would huddle on this center register, hardly large enough for more than six of us (but we'd squeeze together). When the teacher rang the bell at 9:00AM, we would go and stand beside our seats and soon thereafter be led by the teacher in morning exercises to warm us up.

One side of these one-room schoolhouses was almost completely windows, opened in warm weather; no fans nor air conditioners existed even in one's mind. I do not recall any blinds, but it is possible that Hawthorn had them even though the windows faced east.

The single-seat desks were set up in rows and nailed to runners with aisles between each row. Generally the younger children sat furthest from the windows, although I have no idea why. Their desks were lower and smaller and may have had no ink bottle hole. The stationary rows made it difficult to sweep beneath the seat, as I discovered when I began my two years as janitor in Grade Seven.

Each school also had a barn to house the horses and adjacent space to leave the carts or buggies which we farm kids used; very few parents brought their children to school via auto and then very infrequently.

Student enrollment was generally small because of the size of the farms and because the migration populations were just beginning to move in, either from the eastern part of Canada or from the western United States. Regardless of the enrollment in the early days, there was only one classroom for primary grades, and thus only one teacher for all eight grades, and the same structure was in place for the high schools.

This situation gradually changed, at least for the high schools: when I was in grade nine, we still had one room for all four grades, but a new building was erected by the next year. Then grades ten and eleven would be in one room, and grades nine and twelve in the other. The two teachers would transfer according to their teaching ability of the standard subjects. Generally the high school teachers were male, and men and women might be teachers at the lower grade levels. Even in these one-room buildings, the high schools had a small chemistry or lab area, and eventually a small area set aside for typing classes.

Typically in the newer two classroom buildings, there were two small classrooms in the basement – one for Home Economics for the girls, and one for Shop for the boys. We had a female teacher for Home Economics in high school but not for the other subjects, so she was part-time – and probably taught the lower grades in the adjacent public school.

At some time it was ruled that a local doctor would come to the school each year and conduct a minor examination of each and every student. I do not remember such an event until I was at least in fifth or sixth grade, when I was very embarrassed having to remove my petticoat. Perhaps it was during this annual event that alerted the teacher and my parents that I needed further eye examination. Many times I asked Robert, who sat behind me in my row, to read the blackboard writing to me. Yes, I definitely needed glasses.

A School Inspector, provincially licensed, also visited each year, unannounced to the student body (and perhaps also to the teacher, because both positions were evaluated.)

One of the two major differences between Canada and the United States when it came to education was in the final exam system. All grade nine students throughout the entire dominion took the same final exam, prepared by off-site teachers, for all required subjects; the local teachers did the grading and issued the report cards.

However, non-local teachers prepared the grade twelve final exams for all subjects, and non-local teachers graded them. Hence, a teacher in Saskatchewan may have prepared the questions, and a teacher in Ottawa graded the final tests and assigned the grades of Alberta students. One's own teacher was not involved at all. Thus no consideration could be given to the possibility that you actually knew the subject but did not do well that day. Or perhaps it was that the subject was not covered as thoroughly in one school as in another so no exceptions could be considered.

This alone placed the graduation level of Canadian twelfth graders at a higher point, more difficult to achieve than standards in other high school grades, and certainly far above those in United States' colleges. The terms "completion" and "graduation" are not synonymous, though often confused. Some of us might have taken and completed grade twelve but not met the Dominion graduation level from final exams.

The other major factor, which may not have been the situation initially, but was by the time we younger Beards reached high school age, was that grade twelve in Canada was equivalent to the freshman college year in United States. Fortunately or unfortunately, this ranking difference was eliminated later. But for me it meant that my two grade twelve English classes gave me college freshmen credit, and my two college-level courses I completed at home in the summer of 1946, made it possible for me to graduate from college in three-and-a-half years, rather than four.

"And then the whining school-boy, with his satchel
And shining morning face, creeping like snail
Unwillingly to school."
(Shakespeare, <u>As You Like It.</u>)

CHAPTER 12

GRADE SCHOOLS

Herbert Spencer Public School

Herbert Spencer was our first primary school and was four miles across a coulee to the east and a bit north of our home. A coulee is a fairly wide and deep ravine, the result of geological breaks caused by glaciers. A major break was about a half-mile north of our home, and we children enjoyed exploring the area. This was the only "crack" in the Alberta prairies as far as I know. These pictures of our rocks were about half a mile north from the coulee and not on our path to school, but we explored them in the summer time and usually took our lunch in these pails pictured here.

I heard so many tales of sadness and hard times at Herbert Spencer that I kept saying I was going to jump out of the buggy when we got to the coulee and stay there until my siblings picked me up on the way home from school. Some years later Barbara told me that Mama instructed her to sit next to me in the buggy and put her arms around me so that I could not jump out on the way to school. Well, I did not even try. I guess I was obedient – or maybe just scared to take action.

At our nearby geological rocks; lunch pail on Barbara's head

More geological rocks in our coulee

Many of us walked to school most of the time, but we may sometimes have used a democrat—a large buggy that requires two horses, while a buggy or cart took only one horse. A cart could not hold more than two sitting and two standing behind the front seat. To reach Herbert Spencer, we had to cross the coulee and could either keep to the road, which made the trip even longer, or cut across the gully and climb the hill. Elizabeth, just five years older than I, would often carry me, a first grader, across this coulee and up the hill. Many years later I knitted her a sweater, telling her that each stitch signified every step she took carrying me and this sweater was my way to thank her!

If we were late for school, Mr. Ruskin, our teacher, would take Edward to the barn and whip him for getting us there late. Of course when we walked, we all arrived at different times, but Edward would get whipped if he was late. Sadly, he could not leave home until all outside chores were completed or he'd be whipped at home!

Vernon Culp and Laura Drake were in first grade with me. The Drake family had been involved in hiring Mr. Ruskin, and the Drake children were shown favoritism in class. I remember once that we three first graders were called from our front row seats to come up to the front by the teacher's desk—and all three of us were instructed to hold out one hand. I have no idea what we had done, but Mr. Ruskin smacked our hands with a ruler or yardstick. I do not remember crying, but perhaps that was the start of a poor memory, because he always used a stick or a strap; nor do I remember getting any other punishment from him, though certainly other students were regularly punished.

I particularly remember an incident when Paul Clark, an eighth grader, was punished, though I do not know what he had done. He had a boil on the top of his head, and Mr. Ruskin took a huge hardbound dictionary and smacked it down on Paul's head. Male students were usually taken to the barn and whipped with a horse strap.

I don't recall starting the school day by repeating the Lord's Prayer, but certainly we had this ritual at Hawthorn Public School and Kathyrn High School. Mr. Ruskin, who was Jewish, would have had to abide by the provincial rules. I remember that other parents cast aspersions on him because of his Jewish faith, while our parents, strongly opposed to any religious or racial prejudice, gave him support where others denounced him.

Mr. Ruskin taught for two years (1929-1931), but because of his extreme cruelty and perhaps due to other unknown reasons, our parents transferred us to Hawthorn Public School in 1930, four miles away in the opposite direction. The older children had been attending Herbert Spencer for at least six years; I was there only for grade one.

Families had to buy textbooks, which were passed down from child to child. (Eventually I was given our collection of readers for the early grades, which I have now passed on to my niece, Liane, a teacher at Bertchi, a private school in Seattle, Washington.) Here's the first verse in our Alberta textbook for first grade:

"Bow, wow, wow.

Whose dog art thou?

Little Tommy Tinker's dog.

Bow, wow, wow."

(It's hard for me to understand why any first grader would need to recognize the words "art thou," and it was a far cry from the simple language used later, such as "See Jane. See Dick." My nieces, Liane and Gael, both experienced at teaching school, inform me that these initial words were just to introduce upcoming readings and lessons, generally termed as "basal" systems. In short, such words would help young students recognize them in future stories. Could there not be more common words found that rhyme with "wow" than "art thou?"

I can think of "how, now, bow, sow (pig), cow, allow, anyhow, meow," and many more.)

Hawthorn Public School
"The sweet west wind, the prairie school,
a break in the yellow wheat....
A trail with never an end at all
to the eager children's feet.
The frost, the snow! The prairie school,
Where the wild north wind breaks free,
A tiny dot on the white that lies
as wide as eye can see ———-"
(Isabel Mackay, <u>The Prairie School</u>.)

Hawthorn Public School was four miles from our home in a southerly direction towards the small town of Kathyrn, where the high school was located. I well remember our first day at Hawthorn. Edward was now in high school, and we six younger ones were also leaving Herbert Spencer and Ruskin's cruelty behind us.

Daddy drove us to Hawthorn in the big buggy that first morning, and we were late in arriving, because our dear dog, Carlo, followed the buggy and wouldn't turn around and go home when Daddy ordered him to. Daddy got out and whipped Carlo, ordering him to go back home. Carlo slunk away, and we continued on our way to school. But Carlo, smart doggie that he was, went catty-corner across the two fields and appeared again when we had turned the corner for the third and fourth mile route. Why on earth did it matter that this loyal pet was following his family? Daddy's behavior bothered all of us but all we could do was sit there and wait.

As the horse noisily delivered us at the entrance to Hawthorn, the teacher, Miss Durie, came out and courteously but firmly insisted on two things. First, Daddy must get permission from the local school board for us to attend Hawthorn, since our home was in the Herbert Spencer District, and secondly, we must be on time! As it happened, the School Board authorized our enrollment there because much of our property was in their district even though our house was not. I suspect, too, that they were glad to see a higher student enrollment; otherwise within a few years, Hawthorn might have had to close. Provincial rules stated that in order to remain open, a school must have at least six students. In years later, the youngest Beards made up four of the needed six! Most days also, we were on time. Later we learned that Miss Durie viewed the Beards as the best-behaved students in her years of experience.

Paul soon jumped a grade. When we transferred to Hawthorn, there were already students in most of the grades, causing a heavy load for one teacher. Miss Durie realized within our first week how alert and bright Paul was, so she told him that if he answered all the arithmetic questions correctly for the entire forthcoming week, she would promote him to grade four. He succeeded with no trouble and joined Raymond. Paul was now two grades ahead of me, though only eleven months older!

By contrast, my sister Barbara fell behind in grade school at Herbert Spencer to end up in the same grade as her younger sister Elizabeth. Wonderfully strong, Barbara was really the only one to stand up to our Daddy, and I suspect that with a very strict dad and a cruel school teacher, she faced heavy mental and physical strain and undoubtedly days of absenteeism from school. Or perhaps it was the result of illness. We all came down with scarlet fever and missed weeks of schooling, and it is quite likely that Barbara's responsibility as the oldest girl added greatly to her burden. The laws required that after such contagious diseases our mattresses and pillows be burned; and our entire house fumigated and then inspected by provincial and medical officials. (Thank goodness we never got the mumps.) Elizabeth told us later that when we lost these good mattresses, we had to fill bags with straw. I can recall Mama expressing sorrow at losing her good feather pillows.

Two years later, when Barbara and Elizabeth finished grade school and went on to the high school, Hawthorn was left with only these seven students: Marjorie Yates, Warren and Lloyd Haag, and Raymond, Paul, Ruth and Robert Beard. Some years Ronald Deeter was with us, and then Kenneth Yates and Glen Hutchings. But I was alone in my grade from the second through the first half of the seventh. One Longson boy, Johnny, moved into our area for the last half of his and my seventh, and when his family all moved the next year, his older brother, Wilford, joined us in the eighth grade.

Can you imagine being the only student in your class for almost seven years?[7] To make matters even worse, through grades four, five, and six there were only two girls, Marjorie Yates and myself, in the whole school. Marjorie and I had absolutely nothing in common, except that we went to the same church and the same school, and did not like each other. Finally, when I was in the seventh grade, a little Anderson girl started grade one, giving the school a grand total of three girls. Unfortunately, I tried to "mother" her, much to her dislike and our mutual disappointment.

---

[7] Doesn't sound like a twenty-first century school, does it? A major concern we read about today is the need for reducing the class size. Surveys I receive ask me to prioritize this need along with others such as should more funds be allocated to Head Start, Grade Schools, or Teacher Pay.

To start the day, especially in cold weather, we would spend the first ten minutes or so doing exercises. "Arms up, arms forward, arms sideways, arms down," along with other instructions. I believe these came right after our saying the Lord's Prayer.

As to the value of repeating the Lord's Prayer daily, this was an excellent time for high school students to exchange love notes with a friend, or share homework answers! Perhaps some of us would never have passed a test if answers had not been shared. To commence classes, the teacher had a bell to ring; she would ding it a bit when we were already inside but rang it loudly outside. At Hawthorn, a pleasant memory is associated with the first ten or fifteen minutes when getting back to class after lunch. The teacher would read a chapter, usually from a fiction book. Occasionally, older students were given the opportunity to do the reading, and in my later grades I was pleased to be called upon.

At times I can recall some of the titles, but at present only one comes to mind: <u>Ben Hur</u>. I would probably have been in the fourth grade by then. I can clearly remember my mother saying, "I think Ruth is getting more out of this book than Elizabeth or Barbara," a real compliment to me since they were four grades ahead of me. This was one of the few compliments I remember from Mama, though she was very patient and undoubtedly gave more praise than I can recall.

Our first Hawthorn teacher, Ruth Durie, was an experienced and excellent teacher and disciplinarian. Olga Anderson, and then her sister, Esther, succeeded Miss Durie, and both these women developed good classroom skills also. Discipline was controlled in a far more civilized way than at Herbert Spencer. Miss Durie had the mischievous student, Kenneth Yates, stand in a corner so often that his tears removed the wood finish. One could visualize his face there.

I remember Paul telling us at suppertime one night that Kenneth Haag had brought a twenty-two caliber rifle to school and had it hidden in the barn. Daddy instructed him to tell this to Miss Durie, and if he were lying, he would get whipped at home. The next day, Miss Durie left the classroom briefly during the last period, and when she returned she walked in straight and serious carrying this rifle. She placed it upright in the corner by her desk and never said a thing. Of course tension spread throughout the student body.

At the end of the school day, when she dismissed us, she said, very firmly, "Kenneth, you are to remain in your seat. The rest of you are dismissed." I do not know what his punishment was, but I know Paul was greatly relieved that he would not face punishment at home.

When Paul and Raymond were in the ninth grade, they were exposed to smallpox, and so they were moved out to sleep in the chicken house. To help protect Robert and me even more, we stayed in the teacherage at Hawthorn for three weeks. Miss Anderson lived at her family farm that was adjacent to Hawthorn, so the teacherage was unoccupied. My job of sweeping the schoolrooms was easier while we stayed there, but now I had to think about getting meals ready for Robert and me. We would walk to church on Sunday morning, and after the service Edward or one of the parents would take us back to the teacherage by car or cart along with more food supplies.

It was not until I was in the fifth or sixth grade that we got a bicycle. Of course it was a boy's model. It was an ordeal for me to learn to ride a boys' bike, and then to ride it on dirt roads. Sometimes we shared rides to school in good weather and divided the four miles among the four of us: each one rode the bike one mile and then left it along the roadside fence for the next person. What a reduction—our walking now was reduced from four miles to three!

One time Paul did not leave the bike at the posted spot (at the cutoff catty-corner through the field) but continued on the road to the intersection, and left the bike there. The last two children were left stranded without the bike because of his error. I think he heard from his three siblings for years about his forgetfulness.

Riding horseback is one thing; riding bareback is miserable! Saddles were unknown at the Beard farm for many years, so I resolved the misery of riding saddleless by constantly reminding myself, "If Jesus could stand being nailed to the cross, I can certainly stand riding bareback." Of course, Jesus did not survive his ordeal, at least not for long, depending on one's beliefs; but at that time it must have helped. We were also advised to lean backwards, but that advice was hard to follow, at least for a young girl.

Mounting without a saddle was another problem. I have been told that we trained or induced (probably with food) the horse to lower its head as close to the ground as possible. Even as children we could then lean far enough across its neck that when it raised its head again, we could keep our balance and slide down onto its back. According to Barbara, we four younger children did this together. I know the boys did, though I don't remember it myself.

Alternatively, the horse could be placed parallel to a fence; someone would hold him while the rider climbed the fence and then clambered onto the horse's back. This method worked well with a calm horse – both Baldie and Ned on our farm – but not with a nervous or skittish one like our Pet. But even Baldie, who was patient, never jerky, and slower than most of our riding horses, was not a guarantee for a safe ride. Once, Paul, Robert, and I led him into the ditch by the driveway, and all three of us climbed on. Paul, holding the reins, got him to climb up and out of the ditch onto the drive. The ditch was three or four feet deep and at least that wide, and Baldie – whether he simply shook himself, or had decided to get three children off his poor old back – gave a good shake, and we tumbled right back down into the ditch. We weren't hurt, but we were certainly surprised.

If I rode today, I'd use a saddle.

Recreation And Games
Public And High School Days
"Play up, play up, and play the game."
(Sir Henry Newbolt, <u>Vitai Lampada</u>.)

What games can one play if the school's entire enrollment is only six to eight students ranging in ages from six to thirteen years? Not only was I never athletically inclined, but the "game world" was woefully limited while the gopher world was a hundred times larger.

We played "Auntie I Over" at Hawthorn. I do not know whether that was the correct name; it might have been "Annie, I Over" or some similar wording. The teacher picked two children to be captains, who then took turns choosing additional players from the remaining few; thus each side had three or four players. One group went to one side of the one-story school building, and the other to the opposite side. The teacher tossed the ball to the two captains, and whoever caught it got to keep the ball and begin the game. The teacher was not always outside with us so a student might have taken her role at times.

The ball was thrown over the one-story building, and the thrower or captain of that team would yell "Auntie, I over" to alert the team on the other side. When someone on the opposing team caught the ball, one of the players would hide it behind his or her back. Some of the team who now had the ball would run around one side of the building and the others from the same team would run around the other side. As soon as the team who had initially thrown the ball saw players coming around the building, they would try to run to the opposite side without being touched by the one player who had the ball in hand. Any player who was touched by the ball then had to transfer to that team. The team that ended with the most players at the end of recess had won the game. There were standard words we yelled, such as "Auntie, I over, here we come."

We also skipped rope, played hopscotch, and sometimes just stood in a circle and tossed the ball back and forth. These were games that could be done without any teamwork, though the younger children had to please the older ones or they would never have a chance to throw the ball! Playing with kids varying in age from six to thirteen for most of my eight years of grade school taught me that one has to learn to survive as a solitary reaper! Oh, for some congeniality.

I began wearing glasses by the time I was ten years old, and I quickly learned that glasses were always going to be a drawback and competition would be increased in many fields. One time my glasses were broken by a tossed ball, though that wasn't what taught me that athletics and sports were not for me. Even the fifteen-minute morning warm-up exercises were boring.

In fact, it was neither the games themselves nor my glasses that influenced my career, but the need to survive as a loner, and at the same time to be more at home with boys than with girls. While I would gladly stick my head under the Model T Ford to watch Edward clean or replace the spark plugs, I hardly ever played with the dolls given me.

On our farm no creeks were deep enough for us to learn to swim, though the head of one creek was deep enough for simple diving, but we did learn somehow. Nor did we have money for new ice skates—yet the older children had skates given to them. Rubber ice did not occur often nor last long, and of course rubber ice was not suitable for skating.

Dancing and card games were against our parents' religion. Eventually we all outgrew the belief that dancing was sinful, but none of us except Barbara had any dancing ability, or ever danced as far as I know. I was born with two left feet. I did enjoy square dancing at college although I doubt I was very good at it. High school proms were unknown at that time, but an all-student body picnic was held at the end of the school year, and a group picture taken. I have a print of the 1939 high school student body but I can hardly recall many names even though faces are familiar. I never learned to swim, dance, skate, or play "sinful" card games. A sit-down reading job suited my eventual career choice. But that was a long way off.

However, when I left the prairie farm for secretarial college, and had my first job, I did learn to roller skate! If I didn't live in the mountains now, I think I would take up bike riding again!

"Tell me not, in mournful numbers,
Life is but an empty dream!
For the soul is dead that slumbers,
And things are not what they seem!"
(Henry Longfellow, <u>A Psalm of Love.</u>)

CHAPTER 13

CHILDHOOD LESSONS

Dreams

Undoubtedly, all of us had dreams but belatedly I captured those from only two of us.

Dreams by Elizabeth

Elizabeth made a brief note of her dreams, or possibly nightmares. She daydreamed in color, shaped by the natural world, especially by the sounds when sleeping outside at night on the farm. This is where she had full view of the sunrise, stars and the Northern Lights, and of course the beautiful moon in all positions. She noticed the crocuses and wildflowers on the prairie, and listened to the songs of nightingales, meadowlarks, and the call of the coyotes. She dreamed of waves of black wires in the rooms as well as in the sky. She tried to get out but kept getting caught in the wires. The doors were locked and all the lights were out. She did manage to get out one or two times, which was probably an indication she had awakened.

Dreams by Ruth

I have never disclosed my dreams before. They repeated themselves constantly during the early days of my childhood.

I dreamt I had a secret path, known only to me. I placed a doorway at the west and north corner of my parents' bedroom on the first floor. This led to a flight of stairs that opened on the second floor, across the front of the boys' bedroom. This area was sometimes wide open on all three sides, and sometimes walled in except for a small opening. I would stand there and wait and watch to see if Mr. Hutchings came from his farm and drove his car north past our house. That was all there was to that dream. The Hutchings were the most elite family near us, and they were the closest ones to have a telephone. They had only one child, Glen, who did not attend our church but later was a student at Hawthorn while we were there. Mr. Hutchings held a political county position, and one Sunday he even showed up at our church service and asked adults to vote for him. I was afraid of him.

The other dream was far more exciting. I dreamt that my miraculous horse was available and I traveled far with him – until I actually went to sleep! This wonderful horse could fly there outside at the top of the stairs. Seems to me these were the days of "Hi ho Silver." Why not dream of even more miraculous events? It was not long until in my dreams I could flap my wings – my arms – and I could fly. It would not surprise me to learn that other youngsters then and now dreamt that they too could fly.

These particular dreams ended when I left home. Many years later, but prior to seniorhood, I dreamt that I would come back in my second life with two different talents. First I'd come as an architect. In grade school I wrote about Greek architecture and made a little booklet, with a bordered cover, which I retained for many years. My second talent, and the most cherished one, was that I would come back as a highly recognized symphony director and probably an excellent violinist, too. I concentrated on the feelings and sensitivity of the composers' intentions. Was this uppermost in my dreams because this has always been of major interest associated with the musical ability of my children and other relatives? At various times in my life I have not recalled any dreams, although in college psychology classes I learned that dreams occur whether we know it or not. In fact, dreams are deemed to be essential. And one evening in 2006 a doctor on a television program informed us that dreams such as my "flying" one meant that the dreamer had solved a problem and had any depression under control. Well, I can't make that comparison at this late date, but I always wanted to be able to fly and do things that no one else could.

The television doctor also said that we often solve problems or come up with answers during our sleep or through our dreams. I seldom remember any dreams now, but I often tell my friends "just wait until morning, I'll think of the answer about 2:30AM, and will tell you in the morning." With a relaxed mind, the answer often comes to us.

Treats
"And he who gives a child a treat
Makes joy-bells ring in Heaven's street,
And he who gives a child a home
Builds palaces in Kingdom come."
(John Masefield, The Everlasting Mercy.)

A most pleasant memory, especially in spite of the harsh treatment given Edward, is that he was always given the first slice of newly baked bread. Home-baked fresh bread has a fragrance like none other. None of us ever showed any resentment that Edward got this treat and the rest of us had to wait until a regular mealtime.

Calgary has been known from its early beginning for its week-long Stampede activities. When I was ten and Elizabeth and Barbara were living in Calgary, we made our first family trip to the Stampede. It was on a Friday, a special day for children at the Stampede, and the boys and I looked forward to it all week. Unfortunately, that Friday, I woke up sick to my stomach and could not go. What a disappointment! Mama stayed home with me. A number of years later I did attend Stampede, but I remember nothing about it – probably because our farm life provided many of the same activities.

When Mama went with Daddy to Calgary, she brought a special treat home with her. They took the gallons of cream, and any eggs we might have in store, to the Farmers' Market for sale, where they also had a light lunch. Mama always saved a bit of her goodies for me, and I so looked forward to them; a couple of unsalted white crackers! The crackers themselves were certainly nothing special; in fact, today I would view them as tasteless. They were special to me then because they were rare, and they were exotic – all the way from Calgary – and they were Mama's gift to me. Such was pioneer life.

A more regular treat, but one which my brothers and I took turns sharing, was to drink a glass of milk that had first been used to rinse the empty jam jar. What better way to get the jam bits than to rinse the jar with milk? Sometimes we would also be permitted to spread a bit of jam over our peanut butter on our slice of bread. I frequently indulge in these two treats today just to bring back memories – as well as the good taste! (Since reaching adulthood, I get very aggravated that the manufacturers of jam and peanut butter produce jars with a rim at the top and a beveled bottom, so that it is very difficult to scrape them clean. Alas for old-fashioned canning jars.)

Another treat – possible only in winter, but then winters were very long in Alberta – was snow cream. Freshly fallen snow was the basis of our "ice cream," to which was added some sugar, cream, and vanilla. I think this was Daddy's idea to use the clean snow as it was readily available. At many of our church summer picnics, other parents, such as the Wrays and Gumps, would bring their ice cream maker and we would have real homemade ice cream.

Once my brothers caught a seagull, which was very unusual, because we were far from their natural habitat. Daddy, the boys and I, took it to the Calgary zoo. The supervisor wanted to find a way to thank us, and as he offered us various treats, I kept objecting until he said, "Oh, I know, how about an ice cream cone for each of you." I believe that was the second cone I ever had!   As for the first…

Daddy proclaimed we would get the best care at a Catholic hospital and took us to the one in Calgary when all seven children, at the same time, had our tonsils and adenoids removed. I was about five years old. In those days, such hospitalization was at least for many days, perhaps a full week. When we had been released, and were sitting in the waiting room until our parents came to pick us up, the hospital staff brought each of us an ice cream cone! What a wonderful treat, and how appropriate for our "sore" throats!

When I was eight, Mama, Robert, and I went to Indiana for my Grandma Christophel's funeral. I stole a few marbles from my aunt's store, but had to return them when Mama found out. Neither Mama nor Aunt Anna punished me but they explained in detail why my behavior was wrong. When we left to go back home, my aunt gave me a box of new crayons – my very first new ones. Just a few weeks later the Vacation Bible School teacher wanted me to share these unbroken crayons with another child, but I cried and said no. And I clung to them. When you don't have anything new, or anything you can call your own, it is just too hard to share! (See "This I Believe," in Appendix E.)

The very first movie I ever saw was <u>Mrs. Wiggs in the Cabbage Patch.</u> I was about twelve years old; Barbara and Elizabeth were in

Calgary, and I stayed one weekend with Barbara and her family. The movie was about a very poor farm family whose father went away looking for a job elsewhere to earn the money he needed to support his wife, his son, and daughter. The children were tired of waiting but their mother assured them that he would come with some money eventually. He finally did return, before school started, but he looked and acted sad and pathetic. It so happened that the minister was visiting in their home and he realized the true situation and why the father was stalling and not happy to be home. While the farmer's wife and children awaited the show of money, the minister quietly stuck a bill in the farmer's shirt pocket. How surprised and happy were all four of them when the father pulled out this bill—all of $5 or $10 earned for his summer's work!

What an exciting first movie for a twelve year old farm girl! The second feature was as exciting for me as the first: <u>The History of the Canadian Wheat Pool.</u> And how pleased Daddy was that Barbara could explain what it was all about.

Tricks
"Don't believe anything you hear and only half you see!" (David Beard)

This word of wisdom, quoted exactly as Daddy stated it, came from an interesting trick or experience that he had as a young boy.

He was at a carnival or chautauqua event and saw a huge sign on the front of the tent that read "Come see this strange animal! His head is where his tail should be, and his tail is where his head should be." Daddy had experienced and enjoyed little beyond life's necessities, so he was intrigued; he just had to pay the admission fee regardless of the cost.

So he sacrificed his hard-earned money and entered the tent. There was the horse with his tail at the front of the stall, and his head towards the aisle – exactly the opposite position any horse, or cow, is placed in a stall. Ever after, Daddy thought of this phrase as a teaching tool for the need to analyze all issues and differences of opinions. These kinds of teachings bring to mind Mama's telling us that Daddy's reputation, from his early adult age, was "so much good and so much bad in the same man."

Scary tricks

Lacking toys, games, and money for and access to other entertainment, most farm children relied on their imagination for amusement, and we Beards were no exception. We enjoyed playing tricks and creating scary episodes. Barbara was always imaginative, and not only was she the sibling who most often took the initiative whether for adventure or for promoting changes, but she was also the leader amidst the community youth. She enjoyed a tactical advantage over us younger children.

The earliest scaring episode I remember was when I was in the second grade at Hawthorn. Other girls Barbara's age helped her conduct this trick. She kept me out of the classroom, and then blindfolded me before leading me back in. I was to follow her directions, which were to move from seat to seat, to climb up on a chair, and move again. I had to do this many times. Finally I was told I could take off the eye covering and open my eyes. I was terrified.

There I sat on a chair just beneath the high ceiling! How she arranged this without my realizing that I was climbing to a higher level, I did not understand. Probably she was relating a tale all the time to distract me! To get back down, one of the other girls would be on one side holding the chair I was now on, and Barbara would be on the other side helping me move down chair by chair, level by level.

I doubt that Daddy or Miss Durie or any other adult was ever told of this episode. But Mama certainly learned of the following one, not long after.

A team of horses was already hitched to the hay wagon, and a number of us children were present awaiting our trip to the field for some kind of work. Barbara tried to induce Elizabeth to join her on the wagon tongue to ride there instead of in the wagon itself. Elizabeth, being far more timid – or wise – declined, and so my dear sister Barbara talked me into it.

Wagon tongues were narrow, so one foot had to be placed before or behind the other, not side by side. I needed help in climbing up, as the tongue was approximately three feet off the ground, and of course there was a horse on either side. I do not remember which two horses they were. Barbara climbed up and stood on the tongue ahead of me and told me to put my hands onto the backs of the horses rather than hanging onto her. She picked up the reins just as I put my hands on the backs of the horses. That did it! One or both of the horses were frightened by this new posture and bolted! Probably only one jumped, as Barbara immediately grabbed my arm and pulled me along with her as she jumped off in front of this team. Unfortunately, she lost hold of my arm and I dropped to the ground. Just where I was in relation to the horses, I do not know, but I remember my back being hit by something.

Luckily, Daddy wasn't home, or Barbara might have been punished then and there. Mama took me to Dr. Edwards right away. That was eleven miles and again the trip was by horse and buggy. I do not remember any severe pain.

At the doctor's office, Mama and Dr. Edwards had me sit on a potty while they sat nearby and waited for me to dispose internal liquid! I was old enough to be embarrassed even if sitting right in front of my Mama! Finally, they both got up and walked away from me but were still within the examining room, and by gum, I was NOT going to do in public what we had been strictly taught was a very private event.

It finally got through to them why I was not co-operating so they then left the room entirely. I then obliged. It was some years later that I surmised they probably wanted to see if I expelled any blood. I did not, and no medicines or any limitations were given me.

Funny tricks

At church there were Sunday School classes for all ages, but everyone gathered in the main sanctuary for the regular service. Young children sat with their parents, and the older ones sat at the back near their Sunday School room. One week, Barbara found an alarm clock somewhere. By chance it was Daddy's turn to preach that Sunday. Barbara managed to hide the clock in the church, the alarm set to go off during the sermon. When it did, everyone was more than surprised; some were half scared as to what it might mean. The Elders quickly found it, but no one ever learned who the culprit was. (I never knew of this trick until Barbara's husband wrote me about it.)

Another time Barbara went dancing down the aisle to the front of the church during one of the services. The Elders, and of course Daddy, were outraged at this conduct and called for a meeting with her to render punishment. Barbara did not show up at the meeting. This public behavior may have been just one of the reasons she was sent off to Calgary for schooling.

Smelly tricks

Three boys played a trick on Barbara one day at Hawthorn school that got her into trouble with the teacher. I suspect that two of the boys were the oldest Haag boys. To retaliate, Barbara snared a gopher and tied it in the teacher's car. The gopher wreaked havoc by tearing up the fabric on the car seats, as well as leaving its odor. Next day the teacher blamed the three boys and punished them in some manner. The boys knew that Barbara had done it, but they did not squeal on Barbara – because no doubt she would then have revealed the trick they had played on her.

The two youngest boys, Robert and Paul, occasionally trapped weasels and skunks, both at home and when they batched at Kathyrn High School. At school they would put the animals in the woodshed. One night someone tied a captured skunk to the door; when Robert opened the door in the morning, the ice-cold skunk slipped inside. Since it was frozen almost to death, it did not stink. Even if it had, the smell in our kitchen when the boys skinned weasels was worse than any natural skunk smell experienced out in the open.

April Fools tricks (and other sibling activities)

One school day, we could not find our cart so, unexpectedly, we had to walk to school. Not until that Sunday did we find what had happened. The older Haag boys had played an April Fool's trick on us; they had hauled our cart to the church and somehow lifted it to the top of the entrance steps. It must have taken several adults to get it back down.

No doubt the seven of us played many tricks and jokes on each other, but I don't remember many, perhaps because I was next to the youngest. I do recall learning that Elizabeth would pinch Barbara, and when Barbara complained or told what Elizabeth was doing to her, Elizabeth would deny it; then Barbara would be scolded for not telling the truth. Elizabeth was Daddy's favorite, but it was Barbara who had the nerve to speak up to him, so I have to assume that this was Elizabeth's way to "get ahead" in Daddy's eyes even more. Elizabeth resembled Mama far more than any of us, both in looks and in personality, although I doubt Mama showed any martyr attitude as Elizabeth later did.

Tragedies

Farm Accidents

All farm families experience their share of accidents, some tragic and others at least memorable. We were no exception.

Some of our horses were low key, like Baldie, or very high strung, like Pet, or of medium nature like Ned. However, this accident would have set off even the calmest animal. My second eldest brother, Raymond, had his team lined up to hay from the wagon to the adjoining threshing machine. The horse nearest the machine twitched her tail, which suddenly got caught in the machine. The machine pulled her tail and some adjoining flesh completely off! Of course the horse, tailless and bleeding, bolted. Raymond was apparently thrown from the wagon when the horse ran, and a hired man helped get him to the house.

He was in a great deal of pain, and it was obvious he was quite seriously hurt. Mama, who couldn't drive an auto, got him in the cart and drove him the eleven miles to Dr. Edward's office. Raymond's collar blade was broken. I do not know which hurt the most – riding in that cart that length of time and over rough dirt roads, or the broken collar bone until it healed, or the exercises he had to go through to get it back in working order after it had mended. I can remember seeing Mama helping him with the recommended exercises, and seeing the pain on both their faces.

Someone took the horse to the vet for treatment of this horrible wound, or else got the vet to come to the field. Of course the tail was never restored, and the area did not heal for a very long time.

Farm Fires
"How great a matter a little fire kindleth!" (The Epistle of James 3:5)

Twice we faced fires at the farm, one major, the other minor. The lesser, when I was four or five years old, never reached the house. It was a stubble fire that began on the Hutchings field. It jumped the irrigation ditch that divided our properties and was coming across our field towards a haystack fairly close to our house.

Daddy hurriedly plowed a backstop, which is the standard procedure when possible. Mama took Robert and me to the living room, gave us a big can of buttons to play with, and told us to stay there until she came back. Then she went out with the older children and began to dig closer to the haystack just in case the fire jumped the area that Daddy had begun to plow.

After a while, Robert and I got scared because no one else was coming back yet and we had heard someone yelling "fire." We crept to the kitchen and were watching at the window, when, finally Mama and the girls came back in. Fortunately, no serious damage was done except to whatever plantings had been in that field, but it did not get near the haystack.

House Fire – Summer 1940

A more serious fire occurred in 1940. It was 9:30PM and Barbara had come home for a summer visit. She had just put her two young children to bed. Gael was three-and-a-half years old and her sister Liane was six months. My oldest brother, Edward, had temporarily moved out of his small bedroom for Barbara and her daughters.

The door to the stairway was located at the third step from the bottom, and it was always supposed to be kept closed to prevent cold air from coming down into the living room in the winter and hot air in the summer. It also meant those who went to bed early were not disturbed by downstairs noise. But this night the last person using the stairs had left the door open.

Daddy had already gone to bed. Farm work was very tiring for him, especially because of his heavy wooden leg. Barbara and I, having just finished the supper dishes, were sitting in the kitchen when we heard a crackle. Barbara looked towards the living room where the stairs were in view. She screamed, "**FIRE**" and rushed past me and up the stairs so fast that by the time I got past the landing, she was already at the bedroom doorway coming back down. She had the baby in her arms and was pushing Gael ahead of her. She yelled for me to get a blanket and follow her. Our girls' bedroom was not yet on fire, so I dashed in for a blanket and then rushed downstairs. I followed Barbara to the nearby garden where she motioned for me to spread the blanket on the ground. I remember her telling Gael to take care of Liane and stay on the blanket.

She and I rushed back in the house. Mama had already called for my younger brother, Robert, who was the only boy home that evening. "Bring water," she yelled. And, of course, the pump would not start! We used to have to pump it by hand, but about six months earlier, Edward, who excelled in mechanics, had motorized the pump. We did not yet have pipes leading to the house, so having a pump engine was a great advantage. However, as often occurred, the engine would not start: the spark plugs needed cleaning. Robert did not lose his head at all – he had the plugs cleaned in no time and two buckets filled. He and Mama filled and carried buckets the twenty or so yards to the house, then panted up the stairs to throw water on the flames.

Barbara and I were running up and down the stairs carrying clothes from our bedroom. Daddy hadn't time to put on any clothes, nor even his wooden leg. He was hanging onto the open stair door using one hand for balance and the other to hide his privates, and yelling encouragement to us. He or Mama yelled, "someone should run to Low's for help." I said I'd go, so I ran the quarter-mile.

I began yelling when I reached their corner. Mrs. Low was outside and heard me, and she yelled for her husband, "John, John," but John did not answer. Then she yelled, "Beard's house is on fire." Out from the outhouse in a flash he dashed, jumped in his truck and flew down the road. He didn't even see me running to catch a ride with him.

It was some time later that I learned that it was fear that made my bladder feel full, and that no matter how many stops I made on the quarter-mile back home, no relief would come. Fear about the fire and fear that ghosts from the churchyard would come rushing out of their graves towards me. I kept looking over my shoulder for these white figures until I was past the church line.

Now Barbara and I started carrying stuff from the living room out to the garden area. Barbara would call to her children to reassure them everything was all right and that she would soon come to them.

We carried out the big couch, chairs, a heavy wooden rocker, and the Singer sewing machine. We managed to move the tall reed organ over to the outside doorway but knew we would need help to get it down the two steps to ground level. Then we started to move the heavy piano across the room also. The men called from upstairs, "we've got it out, you can stop now." But we kept on. We got the piano to the outside door. Fortunately the men came down the stairs just then and put down their buckets. We knew they could – indeed would have to – help move these last two heavy objects. But we had them right there at the front door. It proved unnecessary to move them outside.

Both organ and piano had casters or we could never have moved them as far as we did.

Later we reasoned that the fire had started from a late live ash blowing out of the chimney. There was no flue plate covering the hole. There had been no fire in the kitchen stove since about 6:00PM, but that red ash was still alive and waiting to escape. There was only a curtain draped over the boys' bedroom doorway, adjacent to the chimney, so this live ash had it made. If the stairway door had been shut, as it was supposed to be, and my sister not seen the flames, the ending to this frightening experience would have been tragic.

"Laws are made for the lowest common denominator. Live as far above the laws as you possibly can."
(David Ray Beard)

CHAPTER 14

TEACHINGS

This was one of the major teachings we heard from Daddy, and since I have never heard that phrasing elsewhere, nor located it by web searching, I would not be surprised to learn that he thought it up.

"Laws are made for the lowest common denominator" forces one to think about, and analyze, our legal system. After all, no one wants to think of himself or herself as the lowest common denominator; being a "good" person means not that you're out of reach of the laws, only that you shouldn't need laws to police your own behavior. Only the "lowest" have to be kept to the straight and narrow by laws. And therefore, raise yourself above and beyond that lowest common denominator: "Live as far above the law as you possibly can." To me, that has always meant following the Golden Rule – "Do unto others as you want others to do unto you."

"Waste not, want not," was another bit of advice and similar to "A penny saved is a penny earned." To this day, I pick up pennies, nickels, dimes – whatever – and unconsciously have my eye alert, whether a home or out in the public, and especially in parking lots. One time, I even found a dollar!

Both at home and at school, we were taught to examine and argue both sides of any issue. At school this could be done with formal debates, a lost art whose revival would benefit us all. At home, debates were informal and generally much shorter than at school.

"There's no such word as 'can't.'" That may sound like one hundred percent good advice, but one should also be taught that there may be some situations that result in very undesirable repercussions and "can't" should be changed to "should not." Of course "should" and "should not" need to be clearly defined or restricted and all terms must be correctly applied and the reasons explained.

I use the term "must" for very good reasons. Let me tell you how I learned the difference. After my hysterectomy, my surgeon said, "You can't lift heavy things," and I up and showed him I could! While still in the hospital, I shoved the heavy stuffed chair in the lounge across the room. It hurt my abdomen. So what? Then within a few weeks of recuperation at home, my husband chopped down the forty-foot-tall old chestnut tree in our Carlisle yard, and I lugged the huge branches about thirty feet to the back of our lot. Fortunately our neighbor lady, who was a practical nurse, saw this and she came out and told me <u>why</u> I should not be doing this, even if I could, and of course I stopped right away. That doctor, a professional man, did not know human nature as well as our neighbor woman! And even today I feel the results of my earlier determination when I iron clothes or when I shovel snow – my abdomen muscles hurt! Thank you, Dr. So-and So!

"Honesty is the best policy" was instilled in us. Robert says he learned that the reason for this was that the facts could be much easier remembered if one told the truth. Some of the rest of us connected that with the Golden Rule. While biblical teachings were often included, I do not recall our parents ever threatening us with "You'll go to hell." Nor did they ever say that about any one else whom we knew.

I learned the hard way about the destructiveness of the word "should." At some Ladies Meeting at our home, when I was at the typical teenager's rebellious age, I heard Mama say to her friends, "Ruth should be a librarian," with emphasis on the "should," and basing that on my love of books, poetry, and constant reading. I also had photographic memory to some extent. I could remember where a statement was made on a page – on the right side or left, clear at the top or further down, or at the beginning of a paragraph or later. That skill was very useful through my school days but gradually has lessened from lack of usage. Mama meant her statement as a compliment and encouragement to me, but I took it as a parental order. And I said to myself, "If Mama wants me to be a librarian, that's the last thing I'm ever going to be." And it was the last thing. How destructive I let her "should" statement become!

Those two words "should" and "can't" are very destructive. From very early teachings, their definitions, limitations and usage need to be explained and understood. That is not an easy thing to do, I realize, since youngsters will generally find it difficult to understand, and the adults, mainly parents, may not have the skills nor insight to see the situation clearly, nor to make the necessary explanation. But this is an issue that needs priority at every level in our society.

With my negative view of Mama's words "Ruth should be a librarian," which she said with pride about her daughter, I pursued the other home teachings of helping others, and so decided I wanted to be a social worker. This goal was strengthened by Daddy's physical condition, and both parents' emphasis on "do unto others what you want done to you." And of course, I really had no idea of what being a librarian meant. We had no library nearby. Our Hawthorn teacher would bring us each a book every week from the Calgary library, but I had never seen nor been in such a building, nor knew what skills or responsibilities were applicable. Mama knew but I did not.

On the other hand, Mama later gave me great encouragement by her repeated words, "Ruth, if you don't do it, who will?" In time, I was privately saying that to myself too. There's an auto repair shop here in downtown Asheville that has quotations or original statements posted on its large street sign, and today's was "Have you told your cat yet about catnip? If you don't, who will?" No doubt, those drivers reading that will get some humor from it – even if not the life lesson I got!

Because of Daddy's physical limitations, he spent many hours at sit-down jobs where he had the opportunity to work and instill teachings at the same time, and he had the drive. Mama would be too occupied with very busy tasks of caring for seven children and was more quiet and soft-spoken. I view the teachings from both of them as being far more prominent and effective than neighboring families experienced. Perhaps I am the one sibling who came to understand both the good and bad, the strong and weak, characteristics, strengths, and aims of both parents, and to accept Daddy in spite of his rather strict discipline. I would note too that he was harsher with the boys than us girls, and more during the earlier years than later when our hardships lessened and we children could do more of the work.

Daddy would never speak the vulgar or swear words that we were not allowed to say, but instead would spell them out, such as "d-a-r-n," "g-o-s-h;" and of course he would never, never utter the "top-of-the-line" swear words, "g-o-d," or "d-a-m-n."

So what's that got to do with the price of wheat? This was a saying that we regularly threw back at one of our siblings when we were losing the argument or wanted to avoid the subject. (I just learned that here in the States, at least in North Carolina – though of New York Jewish origin – a similar statement is common: "So what am I? Chopped liver?"}

The withholding of showing affection to the opposite sex was the rule throughout the entire society for many decades beyond these pioneer days. This was true within one's family as well as the general public. Once, just once, when I was alone in the kitchen, I saw Daddy put his arm around Mama and kiss her on the cheek. She was embarrassed. Today, whether out in public areas or on TV, there is no distinction between what is proper or private and what is not. Greetings might include hugs and kisses between friends, whether both are of one sex or not. Today, I can use the word "sex" – though I did not, at least with comfort, for the first fifty years of my life.

Let me end this chapter by recognizing that the major principle taught us by both parents was to follow the Golden Rule, and that was spelled out to us in multiple ways. If there was any resentment, it was directed at those who were so much better off than we were and would express their feelings by looking down on us. Most certainly none of us have ever had any racial prejudice. We were taught respect for Negroes. So our parents, both from the States, readily respected blacks in the early 1900s, while the United States itself had serious problems in equalizing races as late as the 1960s. Even Billy Graham, a popular conservative evangelist of Western North Carolina, was preaching equality, long before United States took steps to legalize racial rights.

COMING OF AGE

"A little learning is a dangerous thing.
Drink deep, or taste not the Pierian Spring."
(Alexander Pope, <u>Essays on Criticism, Pt II.</u>)

CHAPTER 15

KATHYRN HIGH SCHOOL and BEYOND

Oh glory be, Kathyrn High School, where finally I found a girl friend – Elsie Stuart – who was also in the ninth grade. While I wasn't unfriendly with the boys, except brother Paul, having a friend of one's own sex, and within the same age range, is an undeniable asset, even if I had to wait until I was fourteen!

Edward was the first Beard to attend Kathyrn High School, which was five miles beyond Hawthorn Grade School and near the grocery store and gas station, all owned by Mr. Saunders. Alberta wheat elevators were across the road and adjacent to the railroad. Edward usually rode Ned those nine miles to school. Some times he went by cart, so that he could get some groceries for us, and I would go with him as far as Hawthorn. If Ned was not available, we used the small jumpy horse, Pet. Pet was so scared of cars that when any auto came towards us or behind us, we had to hop out of the cart and hold her tightly by her bridle. Even then, she might jump and drag the cart across the four-foot ditch to be stopped only by the farm fence. Edward completed three years of high school, and took over more farm responsibilities for several years before going to the States. As it turned out, only one of us children graduated from high school, though several attended college and received higher degrees.

Barbara and Elizabeth went to Kathyrn just one year, their ninth grade. During this year, they went across the field to the Yates house for a ride to school, which meant very early rising and caused ill feelings with the Yates if they were late. This situation might well be one of the reasons for their transfer to Calgary the next year. Another reason suggested to me was that Barbara's bizarre dancing down the church aisle had a great deal to do with her being sent away from home. I would give credit to my parents for wanting the best school possible for us, and that they believed the city schools had more to offer and made higher demands than our country schools.

My sisters lived with two different families, earning their keep by doing household chores. No matter how hard they might have tried, it was evident they would not pass end-of-year twelfth grade exams. Barbara went to Edmonton, but soon thereafter came home and married Edward Olsen, and they moved back to Calgary.

Elizabeth and our brother Edward went to Bethany Bible College at Elgin, Illinois, in 1937, and the following year Elizabeth married Ernest Detrick, a ministerial student. Edward attended although there was no thought or likelihood that he would enter the ministry or be a missionary. He was called home in late 1941 and took over the farming responsibilities when Daddy was hospitalized with the cerebral hemorrhage that caused his death shortly thereafter.

When it came time for Paul and Raymond to attend ninth grade, they went to Herbert Spencer. The next year they changed to Kathyrn High School, and at least during the winter they batched with other boys in a house adjacent to the school.

Raymond and Paul were in the eleventh grade when I entered high school. Finally at Kathyrn there were a few more girls, including, as noted, my very first friend, Elsie Stuart. With three Beards at Kathyrn High School, transportation was as much a problem as ever.

Our parents rented a vacant railroad shack for us about half a mile from the school, adjacent to the railroad and the grain elevators. I could stay there even when Raymond and Paul stayed at the farm for harvesting and spring work. The shack was not insulated, and I slept in the living room where there was a small wood stove, while the boys slept in the woodshed adjacent to the kitchen. Once again I was involved in cooking meals, though I was no Martha Stewart! While some youngsters would have been delighted with this responsibility, I certainly disliked it, although my brothers helped a lot, as they had no farm chores to do. Money was still very limited, so meals were not exactly delicious.

After school on Friday, we looked for someone from home to come get us. If weather conditions were threatening, we did not expect them until Saturday morning, which meant a very sparse Friday evening meal and Saturday breakfast. Usually we were brought back on Sunday afternoon, either by auto or by one of our farm wagons.

These trips were not always uneventful. One Sunday going by wagon to our railroad shack, one of my brothers sat with me in the back seat. We not only had some groceries packed alongside us but also several buckets of coal for our stove. All of a sudden the wagon tongue broke right where it was connected to the wagon body. The wagon seat dropped to the ground immediately and all the groceries and buckets of coal dumped down over the front seat and out on the ground. We pulled the wagon across the ditch to leave it beside the farmer's fence, and, of course, picked up the food items and the coal and put them back in the wagon. We rode the horses home, and either Daddy or Edward drove us to school on Monday morning, picking up our food and coal on the way.

The following year Leonard Workman replaced Mr. Hughes as the sole teacher. He was an excellent teacher and disciplinarian.[8] In the tenth grade, Elsie and I took Algebra together, a subject neither of us excelled in. Mr. Workman kept students after school who regularly did not get the correct answers to the homework, and the morning "Lord's Prayer" recitation offered a perfect time for all of us to secretly share answers. Elsie and I spent prayer time comparing answers and changing them to match, so that if one of us had to stay in after class, the other one did too – or we were both free to go home. Boys and girls would also use this opportunity to write notes to each other.

By my eleventh grade, the school had expanded to two main rooms, plus small classrooms in the basement, and two teachers. Mr. Workman became head principal and Mr. Taylor was his assistant. Each taught specific subjects, and they would change classrooms rather than having students move. On Friday afternoons a local public school teacher came in to teach Home Economics, and I remember making my first apron and first petticoat. (We called a slip a "petticoat" in those days.) Frankly, I was more interested in learning how to type, and enjoyed those sessions more than sewing.

Many years later changes occurred at all country schools, and larger buildings and dormitories at high schools were built and busing was provided. Kathyrn High School had a few more students but by grade twelve, there were still only twelve of us in that grade, and about fifty-four in the entire high school. In grades ten and eleven, we had

---

[8]In 1955, Mama wrote me that Kathyrn High School was reported to be the best disciplined school in the entire province of Alberta. Mr. Workman "would not allow pupils to smoke on school grounds unless they brought a written signed consent from their parents. He, however, smoked, and also drank (did earlier at least. Seems he was a Mormon, Latter Day Saints.)" This message also noted that Mr. Workman had recently died of a heart attack.

end-of-year tests both prepared and graded by our own teachers. I did reasonably well in most subjects although it was obvious that I would never pass higher math, physics, or chemistry courses that were prepared and graded by offsite instructors.

"We should all be concerned about the future
Because we will have to spend the rest of our lives there. "
(Charles Kettering, <u>Seed for Thought.</u>)

CHAPTER 16

CAREER DECISIONS

An ongoing responsibility of parenthood is the consideration of the future of each child. Each individual is different, and parents may silently or openly express their wish, or their expectation as to what level of education, what career, and what the future will be for each child. This parental role has lessened with technological advances. Web sites offer career information, educational opportunities, and job options. Children are no longer limited to advice or a push from parents or teachers. There's also testing of skills and aptitudes available to any and all ages. Some high schools require broad testing prior to graduation, and colleges often require them before admission.

Up to the middle of the 20th Century, many farm children continued as farmers, whether in the same community or not, especially in the earliest of pioneer days. A few might anticipate and achieve a very different life than their parents. Both my parents grew up on farms in United States, but their childhood was less harsh in the eastern U.S. than in the western provinces of Canada in the early 1900s. Whether children continued in the same line as their parents or not, society certainly expected that every individual would marry and have children. Even long after my youthful days, this expectation was the custom. Every female was pushed and expected to "catch" a man. It was her fault, or that of her parents, if she failed to do so. Nowadays, women are free not to marry, and even not to have children, if they so wish, and society will honor their individual accomplishments.

So how did we seven children develop and eventually become independent? What career did each of us take? How did the hardships affect our patterns of life, our habits and behavior? And what of our neighbors whose parents had also come up from the States and endured pioneer hardships? Since I left the area in 1944, I am unaware for the most part of the explicit details, careers, or jobs for the majority of our neighbors, although I do know that a number did continue farming. Some of the girls went to Calgary, enrolled in business schools, and found city jobs. Some of them also married farm boys and returned to their childhood farm area.

Both our parents had attended college, and we knew they expected that further education would be the future for some if not all of us. This education might be in the field of additional agricultural and religious training, or it might mean college with careers yet to be decided.

Edward

Edward attended Kathyrn High School for at least two and possibly three years, but not four. He was brilliant in mathematical subjects and very good at mechanical and automotive duties. It was not usual for a teenage boy to be so patient with a nosey younger sister who would stick her head under the car hood and watch him clean the spark plugs, but he always acted glad to have me join him. Sometimes when he went by cart to high school, he would let me go with him as far as my school. He probably would have passed the provincial grade twelve tests in science and math but not any English or language exams, so he quit school before grade twelve. (Because of the different American and Canadian standards, he had the equivalent of a U.S. high school education, but without the diploma.)

Our parents wanted him to have the opportunity to explore other avenues besides a farm life, and he undoubtedly wanted this also. Today he could take tests in mechanical skills and perhaps work as an apprentice in established businesses and earn accreditation in that skill. But in 1937, he and Elizabeth went to Bethany Training School in Chicago with no expectation that he would enter the ministry or train for mission work. In late 1941, Daddy was hospitalized with cerebral hemorrhage and Edward was called back home. I know that Mama had heard before he returned home that he was having problems and not adjusting well to his new life. However, in many ways he was still independent and capable of helping with or directing the farm duties. Raymond had gone to Olds Agricultural School and Paul was already in college by 1941, so Edward was needed on the farm., and his formal education came to an end.

Barbara

Barbara was sent to Calgary for grades ten and eleven and earned her room and board by working for a family with one young girl. The decision to send her away from home was apparently based on some or all of the following: her unwelcome odd behavior at church, her own independent and mature personality, and the burden on our parents of providing transportation to Kathyrn High School. Furthermore, Daddy always stressed professionalism. (He would never take us to an oculist but insisted upon seeing an ophthalmologist when available, and he preferred the highly regarded Catholic Hospital over the Calgary General Hospital; thus he undoubtedly compared school in Calgary with the limited rural offerings of Kathyrn High School.) It was during a weekend visit to Barbara in 1935 that I saw my first movie.

After grade eleven, in 1937, Barbara went to Edmonton and shortly thereafter married Edward Olsen. They later returned to Calgary and had two beautiful girls. A lengthy article in the Calgary Herald, June 25, 1979, entitled "Self-realization the stuff of life in Barbara Olsen's 'turning world'" expounds on all her many skills and multiple accomplishments. (Her daughters, Gael and Liane, have provided details under the ADULTHOOD section.)

Elizabeth

Elizabeth, too, went to Calgary High School the same years as Barbara, but she was placed in a widow's home, which lacked the pleasant atmosphere that Barbara experienced. Once I stayed with Elizabeth, too. It seemed that at every opportunity, whether sensibly or not, the landlady raised the boarding costs, so both she and our parents considered other options.

During evangelist Alvin Brightbill's visit to our church, he suggested to Elizabeth that she consider Bethany Training School in Chicago, Illinois. In 1937, after grade 11, she enrolled at Bethany There she met her future husband, Ernest Detrick, and they married September 2, 1938. Elizabeth was sweet and patient and had talent for singing and playing the piano – appropriate skills for a future minister's wife. (Her sons have submitted a history of her adult life in the next section.)

Raymond

When Daddy and Mama were questioned by the Elders of our church about Raymond going into the ministry, Raymond exhibited fear and reluctance at this proposal. He was a kind, gentle person, always willing to help others, but ministry involves far more than that. Fortunately for him there was no pressure from either side, and he pursued his interest in farming attending Olds Agricultural School after grade eleven. This school was first opened in 1913 and remains the best of its kind yet today. He and Robert ended up taking care of the farm; Raymond moved away first, and Robert moved later when his divorce was filed.

Paul

There was never any thought of Paul becoming a farmer. He was clearly the one to go to college, though just what career he would pursue was still in question. Paul was a collector and a photographer: he knew and collected every kind of mineral, every stone make-up, every breed and part of every butterfly he ever caught and mounted, plus details about photography and developing of photos. It was expected that he would go to La Verne College, in La Verne, California, one of the five colleges of the Church of the Brethren and two thousand miles away, the closest one to us. Many La Verne students became teachers or went into the ministry, but Paul had made no career decision yet. A photo in the college yearbook indicates he was a member of the Student Ministry Association.

Paul was the one and only sibling to complete the twelve grades of Canadian high school. Because of the different structures of Canadian and United States educational systems, he entered La Verne College in 1939 as a sophomore rather than a freshman.

Robert

Robert was a year behind me in High School and did not take any grade twelve courses. His interest was not in college education but rather sticking to handyman type of work. He had hoped to become a policeman but that did not materialize due to his marriage, which status was not permitted at the training stage. Obviously one or more of the boys, excluding Paul, would have had to continue helping on the farm even if Daddy had lived, or else our parents would have had to sell, rent out some acreage, or hire year-round helpers. Daddy could not begin to do either the barn or field work, and his death now led to the need for someone to work with Mama and probably schedule all the outside jobs. So Robert and Raymond filled this need when Edward was no longer available.

Ruth

Our parents certainly worked with us to achieve our aims and were probably aware of which children should be encouraged to continue their education and which ones would be happier doing something else. They always talked about my going to La Verne, too, and of course Mama knew I would need a college education to become a librarian!

Fortunately, the folks knew, as well as I did, that I would probably never pass grade twelve math or science courses and thus I would not receive my high school degree. They also knew that it was more difficult for girls to find jobs beyond waitressing if they had no job skills; it would be especially problematic for me if I were going two thousand miles away. So they worked with me to get secretarial skills first. In September 1941, I enrolled at Mount Royal College in Calgary, staying with my sister Barbara and her husband, and earned my keep by helping with the housework. The upstairs apartment was small and the third bedroom had been turned into the kitchen – a kitchen with no water or sink facilities, which meant we had to go to the bathroom to get water for cooking and dishwashing. Staying with her was helpful in learning my way around this small city, but of course I wanted to get my independence as soon as possible.

By January 1942, several of us students realized that we were not getting the education we needed because the teachers were spending far more time with the military students, so we transferred to Calgary Business School. Daddy was on his deathbed so I did not seek his advice or permission, and I can't remember talking with Mama either, since we had no phone at home. We Beard children were making more of our own decisions by this time, and I still could hear Daddy say, "Examine both sides of the situation." (I still have four "Certificate of Honor" cards from the business school certifying grades of 92% to 93% for Bookkeeping, Business English, Shorthand and Spelling, 1942.)

World War II was ongoing and I wanted, yea needed, a paying job rather than more business courses. Let me correct now an accepted error held by many in the independent country south of the "British-owned Canada." The day World War II was declared by England, Canada took the initiative to join in that fight. Some United States leaders claimed that England ordered Canada to join. This was totally false. Canada joined without any such orders. (In other matters, too, Canada was a free nation even though part of the United Kingdom.)

By late summer of '42 I found my first job: a four-month temporary position with the Great West Saddlery, which distributed dime-store type of merchandise. I was the switchboard operator, quite like actress Lily Tomlin's Ernestine character. Not many switchboards are in operation today where a live voice is heard and where calls are answered quickly and with direct transfer to the individual or department wanted. Certainly the old-time switchboard operator received more appreciation than the current taped responses. When my position ended with Great Western Saddlery, the staff gave me a small china teapot and stand. (I also chose one of their china collie dogs for myself. and I still have both items despite the many household moves I have made since 1943.)

With a job, I could afford now to look for my own apartment, and another student, Phyllis Cochran, from Arrowwood, moved with me into a small apartment in a private home. Later we both moved to the YWCA. I worked for a lawyer for one month, twice as long as the two preceding stenographers stayed with him! This was a most boring job, plus the lawyer was a smoker and the office reeked constantly. I could not stand the smell, nor did I want the responsibility of emptying the ashtrays, so I left there gladly, even though the lawyer was a pleasant person.

Next I went to work for a soap manufacturing company where I used my Pitman shorthand skills. (I still have my secondhand Isaac Pitman Shorthand textbook.)

After Canada entered World War II, food rationing went into effect, and later I obtained a civil service job with that department. By spring of 1944, Mama decided that I should think about going to college soon, and she advised me to check with the American Consul office to determine if I needed a passport or not. I was unaware at that time that she had already been involved in proving citizenship status for Paul. When I went to the American Consul, I told him that Daddy had had all of us registered as American citizens in 1936. The Consul learned that I was working for the Canadian Food Ration Department, and he claimed that in doing so I had signed the Oath of Allegiance to Canada on the civil service application form and had lost my American citizenship. I knew I had taken no such oath. Moreover, I did not want to lose my American citizenship at this point in my life. There was no Church of the Brethren College in Alberta, nor anywhere in Canada, and there was no doubt that La Verne College was where I was to go.

I went home and got my copy of this governmental form and took it back to the Consular official. He looked at it quickly and said, "Well, you've lost your American citizenship anyway." Never one word as to why. I was too naive to consider asking him to explain. After all, I was a pioneer farm girl who didn't know even how to catch a bus ride. I've referred to him as the "Ugly American" ever since. So Mama helped me apply for my passport and alien registration, which I received in November, too late to enroll for the Fall Term. It was best, though, to resign from my job and get to California as soon as possible, so Mama paid my way to La Verne by plane. Mama insisted that I wear hat and gloves on the plane, as all "ladies" did in those days.

ADULTHOOD

"Grow old along with me!
The best is yet to be,
The last of life,
For which the first was made."
(Browning, <u>Rabbi Ben Ezra.)</u>

CHAPTER 17

PARENTS AND MY SIBLINGS

MAMA

Mama moved to Calgary by 1947

When Mama married Daddy, she joined the Church of the Brethren, whose principles were similar to her Mennonite background;

both denominations were considered fundamentalist at that time. Her connection with the Brethren church continued even after she moved to Calgary in 1947 where there was no congregation. While I was a student at La Verne College, she was appointed to the La Verne College Board as the first woman and first Board member from Canada. (In the first "ULV Trivia Book", no date, Question 26 asks, "The first woman to serve on the Board of Trustees was elected in 1950. True or False?" I wonder how many La Verne alumni know the answer. It is false. "Mrs. Martha Beard of Alberta, Canada served three terms beginning in 1943.")

Over time Mama began to question her beliefs; she became more liberal, certainly approaching agnosticism and eventually, I believe, becoming an atheist. Her questions and remarks helped me to continue questioning my own beliefs; eventually I joined a Unitarian church. Mama's letters during my marriage indicate how much advice and help she gave me, always in a most courteous respectful manner. Some of these changes can be seen in her letters, in which she does not sound like a woman who was raised as a Mennonite, married a minister, and joined the Church of the Brethren.

On December 2, 1952, she writes, "Yes indeed if the idea of the divinity of Christ were changed, it would change the world's thinking. I understand quite a few people believe in the natural human birth. That's what the Unitarians believe. Couldn't Christ or Jesus have been divine in spirit with a human birth? I heard a sermon by a United Minister this summer say that while different persons gave the world different things, named a number of outstanding inventions and discoveries, Jesus gave the world a higher ethical and moral social standard. It would change the idea of the atonement, etc. I suppose no one will ever really know the truth of this – just like no one knows how life began and how man came to be. Theories yes, but facts?"

And in May 1953, when considering disposal of estate upon her death, she wrote me: "Don't know how it will go when all the Beard estate is to be settled. But then I'll not be here so probably won't know how it goes. Do departed spirits know what goes on where they had been? Or are there no Spirits? I think there are, but that's about all we know about the subject. I also think they sometimes at least return temporarily and appear in their former likeness and can come and vanish just like that. I have read of cases where this happened. I think that's what happened in Jesus case after the so-called Resurrection. Well, just something to think about."

I'll summarize what she wrote me in early 1955, much of it brought about because my husband and I were trying to adopt a racially mixed child while living in the very conservative religious area of Carlisle, PA.

"Science can neither prove nor disprove the existence of God. Most of us believe there must be a great power behind it all and that is what we revere and respect. How much that Power controls the happenings and doing of people as individuals, groups or nations, I don't know. Can not the standard of conduct, our relationship one to another, be taught without the mystery of Christ? Give Christ credit as a great teacher along with Confucius and Buddhist and others. Science or Astrology has found no end to the heavenly bodies, stars, planets, etc., go on indefinitely into space; some may disappear and new ones show up. Was all this brought about by one Being? And for what purpose?"

And she continues expanded remarks along with suggestions for steps we could and should consider in our adoption attempts.

DADDY

When looking through old letters from Paul, I came upon a poem he had sent me many years ago. It was written by Daddy and published in the <u>Gospel Messenger</u> while he still lived in Westminster, Maryland.

GOD KNOWS

What if life be a mystery,
God understands;
Not only life but everything
He comprehends.

Just why our lives are what they are
The Lord doth know,
If we have really lived for Him
They're ordered so.

The thing that God hath kept concealed
Hath well been done,
When He will have us more to know
He'll tell someone.

For every thing He hath revealed
We should be glad
And not for things He's kept concealed
Should we be sad?

The universe with truths Divine
Doth overflow,
And whatso'er the Lord doth grant
Is ours to know.

The reason much is dark to us,
And much is so,

Is not God's fault, it's simply this
We learn so slow.

Since bright creation's dawning morn
On man did shine,
The Lord has tried to teach us all
Of things divine.

But oft we fail to hear or see
The lessons given,
And so we fail to understand
The life we're living.

Dear Lord, we pray with strong desire
For truth and light,
To guide our footsteps day by day
Into the right.

And grant, dear Lord, that we by faith
May win the way
Into thy realm, where mysteries
Are cleared away.

D.R. Beard, R.D.6, Westminster, Md.

By late fall of 1941, Daddy was in the hospital due to his cerebral hemorrhage, and when we visited him, he worried and asked more about the Pearl Harbor attack on December 7, 1941 than about any other subject. His worry was not shocking but a bit of a surprise, since Alberta had been his home since 1917. He died early in January 1942, and the funeral director arranged for public service to be held January 9. Mama had the courage to object, as this was the date of Elizabeth's birthday, so the service was rescheduled for a day or two later. Mixed memories regarding birthdays must have occurred to Mama, since I was born on the third anniversary of my sister Margaret's death.

As far as I can determine, none of us discussed with Mama whether Daddy's beliefs changed and to what extent. Rev. Harold Michael and Rev. I.M. McCune conducted his funeral service, and burial was in Burnsland Cemetery, in Calgary. I recall clearly that when our minister, Rev. Harold Michael, came to our car at the close of the service, Mama, with tears, said to him, "David is so afraid he is going to go to hell." This decries any theory that Daddy had become an atheist, which has been rumored. I do remember that before I left high school daddy would pace back and forth by the long kitchen table and appear completely absorbed in his thoughts and unaware of those around us. Later I wondered if his thoughts were on how he had treated his children, or if he were projecting what the family's situation would have been had he remained in the States instead of seeking a pioneer future, or just what was on his mind. I would hope that his pacing resulted in his realizing and regretting how harsh he had been with his sons, and that he saw his good moral teachings were accepted by all his children and became their standards in their lives, whether they remained Christians or became agnostics or atheists.

MY SIBLINGS

Edward

Edward , some time after high school, ca 1938

The physical and mental demands made of Edward in his childhood caused him serious problems later. When Raymond took over, and he no longer had to run the farm, Edward hired workers for fall threshing jobs and he did the cooking. His responsibilities also included bookkeeping and banking duties, but when the banking officials required certain action or forms from him, he refused to meet their demands or get the information they wanted. This was the first time he ever stood up to authority. I do not know all the details, nor dates or persons involved, but I understand he later talked with Mama, and she encouraged him to receive help by entering Ponoka Mental Hospital. By committing himself, he retained the right to leave the hospital. Eventually, he took the initiative to enter the hospital, and he did leave within a short time.

Later, he came down to see me at La Verne College in 1946 and took my roommate and me to Tijuana, Mexico. The lengthy drive and hunting for directions in a new territory caused him some confusion, which I recognized as unusual for him, though I did not tell my roommate about his situation. She was a worrywart to begin with, and I certainly did not want to deal with two nervous, high-strung people simultaneously.

A letter from Mama, dated August 23, 1954 tells of Edward's ongoing problems:

"On 10th August, I received word from the Provincial Public Trustee that J. Edward Beard had been admitted to the Mental Hospital on the 2nd of August, and would I fill out the enclosed questionnaire. That's the first we knew anything of it; we had known for several years that he was not as good as he had been but that he had gotten into trouble, we did not know. The 13th of June he was here in evening when the others were all here and we divided the quilts and rugs that Aunt Susie had sent up. He appeared quite good, quiet unless on certain subjects.

"It seems he got into trouble with the police and Provincial Traffic Board over a traffic violation, caused an injury to a car. No person was hurt but car smashed, then would not give up his driver's license and became very confused, etc. result was that a psychiatrist was called in. Edward would not talk or answer questions so Dr. recommended he be sent to hospital for his own protection. He might cause or get into a worse accident. He will be there till hospital considers him recovered enough to be safe in society again.

"The police violated their ethical rule by not notifying us as they are supposed to do. Said it was just an oversight."

In January of 1955, Mama reports that the doctor says Edward does not seem to be improving. He was in this mental hospital for many years. Raymond and Robert visited him there even though Ponoka was many miles further north of their homes, just south of Edmonton.

Edward was not rude, nor antagonistic, nor demanding; he was even assigned to kitchen duty where he had access to knives. His quiet, peaceful nature gave authorities assurance that there was no danger to fear from him.

In August 1955, Mama wrote me:

"We had a shock this evening. Raymond phoned Barbara saying Edward phoned and Raymond picked him up at hotel. Edward said he told them at hospital he was through with them, said goodbye and walked out. We knew that if he walked away on his own and we knew about it, we would have to notify his hospital doctor. So Barbara phoned the doctor, who said Edward was better and they had let him outdoors without guard. They had not missed him yet and Dr. said this would not be held against Edward. RCMP [Royal Canadian Mounted Police. R.B.] were notified where Raymond lived and they went to get Edward. Since Edward refused to go back to the hospital, the Mounties took him to police station. He consented to go there and try to fix things up and come back to Raymond's to sleep. Too complicated to tell on paper. Edward will have to be officially released from hospital. Barbara and I found him just as badly confused as ever and we again resign ourselves that he is still a very sick man."

Just when Edward was officially released, I do not know. However, some years later he held a local sales job in a men's store. Perhaps the storeowner kept the hospital alert to how Edward was doing. Eventually, though, Edward was entirely out on his own. He established his own small consignment shop, and did all the office and banking work himself. At this same time, he undertook a mail-order course in locksmithing. His consignment shop is where I visited him when I took a trip home in the late 1970s. Unfortunately, though, after a half-hour of congenial talk with anyone, Edward would show dissatisfaction with Mama and blame her for his situation. Of course all of this hurt us, and we knew how strong our mother had to be in order to commit Edward and to withstand his ill feelings towards her.

In 1981, Edward wrote me this letter, and it shows how well his mental condition had improved (or had never been seriously affected) in certain areas.

"Thank you for the Birthday Card. My, my but you do remember well to recall seeing me tinkering with our first Model T Ford! Please let me tell you something you never likely knew. Did you know we had a Model T Ford while we were still in the USA way back before 1917. Dad sold it before we came to Canada, I think, as some years later he heard from the man who bought it and then paid for it later at this time. Along about 1922 we had one then traded it for another about 1926, then we had another – a coach, then another with red wire wheels. The last Model T after some other makes of cars in-between was about 1936 when I gathered up enough parts to put one together. Crop failure that year and no money. Now which Model T did you see me tinkering with? Love, Edward."

I was only three years old in 1926, so it was the 1936 car I "examined" with him at age thirteen.

In 1982, Edward wrote and asked me why I hadn't taken back my maiden surname after my divorce. He knew that this choice was not uncommon, while I had no idea it could even be done.

Edward ran his shop until his death in 1986. By a coincidence, his death occurred on March 23, the same day as sister Margaret's death in 1920 and my birth in 1923.

I have many good memories of my relationship with Edward. He was very patient with my questions and actions.

Barbara

Barbara, age 69, 1985

(Gael Edmonson, with assistance from her younger sister, Liane, wrote this summary of their mother's life and has given me permission to include it here. As a Canadian, Gael's spelling of certain words differs from that in the United States, but she is correct.)

"Barbara grew up on the farm like her siblings, knowing what hard work was. Being the oldest girl she was responsible for many chores which also included helping her mother with the younger children.

Whether going to school or helping with the thrashing of the grain, Barb handled the horses with determination and spirit that earned her the reputation of a tomboy.

"All through Barbara's life she demonstrated her basic belief to stretch yourself mentally and physically, to constantly challenge yourself. This showed in her determination to get more schooling. She left her family and the farm to go to Calgary where she obtained a high school diploma. The only way for her to attend high school was to do several housecleaning jobs for her expenses including room and board.

"When her daughters were in school Barbara became active in the community by becoming president of the Home and School Association. At the same time she took a three-year course in dressmaking and tailoring. This led to making clothes for her family and other people as well as a position at a sewing centre teaching lessons in sewing skills. To further challenge herself, Barb even had her own sewing show on a local TV studio in the early 1950's, when television was just beginning in Calgary. [Note: Mama wrote me that in October 1954, Barbara was demonstrating the new zigzag sewing machines at the Hudson Bay store in Calgary, perhaps on TV, as Calgary now had TV.]

"However, Barb felt that she wanted to further her education into another field, as she was curious about why people behaved the way they did. Even though society frowned on older women going to university at that time, she went undauntedly ahead to Mount Royal College and later the University of Calgary to take courses in psychology and sociology, earning a degree in Social Work. This led to counseling work in various fields including alcohol and drug abuse and rehabilitation work for people with mental disorders. Later she would become the executive director of the Volunteer Centre helping establish the philosophy and policy of the organization.

"After an amicable divorce from her first husband, she saw a need in the community for people who had been through a divorce, and she wanted help to understand the stages one goes through after a divorce. She developed a six-week course that helped those divorced less than 2-1/2 years grow from the experience and move forward in their lives. During this time as she taught the course she realized that what would also help recent singles was a place they could drop into for more information and discussion. Along with other like-minded friends she assisted in beginning The Calgary Singles Council Society, which is still active in 2006.

"When Barb and her husband, Doug Howell, moved to Vancouver Island, British Columbia, Barb quickly became involved as a board member of Peninsula Volunteer Services for several years. She helped them with developing some of their aims and goals for volunteers in the area.

"There was always a creative side to Barbara. From an early age she liked to draw what she saw around her. Over the years she took various art courses and attended classes at the Alberta College of Art. She particularly enjoyed oil painting and clay sculpturing. She had a wheel for throwing pots and a kiln to fire the objects made at her homes in Calgary and in Sidney, BC. She created clay pots, animals and geometric shapes and placed them throughout the house and garden. One never knew what treasure would be around that bush or near that flower.

"Many of her oil paintings were of nature, particularly the prairie where she grew up and various elements of the coastal forests she explored when she retired there. Portraits of family members and friends she admired were hung throughout her home or given to the person painted. She gave lessons to family and neighbourhood children, delighting in watching their creativity grow under her instruction.

"Perhaps because she grew up on a farm she always had an interest in nature. This showed itself in the creative gardens she developed at each home she had. The gardens attracted many birds that Barb learned to identify by seeing them and by their songs. This led to hikes where she could increase her bird watching skills and take photographs for later paintings or sculptures.

"Barbara lived her life exploring her creative side and the desire to constantly challenge herself mentally. She touched many peoples lives and in turn grew emotionally through all her explorations of her world."

Elizabeth

Elizabeth, in her Wisconsin Home

Though she was far from home, Elizabeth's warmth and caring attitude continued throughout her adult life. Her sons compare her life to the teachings of Apostle Paul in his letter to the Galatians, where he encourages them to live into the fruits of the spirit, the qualities of love, joy, peace, patience, kindness, generosity, faithfulness, gentleness, and self-control. She and her husband not only had three children of their own, but they gave a home to eleven foster children, even taking in four at one time and fostering some of them for many years.

Her youngest son described her kind nature this way.

"One particular incident that is etched forever in my mind is the 'smoking' incident. My older brother, Ralph, set up a cigarette-making factory in his room. We three boys would pick up cigarette butts along the road from the church to the house and take them apart to roll in paper, or put in a corncob pipe. We smoked them in a corn-shock 'teepee' type structure out in the cornfield. I was five or six years old and John would have been about eight and Ralph about ten.

"I apparently heard somewhere that smoking would stunt one's growth, and we were found out when I announced to mom that I was not going to grow any taller. When I said those words, I immediately knew that I had 'spilled the beans.' Mom asked 'Why?' I had to tell her that I had been smoking and about Ralph's cigarette factory. I showed her where the 'factory' was – in Ralph's room. Mom's punishment for me was that she made me smoke a whole cigarette, at least a few good puffs until I was half-sick. Then she destroyed all the contents of the 'factory' housed in the back of Ralph's desk. What was surprising about that incident is that Mom did not yell at me, she did not spank me, nor get angry. She did say something about smoking not being good for one's health and to not do it again.

"What I learned from that early episode was that mom was more of the grace-giver and dad was more of the law-giver."

This incident, which I just heard at this writing, truly expresses the nature my sister has always exhibited, both as my caretaker and teacher decades ago, and later towards her own children. However, this wonderful patient woman endured numerous episodes of depression, and her dreams of dark clouds and utter blackness returned as they had during her childhood.

In 1974, Elizabeth was licensed to the ministry, and in 1977 she was ordained and became the only woman at that time to pastor in the Church of the Brethren in the state of Wisconsin. She was involved in a team ministry preaching on a rotating basis at Rice Lake, Menomonie, Chippewa Valley, and Stanley Congregations. Later she and her husband served as a team at their home church in Stanley, Wisconsin.

Over the years her talents and love of music expanded, and she eventually learned to play at least six instruments; she also composed twenty-two pieces of music, and gave piano lessons for many years. That bag of potatoes that bought our first reed organ in early childhood, on which Elizabeth learned to play, certainly was worth every gardening muscle involved and much more!

Here are some excerpts from her letters to me. During a trip back to Alberta in 1983, Elizabeth read a book <u>The Little White School House</u>, and found out that others in Alberta had it worse than we did. "Why didn't we take the clothespins off the line during dust storms?" she asks.

"1987: Says she was attending classes on health and directing the exercise program. "I took the accordion and we exercised first with waltz music, then faster march type, then slower for cool down. Everyone was smiling and many said afterwards that they would like to do the same again. I'll make a tape using organ and accordion – then it's easier to direct with hands free.

1988: Remarked on my using over 19 idioms in my note, which is alerting her to look up Brewer's <u>Phrases</u> in library. She tells me "I say get off your duff and start writing a book. You have a flair for words. The truth of the matter is, you were born a tiny little princess yourself and your wit and charming smile and sense of humor have helped carry you along with the breeze. Off the cuff I'd say some mighty fine qualities came from this little premature infant as she blossomed over the years.

1989: Wisconsin – Says that "Irvin Stunt & Wife Cecil lived on the Haag's place for about one-and-a-half year….I met him this fall, 1989, in museum where he had a booth and Indian beads from Alberta. I said I was from there and one thing led to another and when he discovered I was one of those Beard girls, he hugged me and was so glad. I hadn't seen him since I was age 5 but have often wondered where they were. He said our folks left you and me at their place while their mama and daddy went to Annual Conference. That was 64 years ago. He also said our Mama went to their place when his first wife was expecting, while he went for a women's doctor but baby was born by the time doctor came. That woman doctor also set my broken arm.

1990: letter to Barbara, Paul, Ruth and Robert: "I wish to thank you for the most thoughtful invitation of the "5 Beards" having a reunion in beautiful BC at your lovely home. Due to the nature of the situation of the proposed family gathering, a discussion of events pertaining to our early life on the farm would be unavoidable, and as a lot of it was unpleasant, it would trigger an emotional stress problem too great for me to bear. My long history of "paroxysmal Tachycardia" or heart palpitations, grows more severe with age and I dare not allow it to happen by focusing on these past memories. Please do not exacerbate matters by further persuasion.

1991: Long horned cows, not buffaloes, attacked Daddy's tent in 1910. In grade 9 – I drove old car bought from C. Cawley. Drove to Kathyrn HS & also went with Yates. I remember driving that old car one day and believe Barbara, at least, and maybe Edward, was with me.

1995: Today in chapel I did something for the first time. I gave a program using most of my original music. Used it for prelude, seven pieces for program; had four people sing four of my songs.

Am down for another chapel service today. Will dress in long navy skirt, white blouse, navy shawl that is over 100 years old and head covering with ties. This is in taking the part of Sarah Major, the first woman preacher in the Church of the Brethren in the 1800's. I'll talk about the things I've learned, ie values in life, our relationships one to another, and aspects of positive living, etc."

Ernest and Elizabeth lived at Timbercrest Center, North Manchester, Indiana for a while, and eventually Elizabeth was moved to the Crestwood Health Center. Immediately upon the death of Ernest, Elizabeth exhibited a great relief of stress, and though she could not express her feelings, her sons believed she now knew she was no longer needed and thus she released herself from life. The Detrick grandchildren were pallbearers at both funerals and also gave violin meditations.

Words and music of the hymns sung at both funeral services were composed by this couple: Elizabeth wrote the music and Ernest the lyrics.

Raymond

Raymond, ready for Olds Agricultural School

In 1941 Raymond attended Olds Agricultural School, which school is still considered the best school in its field. In 1942, he and a friend made their way south to California working in orchards and threshing crews, and back to Alberta in time to harvest the crops he had helped plant. Stories that I'm told vary as to how the decision was made whether Raymond or Robert would remain on the farm and run it. One descendant tells me that they pulled straws; another says that Mama made the decision. In any event, Robert stayed on the farm, and Raymond worked for farmers in southern Alberta, where he met Lorraine, his wife. Later he moved closer to the homeland and bought his own farm, where he set up a bee colony along with the typical field crops. He also set up bee colonies at neighbors' farms. About 1952, he became secretary of the Calgary and District Beekeepers' Association. Mama sent me an agenda of their annual meeting that Raymond arranged. She thought his notice was very well written and she was proud of his efforts. He was the co-founder of the Fort Calgary Wheel and Runner Association. During Calgary Stampede week he would offer wagon rides to visitors. Among other jobs, he worked for Texaco for twenty-five years, retiring in 1979.

A last request

Raymond Beard was a lover and collector of old horse-drawn carriages. On the day of his funeral, Monday, at the Irricana United Church, he was brought to the church in this old-fashioned hearse. Mr. Beard died when the tractor he was driving overturned in a ditch. He was 83.

Raymond's wagon, carrying him to cemetery

Raymond remained the congenial adult as he had been as a youngster, and truly had no enemies. He loved horses, music, dairy cattle, and people. It was ironic that he visited our old Irricana church just three weeks prior to his tragic tractor accident. On the day of his death, though he was not feeling well, he insisted on finishing his tractor work. He accidentally missed the roadway and the heavy tractor went over into the ditch and fell upon him, causing his death.

Baby Margaret and Raymond are the only two Beards buried at our home church. Two of Raymond's favorite horses, Cindy and Sprite, pulled his hearse to the graveyard. How emotional it must have been for his close friends to be his pallbearers. One honorary pallbearer was Eugene Heinz, a very close neighbor all during childhood and youth; was only four days younger than Raymond, and they were like twins during the years they lived close to each other. Two of our favorite childhood hymns, "I Come to the

Garden Alone," and "Bringing in the Sheaves," were sung by the congregation at his service.

Paul

Paul, during La Verne College days

When Paul enrolled as a sophomore at La Verne College in September 1939, he had a notarized certificate signed by Mama stating that he was born in Canada. But because our parents never gave up their U.S. citizenship, and Daddy had had us all registered in 1936 as American citizens, he was considered an American, though being born in Canada, he also was a British subject. Thus the four of us born in Canada had dual citizenship. When he turned twenty-one, he was given his choice of nationalities, and the cold Alberta winters influenced him to remain in the States. I have a copy of his Certificate of Citizenship, No. AA-5396, dated 3 July 1946.

After the United States declared war in 1941, the US Army notified Paul that he was to report for duty, and he appeared at the office as requested. When the attendant told him to sign for military duty, Paul tells us he replied, "If you're going to call me for U.S. duty, then give me my U.S. citizenship." The government did so, and the U.S. Army followed up by telling him to now sign up for duty. Paul answered, "No. I'm a conscientious objector." As a result he was given alternative service assignments, including being a guinea pig for medical tests at Bethesda, Maryland for several years. Thus I graduated a year ahead of him. Many La Verne students became teachers or went into the ministry. A photo in the college yearbook indicates he was a member of the Student Ministry Association, but we all would have been surprised had he actually entered the ministry. Instead he was certified as a teacher and taught for thirty years in the Monterey, California area. Long before his death, his photographs of nature were assigned to a dealer to handle on a web site.

In 1993, Paul wrote that his memories included Santa, at the Hawthorn Christmas program, calling out "Ruth Whiskers" when handing me his package. Even at an early age, Paul says he was more fascinated with the knots and miles of sting to hold the parcels together than the gift of used clothing as our gifts. One of his earliest memories was "we all dressed up in old clothes and paraded in the Irricana Chatauqua parade. I can still see the big tent and the magician sawing a lady in half."

I too remember that, and can see Mama tying a stuffed bag on a pole that Raymond held over his shoulder to resemble a homeless man, or a "vagabond" as we called them.

As to his religious beliefs, Paul writes, "I am naturally very curious and ask myself 'why do humans believe in a creator?' I see so much wishful thinking and subjective observations that I consciously go out of my way to try to be scientifically objective…have seen and studied the wide range of living creatures on earth, from simple viruses to complex humans, studied inorganic universe…this knowledge is reaching a smaller percentage of the population, due to fears and short sightedness of religious proponents. Humans are animals that are programmed biologically through our genes to perpetuate our species just as are cats, dogs or small pox bacteria on trees….I subscribe to the Golden Rule only because I get a warm fuzzy feeling in my being when I make other people's lives more enjoyable…am an Indian giver. Elephants, as a group, are much more compassionate to each other than humans are to each other. Are we up to taking the challenge or shall we keep on killing ourselves in selfish endeavor?"

I think without a doubt Paul analyzed the world's religious philosophies from a scientific viewpoint and is another result of "questioning everything," as we were taught.

Heart attacks resulted in his wearing a defibrillator from 2000 until his eventual death on March 21, 2005. His obituary states that "Paul was a gentle and kind man, intensely interested in life, nature of things, children, animals, minerals and photography, was active in many community organizations including the Gem and Mineral Club, Mining and Mineral Museum, Mariposa Photo Club, and a Courthouse tour guide. He created extensive and imaginative science learning environments, including butterflies and other wild creatures, while teaching grade school, kindergarten, and at the Alternative School for the Monterey Peninsula Unified School District for more than 20 years. He helped establish Camp Unalayee, a wilderness camp for kids, his collection of skeletons of many reptiles and animals were carefully identified and shown to students, he gave his large butterfly collection to Mariposa Elementary. Never one to seek recognition for his many activities, nonetheless the value of his presence was always apparent. He added greatly to the quality of life in Mariposa, especially for children."

Robert

Robert, some time after High School

Robert writes the following: "In winter of '45, I wanted to get off the farm for awhile. Went to Calgary and got a job with Dominion Steel. That lasted about a week. I could not stand the supervisor slinging orders but not lifting a finger to help. Went to Alberta Ice to cut ice for fridges and trainloads of ice for shipment to other towns. Stayed there till spring work. While in Calgary, I stayed at Barb's mother-in-law, Mrs. Clark. Came back and farmed and I think that summer Raymond left to work elsewhere in Calgary. Just Mom and me now. In fall of '46, I tried to join the R.C.M.P. They may still have my fingerprints, for all I know. I backed out – not them refusing me. The reason was I got married that spring and you could not be married at that time and join the Mounties.

"Mom moved to Calgary that spring, 1947. I rented farm from Mom on a share basis for about 12-13 years. By this time we had 3 children; Bligh, Bruce and Patty. I wanted a place of my own and was looking around. Mom asked what would she do. I said Ray would be back in a minute. She said <u>"No, no, no."</u> Then we made a deal where I would buy it. I would get a good price and she would get her share as long as she lived. It turned out okay. The year it was paid for was the year Mom died.

"A few years after marriage, I took a mechanical course in Edmonton for 7 weeks. Didn't learn much as past experience is better than books any day. My final test scores were better than those of a chap I bunked with, which guy was a licensed mechanic.

"Stayed farming till spring of 1977. Then rented to neighbour. Wife and I had difference of opinion and separated. Took 7 years to get a divorce.

"Friend and I moved to Medicine Hat in spring of '77. Got a job at a Farm Machine Dealer, repairing, setting up new products and delivering them. Was their last employee when they sold out in December 1990. Worked for different dealers till I was 73 years old. Some time in here, we moved to Redcliff, near Lethbridge. To spend time I would make garden sheds, my style, and utility trailers, and now dog houses that look like a barn.

"My good friend, Lou, had four children, who went with us to Medicine Hat. My three stayed with their mom. Lou and I got married in 1990 and all is well. Her children moved out, some married, some don't want to.

"Now I make the dog houses, hoping to sell. Sold three this year. Only make on order. I read a lot, mostly true crime and western. No fiction.

Retirement hobby for Robert

"Am in reasonably good health, but have spur in hip and shoulder near or in backbone. Can never recall having a headache. Wear glasses to read. Way back in time I was called 'Robert,' and don't know when or where folks began calling me 'Bob.'"

(Daddy would <u>never</u> allow any of us to be called by nicknames, or adding the babyish ending of 'ie' such as "Ruthie." The one exception was the one he made by calling his favorite daughter 'Betsy' at times, instead of 'Elizabeth.' To this day, I refuse, hopefully in a polite manner, to answer to "Ruthie." Coincidentally, my ex-mother-in-law and my successor were both named "Ruthie." R.B.)

"No matter what my birth may be,
No matter where my lot is cast,
I am the heir in equity
Of all the precious Past."
(Abbie Farwell Brown, <u>The Heritage</u>)

CHAPTER 18

AUTHOR'S JOURNEY

RUTH

Ruth, in Portland Oregon, 1949, after College

My "alien" status meant I had to register every year at some U.S. office. The first year I took a bus to Los Angeles. Even though it was not as huge a city then, it was frightful and downright scary for this country girl to find bus service or taxi, locate the agency, and then make the return trip. It's a wonder my black hair didn't turn white on the spot. The following years I went to the office in San Bernardino. While it was still frightening, it was much better than metropolitan Los Angeles.

Perhaps a few remarks that fellow students wrote in THE 1945 AND 1946 LAMBDA, our La Verne College yearbook, will describe how fellow students viewed me when my background varied so much from theirs. How many other girls had no friend until the ninth grade? Were any of them the only student in a primary school grade for over six years.

They wrote:

"Things have been more lively since you moved in." "Keep that Canadian smile." "You're a pretty good kid even though you are from Canada." "Truly, I've never had such a friend as you. As a tease, Ruphus, you are really super." "Do you realize what queer individuals we all are? That's why I enjoy people like you." "Ruth, when you become civilized and learn to eat with a fork, you'll be ready to graduate." "You're really a swell kid, and the fact that you've come from Canada isn't a set back. You've been a lot of fun and you really have some great possibilities in the field of speech—even if you wouldn't give your philosophy of life in chapel."

"This year has been extremely interesting…With all of your interesting additions and questions in both Psychology and Sociology the classes have never been dull." "Boy gal, what a screwball (that's pretty good spelling huh!) you are. Ha! Ha! Seriously, I like you very much, chum." "Being from Canada, of course you're first a foreigner." "Canada has some very fine people and you are one of them." "It's been fun knowing you and being able to tease you. You have a great sense of humor. A lot Canada can be proud of its little Ruth." "Well, Paul said that you were a chip off the same block—just something about these furriners that distinguishes them."

So it would appear that I was not a quiet unfriendly type gal, but evidently fit in with these students from many areas in Washington, Oregon, and California, and from a wide range of backgrounds. A cartoon captioned for me as "ornery creature" showed one cow turned around in a row of many cows. Clearly I had changed from the lonely isolation of my grade school days.

Referring to the above remark about learning to eat with a fork, the English hold the fork in their left hand and the knife in the right, eliminating the need to transfer utensils as is our practice in United States. While on the farm, we all used the American way, but when Barbara and I lived in Calgary, we both accepted the English custom.

Since I entered La Verne College at mid-term and had some credit for my Alberta High School courses, I was not eligible for a specific class year until I completed two additional courses during the summer of 1946. Then I was eligible to be classified as a junior that fall. Activities during college include:

Membership in the newly formed Visitation Group

Co-president one year of the Student Christian Association

Minor role in The Rivals.

Leading role of Jo in Little Women.

Speech Contest, Junior Year. Placed second with four participants.

My disappointment in not taking first place in the speech contest was greatly eased when others told me my delivery was the best, and I should not feel bad because the first place winner was a senior and an honor student! The topic assigned for this contest was "Should Palestine be a homeland for the Jews?" I also recall just before this topic was assigned that a guest chapel speaker opened his talk with this statement: "The turmoil in the East is based on the term 'oil'." So what else is new more than six decades later?

Practically every student worked their way through college, perhaps limited to fifteen hours per week, as is true today at Warren Wilson College in Swanannoa, NC. I arrived at La Verne in January 1945, my initial job was with Fred Butterbaugh, Field Representative, who wrote in my '45 Yearbook "You're a good secretary, Ruth, Nuf said!" In the fall, I accepted a library position and ended up typing catalog cards!

Today with all collections entered on the computer, these cards are obsolete. Typing on three-by-five cards, before any erasable ribbon was invented, took really good skills and was a headache. One corrected errors with a special knife, and to my pride and joy, I still today, sixty years later, have that special knife that I bought. I do not use it for typing corrections, but it is perfect for many jobs that no one would ever think appropriate for most knives. The two-inch steel blade is very strong and the yellow bone handle is both strong and beautiful.

In the summer of 1945 when all the other students went home, I could not afford the two-way trip back to Alberta, nor was it likely I'd find a job for the short summer break. One of the older girls, Alveta Shively, invited me to go home with her to Bakersfield, California and find a job there, which I did. I was very grateful that she suggested this and that her parents not only were receptive to the plan but treated me as a family member.

That Christmas all but three students went home for the two weeks when the college was closed. So Johnny Johnson, our one Negro student (we never referred to that race as "black" in those days), and a very heavy, tall student nicknamed "Tiny," and I spent our leisure time in the evening walking around singing, "We are three little lambs who have gone astray, bah, bah, bah." Johnny was the only one who could sing, in a beautiful tenor voice.

I was proud – and lived up to Daddy's beliefs about race relations – when I later learned that Johnny Nelson Johnson, from New

York, told college officials that I was the first white girl who ever asked him to be her partner. I had asked him to be my partner and roller skate with me, though we had very different styles of skating. I would pick up my feet while Johnny just leaned his body left or right and bent his legs, but we enjoyed the event and each other! We all were sad that Johnny did not return to La Verne the next year.

When it was time to decide what career I wished to follow and choose major courses, the early statement from Mama that "Ruth **should** be a librarian," impelled me to tell myself "If Mama wants me to be a librarian, that's the last thing I'm ever going to be!" Mama never knew her remark burned in my soul for decades; in fact I feel sure she never learned how much I let that comment harm me. There was no recognition by society in those days that teen-agers had specific age-related problems and parents could ask or suggest but never tell their child what they "should" become. Had Mama worded her statement as "Ruth would make a good librarian," or "I think Ruth would enjoy library work," rather than the word "should," I suspect I might have had a more positive reaction. I favored social work because we were always taught respect and care for the less fortunate and physically disabled folks, and no one had said "Ruth should be a social worker!"

How many hundreds of years was society obsessed with the strong expectation that every adult would marry, with the implication that it was up to every female to "catch" a male. When I was home in 1946, one of my older neighbor males approached me to ask "What's the matter? Can't you catch a man?" There was that word "can't" again! And I still had not learned to put it in its proper place, or to defy society's expectations. When a male friend came from my home area to visit me at college, I very reluctantly declined his request to marry him. Having endured the hardships of farm life and the kitchen responsibilities, and all the farming inconveniences, I told him "I could never be a farmer's wife." I might very well have been happy with him, but the thought of a farm life was unbearable. But if someone had said to me "Ruth, you 'can't' be a farmer's wife," I might very well have married him to show them that "I could!" Hmm, today I wonder if I could have persuaded him not to be a farmer! Probably not.

The Student Advisor, Dr. Lorell Weiss, discussed with me what plans I had upon my graduation. The question of my citizenship never came up, and I wonder yet today if he was aware that U.S. citizenship was required for any state social work or if perhaps he knew that a Master's degree was essential for private service agencies. I do not recall any advice or definite decision at that time.

I graduated in the spring of 1948 with limited options. I might be called back across the line by the Canadian officials, or worse yet, ousted by the American ones, so what should I do? Fortunately the college had planned and was financing a Peace Caravan Tour lasting most of the summer months, which would tour close to the western Canadian border. I applied and was included with four other students. I had no job and knew I might be deported at any time, so I planned to remain as close to the border as possible, but still without any job or living accommodations in mind.

From the denomination's Gospel Messenger of July 31, 1948: "A peace caravan, composed of five La Verne College students, is touring Oregon this summer. Members of the caravan are Ruth Beard, Mary Esther Glover, Calvin Tooker, Wayne Gibson, and Stanley Sutphin. The caravaners spent one week at the Tonganoxie Peace Institute in Kansas in June, then they spent ten days at the Friends Service Committee Institute on international relations at Whittier, Calif."

During part of this trip, an additional student, Philip Zinn was with us. I kept a journal of our travel, a portion of which follows:

"Early June, 1948: Remember our hot stop in Needles, CA, at 8:00AM, when we stopped to have the car fixed and buy a water bag. We ate under the sprinklers in a little park and moved the hoses when the custodian turned his back, so we could wash our lettuce, etc.

"And the 2AM incident out on the wide open spaces where the lavatories were operated by the same key and we drove off with the key in our possession – finding it in the glove compartment next day, put there by Philip Zinn.

"Shall we mention our flat tires here or wait and give them altogether. Out in the desert, of course! Let's not mention the 3 flats we rode with all summer. Ouch.

"Our buzzing door must be next. Oh wonderful music to my ears. Remember how I looked through the slats of the women's lavatory door to see why no one answered our knock and how they could make such unearthly noises in such a small confined space. And how we lunged for the door after the attendant told me it was electrically controlled. The blessings of this modern age!

"Poor Wayne and Phil. I guess we 3 girls (originally there were 3 girls and 2 men, but plans were to become 2 girls and 3 men) did keep them waiting at gas station stops. But not as long as we all 3 took showers in the men's room when the ladies' was being painted and Zinn took guard at the door. Such a small area too.

"Of course, I shall never forget Colorado Springs – nor shall Wayne. As Cal would say "our shodesty was mocked when first Wayne walked in on me and then I on him. Have you ever seen a pair of shorts go dancing?" And then the night you woke up, Mary, and found Stan had moved his sleeping bag in our rain-soaked tent beside yours.

"June 13 – July 14, attended various training conferences prior to our own program presentations.

"July 14 – Waterford Church of the Brethren. Modesto and Empire congregations included. Moderator: Stanley Sutphin. Theme: Russian-American Relations. Comments: We were advised that the people would probably want to see us all in action. Four of us gave short speeches and Stan opened the discussion. We felt that the audience presumed that they were to criticize our methods and answers in light of the rest of our trip, and we are not holding the meeting for their benefit. Their questions indicated that they thought we were experts and should give definite statements. We failed to make our purpose clear at he beginning of the meeting.

July 18 – Medford, Oregon. Calvin led the discussion on "Causes of War" with an audience of Methodist young people. Half way through the discussion one fellow asked what the purpose was of such a talk and remarked that the causes mentioned were outmoded. He was outnumbered by the rest who demanded to know what causes did not have part in today's problems, and before long he was on our side, talking very intelligently on international problems. The Sunday School Superintendent advocated that U.S. carry a big stick and speak softly to Russian."

We traveled through adjacent states from Kansas and then northwest through Idaho before ending in Oregon. While Idaho was a bit closer to my Alberta home, I knew no one there, so I decided to go with the tour group all the way to Oregon and stay with my former dormitory roommate until I found a job. I stowed away $30, sufficient at that time for bus transportation back home to Calgary.

So now here I was in Portland, staying with a college roommate while searching for a job. I was not eligible to be a social worker since I was an alien, but I could work with the State Welfare Department as a secretary. Within a few months, I knew this choice of career was not what I'd hoped it would be. There was too much bureaucracy, too long before providing service to needy folks, and the social workers' hands were tied. I left within three months. Now what? I could not afford to even think of getting my Master's degree in order to seek similar employment with a private agency, and perhaps my negative reactions would have surfaced there too.

I took a memorable job as secretary with the Portland YMCA. There was a window on the back wall of my office space that opened directly to the swimming pool. The window blind could be opened or closed only on the pool side, and someone had left it open. One day I heard someone calling out a question, and I naturally stepped to the window to answer. There was a man coming along the side of the pool – completely naked.

In November of 1949, out of the blue, my Certificate of Naturalization arrived. That $30 I had hidden came in handy to take a surprise trip home at Christmas. I had told Barbara and we were keeping it a secret. Mama had previously bought a house and was living in Calgary. I arrived and simply knocked on her door. Not only was she surprised, I was taken back by her quick and unexpected greeting of "You've got bangs!"

During my time in Portland, I attended the Church of the Brethren; when a group of the denomination's conscientious objectors was assigned to a project in the area, I met Joe, one of the young men. Within a few months he asked me to marry him. I was almost twenty-seven years old in a society that looked critically at any girl of that age who hadn't "caught" a man, so I accepted; but as many potential brides experienced then as now, I endured anxiety for weeks as to whether this was the right decision. I hadn't known him very long, I was a good bit older, I had finished college and he had not even started, and he had serious eye problems that might result in his early blindness. I argued with myself that caring for others was what I had been trained to accept and what social service was all about. I could take care of him, and since he planned to be a minister, I would have the opportunity to prepare the worship portions, which planning I always enjoyed. A discussion with one of our ministers still led to indecision. However, I decided to go ahead with the state-required medical exam, as I had not seen a doctor since leaving home in 1944, and I felt I had reasons for a physical examination. I would make a final decision later as to marriage. (In 1999, Barbara sent me a photo of mama, and wrote: "It saddens me when I see her so full of life and intelligent. To think she ended up living in a cold shack for most of her life. I once asked her why she married father. She replied 'It was less of a shame to be married to someone you didn't love than to be a maiden lady.' How society has changed.")

The doctor kindly told me that my condition indicated that very likely I could not have my own children, and that we take that fact into account in making plans. Every married female was expected to have children, and so did I, despite not being at home with babies. Furthermore, there was that word "can't" again. It also came to my mind that I had learned in college that adoption took many lengthy years. I put aside all doubts of this partnership choice, and we were married shortly thereafter.

That spring Joe started college at La Verne. I moved down by the end of the semester, and by midsummer we decided we must go back to Pennsylvania to take care of his parents. My brother Paul gave us his old Model A Ford for a wedding gift. I was very thankful, though, that he lent me his automatic steering car to take my first driving test, which I passed.

During our drive from California to Carlisle, Pennsylvania, when Joe was driving, a cow started across the highway. At the last minute I yelled as it was obvious Joe could not see the animal coming from the side of the road. That really woke me up to the seriousness of his condition, and my marriage to him.

His father, Joseph, was in his eighties, his mother in her sixties and almost blind from cataracts. A blind uncle also stayed with them sometimes. His parents' home was half of a double house, built by his father, an architect and cabinetmaker. In fact, Joseph Sr. designed and built the first Indian School, which was right there in Carlisle. (I must mention that because I kick myself every time this comes to mind. I know now that all of his dad's sketches, final drawings, and all the bookkeeping details, including copies of bills and receipts, would be extremely valuable today, as one learns by watching <u>Antiques Roadshow</u>. Unfortunately, after my mother-in-law died and we made plans to move, we naively threw them all in the trash!)

His mother's name was Ruth but everyone called her "Ruthie," or "Little Ruthie," and my Joe was referred to as "Little Joe," so we could avoid confusion as to who was being called.

Joe enrolled at Elizabethtown College, near Harrisburg, PA, another Church of the Brethren college, but after two car accidents, he got cataract examinations from a highly reputed ophthalmologist in Philadelphia. His cataracts were congenital and surgery was planned. Different neighbors drove us those one hundred fifty miles several times, but for the last trip we decided I would drive – a very different experience than driving the country roads nine miles to high school! During this time, Joe had to give up college, but he found various jobs there in Carlisle.

I worked at the Bedford Shoe Factory across the street from his parents' home. At one minute after 5:00PM, as I walked back across the street to our home, my mother-in-law would call to me and say, using a typical Pennsylvania Dutch expression, "You dare set the table now." No break of even five minutes for any relaxation. Since supper was no later than 5:30PM, we all had a snack of ice cream before bedtime, beginning my lifelong habit of bedtime snacks.

Early in 1952, I had a hysterectomy, and now birthing our own children was out of the question. That part I did not mind since I was terrified of babies, and it would be a double worry for me living with an almost blind mother-in-law and a blind uncle. (Princess Elizabeth became the queen when I was in the hospital; another connection which aids in memory of events.) Joe's dad died in the spring of 1952. Knowing that the wait could be very long for adoption, we applied within a couple of years to the local adoption agency, requesting a girl, one at least two years old.

Joe's mother was eligible for a blind pension; its denial caused her such trauma that she had a heart attack and died within several months. The State income formerly given her due to her blindness was our basic source of everyday financing for all of us.

Sometime after his dad died, when Joe was working as a sales person, he surprised his mother and me by bringing a young pup home from the pet shelter. The puppy was totally black, a part schipperke whose long tail had been cut off. (Schipperkes were the breed used in Belgium on ships to catch rats.) We named him Pogo. Since the yard was completely fenced in, Pogo had the run of the outside as well as inside. His favorite nesting place was the old living room couch, and I can still see my mother-in-law trying to sit down on the couch when, naturally, Pogo would be in the very spot she had chosen to back into.

It was not long before he exhibited great curiosity and would scratch the wall in an attempt to reach a light switch—not to turn it on, but to check out what that thing was. He barked at every new object he found.

One morning as I came down to the dining area, I found Joe's blind uncle feeling all around on the table and half muttering to himself.

When I asked him if I could help him in any way, he said he thought he had eaten only one piece of toast and he couldn't find the second. He'd already rechecked in the kitchen and didn't find it. I then also checked the kitchen area and assured him it was not there nor was there a piece on the dining room table. So he said he must have eaten it without realizing that he'd done so.

By then I needed to go upstairs to waken Joe and I went up the back steps rather than the front ones. There was no stair light on and I almost reached the top step when I came upon Pogo, nosing around something on the step. A closer look and I saw he had half a piece of toast. Of course I never told any one except Joe about this incident.

Later we also took in two Spitz pups but retained only the female, whom we named 'Susie,' and gave the male to another couple. Susie liked attention and petting always. Years later I realized her personality was like Joe's and Pogo's was independent like mine, and why these two pets would choose the company of their owners who had their same characteristics. This is often typical of humans but was surprising to us from these animals.

Our financial situation was very poor so I again went job hunting and found a job at Dickinson College as Acquisition Librarian. Exactly two days after starting this job, the Carlisle social worker called and asked us to come in. I could do so on my lunch hour and went by myself. She was offering us a two-day old baby girl! I told her I could not possibly handle so young a child and reminded her that we had asked for at least two years old. So what did she do? She immediately tore up our application. This social worker was a spinster of approximately seventy years, and I doubt if she had ever had any official training in this field.

We knew that social agencies in this conservative Pennsylvania area would not consider us for adoption if we were not strong churchgoers, so we stuck with the Carlisle Church of the Brethren. We filed an application with the Harrisburg agency but sensed little acceptance due to our willingness to adopt a racially mixed child. We applied to an interracial agency in New York but could not afford to travel there for the required personal interview.

From the time that we knew that adoption was the only means by which we could have a family, Mama made helpful suggestions in all her letters to me. In April of 1955 she asked, "In getting a baby from a welfare or adoption board, is it possible to know any thing of the child's background? What kind of parents, etc? I am wondering whether Welfare people will adopt those children out before they know whether one or the other or both parents might recover, and want the child back, especially a baby. Isn't it possible to get a child from intelligent parents who are not married or even where the father might not be known? "

And another letter that month, she suggests "How about contacting your doctor or the Salvation Army for finding a small child? Is there an age limit that foster parents have to be? These children that Pearl Buck writes about that she adopts out come through the Adoption Board. They are the children of mixed race parents – and neither race wants the child so she get them and finds foster parents who are willing to take and love this child even if it should have slant eyes, etc. They are often clever and quite intelligent youngsters. Perhaps you couldn't bring one like that into your family circle? Just as long as any child you get is physically and mentally okay, race doesn't matter."

And on May 9, 1955, she wrote, "Barbara knows the woman at the head of the Calgary Welfare Board so she talked to her. The reply was that the Welfare Boards were not eager to send children to the U.S. However, she gave Barbara the address of the Superintendent who is at the Head of the Provincial Board.

Here it is, you can do as you wish about writing him, telling who you are, being born and schooled in Canada and that your family still lives up here, etc. We thought all that might help.

"Now just in case you are unable to get a child, you won't get too despondent; there are many other things to be done. Those old cities are so set in their old pattern, no reason for them to be up and doing. The West is younger and more ambitious to get ahead. The whole East is more conservative; try and see it from their angle and you can understand them better."

(On an entirely different note, Mama informed us that in June, 1955, Alberta and Saskatchewan were celebrating their 50th Anniversary of becoming "Provinces," and the events were called Golden Jubilee Year.)

Although I had known about Pearl Buck's adoption agency, near Philadelphia, I did not give that source serious thought until Mama wrote about it. We were so tired of getting the runaround that we decided to take the one-hundred-fifty-mile trip near Doylestown, Pennsylvania without calling or making an appointment. Fortunately the Welcome House staff talked with us for about half an hour, and then said they would schedule an appointment with a social worker and we would need to come back. Not only did they not turn us down, they were very courteous and cooperative, and especially receptive to our desire for a racially mixed child. John Holt's agency in Oregon dealt mainly with Negro adoptees and Welcome House with Orientals. We applied for any racial child, but knew that it was very likely to be of mixed Oriental race, which was quite okay.

Before any child was available, my mother-in-law died. We wanted to move from that home near the Bedford Shoe Factory. In the late 1950s, we found a home in the country setting of Shepherdstown on old Rt. 15. This highway ran from Harrisburg to Gettysburg, but there was minimal traffic as the new Rt. 15 was now completed a quarter of a mile east.

Shepherdstown consisted of a post office and a grocery store, located on the top of the hill almost across the road from our new home. Our home, a four-bedroom building, was lovely, although some improvements were needed. We were on the southern hillside, and the former Shepherdstown Hotel was on the northern side. Originally named the Union Hotel and built in 1860 by Abraham Zook, the hotel was a 20-room Georgian inn. It sold in 1887 at an orphan's court sale for $1,206; in 1897 Adolphus Busch bought it for a place to sell his beer. When American went "dry" in 1918, he sold it for $750, and for two decades it became the Hilltop Inn. From 1940 on, it has been a private home, and the present owners soon became our friends.

Our next door neighbors, Katy and David Dobbs, were a middle-aged couple who sometimes needed our help, but who also helped us when we needed them. They accepted our two dogs almost as their own, and we would often find them, especially Susie, sleeping on their back porch which faced the south side of our home.

On one occasion, David needed help to repair his high barn roof, and Joe not only helped place the two-story ladder to the roof but was up there helping with the repairing. Can you imagine how shocked I was when I went outside and saw that Susie had climbed this ladder and was almost to the top step! I held my breath.

Then I yelled to Joe. How could Susie get up that last step onto the roof? And how could she manage the sloped surface? And worse yet, how could she turn around and climb back down? Fortunately she did not try to turn around but kept looking upwards and putting one foot up, then back down, then up again. By this time Joe realized that the only solution was for him to carry her back down. I can still see him, crowding around that big hairy Spitz to get his feet down on the ladder step below Susie and then holding her in one arm and bringing her carefully down as he himself had to balance for this unusual experience.

And did it ever happen again? Even when she had been told NEVER to do that? A few days later, not only was Susie almost to the top, but there was Pogo ahead of her. I grabbed my camera, got a shot of them, with Joe again at the top bewildered as to how to get both of them down. One can only imagine his fear—he could manage only one dog at a time, and how could he safely leave one while working around the other? He was successful, but I don't know how he did it. We did solve future misbehavior by blocking the first several steps of the ladder so that neither could climb nor jump to a crossbar.

Pogo and Susie climbing the ladder

CHAPTER 19

OUR CHILDREN

Carol – Our First Adopted Child

Sometimes extreme happiness can cause as many tears as the most tragic sadness. It was in the early 1950s that my husband and I applied to several adoption agencies for a child at least two years old or older. Since having children of our own was impossible. Our choice was for a racially mixed child, although any single race child would have been quite acceptable, but few such children were available in those days, and the few adoption agencies that accepted non-white children were dealing mainly with mixed racial ones. We finally turned to Pearl Buck's Welcome House in Doylestown, PA.

We had a most pleasant office interview with Welcome House staff, followed up by almost three years of phone calls, more visits, and letters. Finally at the end of May 1957, Miss Scott from Welcome House came to our Shepherdstown home, bringing a little girl who was available for adoption. Virginia was five years and nine months old. Her biological parents were American and

Filipino, but this young child was born in the States and had been in foster care for over four years.

Virginia was to stay with us for a week before we needed to make a decision. We spent several hours talking with Miss Scott. I took Virginia upstairs to see her new bedroom, and she played up there while the three of us were downstairs in the living room. Eventually I went up to see what she was doing. There she was, down on her knees pulling back the bedspread and looking under the bed. I asked, "Virginia, what are you looking for?" and she answered in an anxious childish tone, "I'm looking for my new Mommy and Daddy." She had been in foster care for almost five years, and did not know what a Mommy and Daddy were! This foster care had been provided by an older unmarried woman, "Aunt Sarah," who cared for her elderly father, called "Grandpa."

The child was very sweet, and of course we wanted to adopt her; we named her "Carol." During the next few weeks, we found out that she could not count to ten and knew only three colors, yet she had been in kindergarten for ten months. What she liked best was playing with the dog, climbing our trellis, and singing repeatedly, "Go tell Aunt Grodie." The few times we had her sit in a chair for misbehaving, she would just sit there and sing that song over and over. We spent time trying to help her catch up in the many areas so long neglected.

Since she had been in kindergarten a full year, we enrolled her that September in first grade in our local Shepherdstown school. At the close of the second school day, her teacher called me and said that Carol was not ready for grade one. I reminded her that Carol had had a full year of kindergarten and should certainly be eligible for first grade. The teacher wisely invited me to come the next day and view this situation myself. I did so. It was obvious that Carol was totally out of it. Her eyes became totally glazed. Nothing was sinking in. There was no sign of paying attention, or interest, nor recognition of anything being said or asked by the teacher – just that totally glazed and inattentive appearance. Sadly, it was apparent that no further discussion was needed, and I agreed that another year of kindergarten was essential.

Several months later, just a few days before Christmas, a friend of mine offered us her son's excellent top grade upright piano. We accepted eagerly, and it was delivered immediately on Saturday. On Sunday, we went to church where children had their own Sunday school class but then came to sit with parents during the sermon. Most of the children would spend that time coloring or reading. While my husband sang in the choir, Carol sat beside me quietly, sometimes swinging her legs but never asking to color or read.

When we returned home, Joe went upstairs to change his clothes and I went to the kitchen to prepare dinner. Carol was in the living room playing with Susie, or so I thought. All of a sudden I heard a noise from the living room, and I stopped short, "that's not Joe!" Immediately the sound came again from the living room, and I dropped the paring knife and stepped into the living room. Just as I crossed the threshold, I saw a shadow to my left from the window landing and glancing up the stairs, saw Joe staring down with eyes and mouth wide open – a look of complete awe. I turned quickly to see what he was staring at, the spot in the living room area where the sound was coming from.

There sat our little girl on the piano bench. Both her hands were on the keyboard – no hymnals or music facing her. But she was playing – playing the carols we had heard at church that morning. She played several measures from one hymn and several from another, but we could easily determine what she was playing. Joe came down the steps and we both sat there, our mouths open, tears falling, and not believing what was obvious. There was our little girl, playing by ear! This little girl who had to repeat kindergarten, had this unique, wonderful, and unforeseen gift.

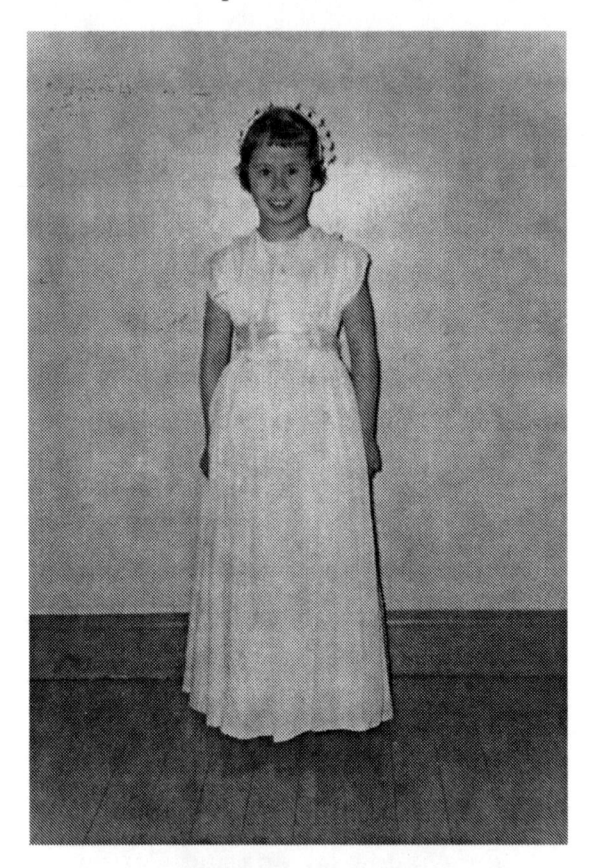

Carol in Kindergarten, Spring 1958

And as her parents wept, she began playing the morning Choir anthem, playing this piece from beginning to end. It was a simple tune – "Come, come ye saints." And wiping my tears, I thought, "yes, there are saints in this room, there are even angels here today." Our little girl, who was still learning what a Mommy and Daddy were, could play by ear.

It is a talent so unusual, so unpredictable. Later a psychologist suggested that this skill was probably founded in the loving treatment of her foster "aunt" who repeatedly cautioned, "Be quiet, don't waken Grandpa." So what she heard was retained because she could not be active, noisy and talkative like typical young children.

It was the happiest day, and it is still the most joyous and unexpected experience, of my entire life. The tears of absolute surprise and joy then turned to hope and confidence about what our little girl could accomplish and share with others.

We received the official adoption papers at the end of her first year with us. We were so thankful that we had found an agency that graded honesty and ethical values above the conservative stance of the Carlisle society." Since our religious beliefs were becoming more liberal, we did not feel at home in the conservative local Church of the Brethren. Shortly thereafter we joined the Unitarian Church in Harrisburg, Pennsylvania.

Nelson – Our Second Adopted Child

Now it was time to meet with Welcome House and apply for adoption of a second child. Anticipating the possibility of adopting three children, we asked for another girl, stating that we would then want the third child to be a boy. In early November I received a phone call from our social worker asking if we might consider a boy from Seoul, Korea. When I quickly answered, "Yes," she interrupted with the suggestion that I might want to talk with my husband first, but I assured her he would be in full agreement. I wonder if the worker had earlier sensed that I was the one who generally took the initiative in decision making. Joe always did the reasoning and questioning within his own mind, while I was used to blurting out arguments, as learned earlier with my siblings, especially with Paul.

We expected this two-and-one-half-year-old Korean-American boy might arrive by Christmas. I cannot describe the excitement and then anxiety we endured when we were not called until mid-January to meet the social worker at New York Idlewild (now Kennedy) Airport on January 17, 1959, 11:00AM, Northwest Airlines, Flight #8. She was bringing five children from Korea and ours, Lee Yong Soo, was the last one to be picked up by his new parents. He was one of many "street" children who survived even at his age out in the street. Of course he could not speak one word of English.

All three of us were anxious as we waited at the airport. While we were high with anticipation, the social worker was in tears as she turned over the last of the children she had rescued. While Joe went to retrieve the car for our homeward trip, I took both children to the restroom. When I pulled open the commode door, as soon as Lee Yong Soo saw where we were, he became overly anxious, grunted sounds, and pushed us aside as he hurried in. There was no doubt he had to go first. On the drive home, all of us jabbered constantly without our understanding each other! We named him Nelson Lee, honoring his own name as well as that of some of our special friends.

**Nelson joined us in 1959.
Carol and Nelson by our fireplace**

I wrote our Welcome House social worker on January 29, 1959, just thirteen days after we got our Nelson:

"Dear Miss Scott: What do you mean that it will be about two weeks before the children generally start talking English? I wish you could hear Nelson tonight trying to sing "Twinkle, twinkle little star." He is just as sweet as can be. I think we hit the jackpot again. He was attracted to the radio right away and would stand in front of it and jazz it up. So we played Carol's records about 4 days ago. That was our mistake. I now change records from the time he gets up in the morning till he goes to bed at night and he is just heartbroken if we turn it off. Carol sang and played the above song soon after he came and he does his best to follow. Maybe he's doing so well because Joe started him out saying "Massachusetts Institute of Technology." He says the following words knowing what they mean: Carol, kitty, doggie, baby, and car.

"No longer is he the shy little fellow we met at New York. He is a little reserved with others but with just the two of us he and I talked so much – before he discovered the record player, that is. Yesterday he learned to kiss. It's amazing the way he can read inflections and hand signs. We still have difficulty making out his wants at times but when he starts hollering when I carry food off the table, I know he wants it even if it is leftovers from someone else's plate. I think his appetite has tapered off a bit. For awhile I thought we would never fill him up.

"Carol is quite pleased with him. She thinks she ought to have time to play with him before leaving for school. They play hide and seek. He pulls her over to the music to clap hands along with him. She's been helping him up from his nap and cutting his meat, etc. Sunday, they got up first and went downstairs. Pretty soon I smelt toast! He had his buttered piece fixed by Carol. The last time Carol sneaked downstairs to surprise us with breakfast, she didn't get anything done but putting the teaspoons on the table.

"I thought you meant Carol would have to realize that her parents had two arms each for them. One night last week I put my arm around Carol as she stood by my chair, she and Nelson already having eaten supper. Nelson howled at this and cried to get down. He immediately came to me begging to get up on my lap. Then he proceeded to help me finish my supper! The first few days he didn't welcome his daddy home at all but now he's about as anxious as Carol to greet him.

"Of course he's had his pouty times too. I'll be happy when he keeps his bed dry at night as well as at nap time! He's beginning to lose his fear of the pets. I caught him pulling the cat's tail so I can't feel too sorry for him when she turns on him.

"Do come see us whenever you can. Sincerely yours,"

The Shatto Family: Joe, Ruth, Nelson and Carol, ca 1959

We had been told that in Korea most orphans or abandoned children were "street" kids and resorted to self-survival actions, and that they all wanted to learn English. Of course we started immediately to teach him – just a few words at a time. We also introduced the alphabet and began by showing him one letter at a time. He would hunt for this letter on any piece of paper, or yardstick, or canned goods that he could find. He would also stand beside the record player and listen without saying anything, but would cry if we turned it off. But when my husband taught him the most important and essential words that any two-year old should know, "Massachusetts Institute of Technology," he would join us in laughing at his fumbling endeavor. Since Nelson and I were alone most of the weekdays, we had lots of time together to undertake his indoctrination to America.

One day for lunch I had an open can of tuna on the dining table and had to go to about four feet to the kitchen for a fork; when I returned within just seconds, the tuna was gone, dribbling from his mouth and still being stuffed in. He looked guilty. His surviving on the street came back to me. It was heart rendering at supper time when he would try to grab food off the table, and he was soon crying out in garbled language, "don't take all, that's mine," sometimes reaching across the table to grab the dish.

When Nelson was seven, he received his American citizenship, and I still have the little American flag that was given him.

Our new American citizen, 1961

Since we now had a girl and a boy, we did not apply for a third child. Our two children were of opposite personalities, as were their adoptive parents. However, both children liked to entertain themselves. Carol sang, climbed our trellis, played the piano, and petted our dogs. Nelson read, stood attentively to listen to the cassette player or radio, and would come jabbering and practicing his words. We arranged for music lessons for Carol as soon as we found she could play by ear, and her teacher was a kind, low-keyed, middle-aged woman. I wish I had a picture of Carol playing her first duet, a simple tune, with her daddy. She learned the left hand first while he played the melody, then they switched. This joint music playing put a cement bond between the two of them.

Nelson later began lessons with this same teacher. Later still we transferred both children to Carlisle and chose different teachers for both of them. When Nelson reached fourth grade, the school offered music lessons and choice of instruments. Of course our boy chose the violin because "it is the hardest instrument to learn and to play," he said.

One of the neighborhood parents, whom we did not know, alerted us to a Harrisburg private academy, and before we knew it, we were offered a scholarship for Nelson, and the neighbor provided him with transportation. One of the teachers at this Academy, Mr. Richard Bickford, appreciated Nelson's efforts at writing poetry, especially haiku, and the two of them shared their writings. [See Appendix E.]

Those eyes say it all!

Family Gathering At Alberta Home

In the spring of 1960, Paul and his family, now consisting of two young boys, and his wife, Mary Esther, who had been a friend of mine at La Verne College, were planning a trip home to Alberta to visit Mama and the others. Paul wondered if we could also plan to come up. He said he hoped to be up there July 15. We told him we would also plan on that. That was the last word exchanged regarding the trip and the timing. We had our two children also; Carol since May 1957 and Nelson since the present January.

On our way to Alberta, we stopped in Wisconsin to pick up Elizabeth and take her with us, and on July 15, we duly arrived at the home farm about 6:00 PM. Paul had arrived about 4:00PM. Our timing jibed perfectly, despite our having had no contact with each other since the initial spring plans were made.

So this new generation of cousins now met and played with each other, while their parents and Aunt Elizabeth caught up on news and shared memories of our farm days together. I know Mama was pleased to see our children. It was also the first time she had met Paul's wife or my husband. I wonder what Mama thought of our choices. Parents often have an objective view of their offspring, especially when they have been separated from their children for some time. When I thought about this years later, I suspect Mama wondered about the stability of my marriage because of the great differences between Joe and me in personality and temperament as well as age and education.

"Multiplication is vexation, Division is as bad;
The rule of three doth puzzle me, And practice drives me mad."
(Elizabethan MS, 1570)

CHAPTER 20

TRANSITIONS

Recently a radio announcer remarked that "many couples marry out of weaknesses," and by the mid-sixties, it was obvious to both Joe and me that our marriage was weakening. I desperately needed to plan my future and gave serious thought to working towards a Master's degree at the local Pennsylvania State University. But in what? I argued back and forth with myself, as well as with Joe, as to whether I should work towards a Master's in psychology or in librarianship. Mama's words haunted me again, but neither did I approve of society's current acceptance of very lenient sexual behavior that would be a factor in psychological counseling (though nothing compared to the "anything goes" habits of today.) Joe finally and wisely said, "Well, the happiest I've seen you is when you worked for Dickinson College Library." And it hit me, "He's right, why am I fighting my mother? I want a library degree."

We were apart for a year before we decided to divorce. For various reasons I told Joe he would have to tell the children. Just after Christmas in 1966, we sat them down and when their dad told them that we were divorcing, it was Nelson who spoke up and answered, "We're disappointed but we're not surprised." How mature this little eleven-year old boy was!

As luck would have it, I found a library job in a Junior High School in New Jersey, and a house to rent nearby in Sewell. Both were within close highway routing to Drexel University at the edge of Philadelphia. I signed up for evening classes in Library Science. After the first year on the job, the State required that I obtain a Teacher's Certificate, so I immediately looked elsewhere for work. I found a cataloging position at Haddonfield Public Library. Again my luck changed: the owner of the rented house was returning so we had to move again. By this time, Joe and his new wife had moved into our Shepherdstown home and Joe had paid me my share. So I bought my first home, in the late 1960s, at a price of $14,000. It was a two-story half of a double house in Haddon Heights, New Jersey, about three miles from my job. (The seller, Mrs. Laub, gave me her beautiful oval china soup tureen that I have just this year given to my nephew.)

So now I was working in a beautifully small historic town taking a course in cataloging at Drexel at the same time that I was the cataloger in a public library. All the previous catalogers there had been non-professionals, but I was told that I was being more consistent with the subject and call number assignments, and in fact, the entire card formatting, than any of the previous staff. While I did not particularly enjoy that type of library work, I did enjoy the staff and the environment.

At the end of June 1970, Carol graduated from high school and I graduated from Drexel with an MSLS degree.

Carol and her mother, Graduation, 1970

Now I wanted a professional position, preferably in Reference or Acquisitions, but not in cataloging or interlibrary loan service, and preferably not in New Jersey. I moved to Cumberland, Maryland, and my first professional job was in Reference at Frostburg State College about ten miles away in western Maryland. Carol was at a loss as to what the future held for her. She also moved to Maryland about one hundred miles east of Cumberland and made use of her capabilities, including her pleasant personality and her unusual musical skills.

My future positions were all in various library departments: Pennsylvania State University, York, Pennsylvania; Lancaster Public Library, Lancaster, Pennsylvania; Warren Wilson College, Swannanoa, North Carolina. Except for cataloging and interlibrary loan duties, I enjoyed Administration, Reference and Library Instruction and Acquisitions. I prepared student library manuals including explanations of the Dewey Decimal System and the new Library of Congress Classification System, as well as held classes for Freshmen students and prepared booklets of homework assignments. I was the first professional at Frostburg State to plan orientation for incoming freshmen and produced a forty-seven-page Student Handbook for this purpose. I wrote articles for local newspapers, especially when I was employed by public libraries, and in fact prior to graduate school.

Rather than living in the small town of Frostburg, I bought a house in the nearby city of Cumberland. Soon after we settled there, Nelson got a job as a newspaper delivery boy for the weekly morning paper. The cold mountain temperature turned his skin far bluer than the ordinary person experiences. Had I known this area would be as cold as my childhood country, I never would have accepted a job there. Nelson was in the 10th grade and found the public school inadequate for his very high scholarly needs, so at the end of the school year, we agreed his needs would be better met at the Catholic High School in Cumberland. We talked with one of the Sisters, and Nelson made the decision that he would like to enroll there for the fall of 1971. His positive experience with the former private school affected his decision.

Since leaving Shepherdstown, Nelson had had no music lessons, but he kept practicing the violin. I sold our piano before we moved to Cumberland so he was now without one. (The reed organ did not exactly fit his needs except as a great family heirloom.)

On this summer day Nelson was to decide whether he wanted a new piano or the school electric organ that was to be sold. I was leaving the decision to him once he found out why the school was selling it and if it needed repair, and the approximated cost of repair work. My hopes were that he would choose the organ because of his ability to express himself more beautifully through an organ than a piano.

I was at work ten miles from home when I got the last phone call any mother ever wants to get. Cumberland hospital called me and said Nelson had had an accident and could I come to the hospital, and did I want some one to come get me. I thought, "I bet he's fallen off the balcony that he was to be painting and perhaps injured himself." I told the caller that I could drive myself. When I reached the hospital entrance I saw the Chaplain, with a second person, awaiting me, and I was immediately filled with suspicion that "this may be a more serious accident than I initially thought." As we entered, I was asked to step into a side room. My heart was pounding. I suspected immediately that this was going to be very serious.

The worst had happened. Nelson had gone swimming with some of his friends. Swimmers with long hair could not get in the city pool without wearing a net or cap. So Nelson and two or three of his friends, who defied such rules when no reasons were given, went to the nearby unguarded, unfenced, mountain quarry.[9] An ice-cold mountain quarry about thirty feet deep! Bravely, and innocently, Nelson had dived into this thirty feet of ice water.

The chaplain let me see him for a brief moment, then took me aside and had me drink some medicine to keep me alert, and he asked for a contact number of Nelson's dad. He also assured me that Nelson's friends had done all they could, even CPR, to save him. Hypothermia, playing on a genetic susceptibility to cold, and his daring attitude, took his life.

I knew he would want his body used for a good purpose and not burnt or put in the ground. There was a request on television for an organ transplant needed for an adult male, and I offered my son's; unfortunately the blood type was not compatible. Nelson's body was then donated to a medical school in Maryland. I cannot describe my loss; nor can I count all the letters and cards I received from every place we had lived. He was so well-loved, so great a youth. The responses amounted to far, far more than are even sent to famous people. When I read them this last time, as I now downsize my holdings in my senior years, I will – I must – dispose of them – and I will cry. And I cry when I open the little book he gave me with his brief note on the inside cover. The book was <u>The Bluebird Carries the Sky on His Back,</u> by Henry David Thoreau, and Nelson's brief note reads: "I knew it was yours."

---

[9] This year, 2006, in Western North Carolina mountains, a hard-working mother was tried for murder because she had no one to care for her son and so left him in her car, where he died from the heat, while she worked long hours at two jobs. I cried for her. And I felt a blessing for the jurors as they acquitted her. Society failed her as they failed me. She had no available care for her son within her meager income while our government gives so much to the rich and denies decent wages for the poor.

In my case there was no national, state or county law demanding that the quarry owners take all necessary precautions to prevent entry to this dangerous area. There are many instances where government fails its citizens, and it is our government officials who should be tried for murder.

The winters in western Maryland were as cold, although not quite as long, as my childhood ones in western Canada. There was no Unitarian Church, and social life was limited. A few years later I accepted the head position at the small Pennsylvania State University campus in York, PA. This was a most unsatisfactory job, so I became head of the Adult Department at the Lancaster Pennsylvania Public Library.

In 1984 a library position was offered me at Warren Wilson College in Swannanoa, North Carolina, near the city of Asheville. I did not want to sell my York home until I knew if I would like this Bible-belt atmosphere, so I rented it to a friend. After the first winter in North Carolina, I was certain I never wanted to return to cold Pennsylvania, so I immediately sold my York home. This college position included housing, some on campus and some, including mine, off-campus.

Few colleges existed in this mountain area. Three professional librarians, including me, left this wonderful college because of personnel problems with leadership. I accepted a position at Western Maryland University with its Center for Improving Mountain Living. A grant had been received to analyze the effect or changes that children experienced when seniors worked with them in after school program: "Would their view of seniors and their own age change after years of such care?" I interviewed the senior volunteers, the children and their parents, and entered the results on computer. Fortunately, I learned computer skills from a retired IBM instructor while at Warren Wilson College, and had bought my first computer and printer by 1986.

At the end of the year, the University Grant unexpectedly ended. I gladly returned to Asheville to work with United Way's First Call for Help. I enjoyed helping the callers, but management was trying to dispense with some of the services of United Way: instead of showing leadership, they were so indecisive without keeping in touch with this entire division that I left.

I was past sixty-seven years old. I sought part-time work for the next three years, and some on a volunteer basis. So I was seventy-one years old before fully retiring the end of 1994. Perhaps that has helped keep me as young as possible, and to make me believe that the retirement age of sixty-five should be greatly extended, with exceptions where needed. Volunteer positions can be as much of a headache – or give as much satisfaction – as any paid job. Some I enjoyed; some I did not.

In late fall of 1994, a friend in Pennsylvania told me how she had resumed her maiden name after her divorce, and I suddenly decided I would do the same. I immediately wished I had done so long ago and particularly when I moved from Pennsylvania to North Carolina, where no one knew me. I was surprised to find that within a year or so, my long-time friends could not remember my married name!

Today, it is not unusual at all for a woman to keep her maiden name and even include both surnames as their children's surname. Of course, it does take some familiarity or friendship with these individuals before a person knows whether the companion is a partner or a spouse. And children are often conceived outside of marriage, or at least before a union. Over my eighty-plus years, there has been a complete change of societal behavior and acceptance of any and all variations.

What have I done with my life since my last official volunteer job? My church has always been of primary interest. I have served in the following areas:

President of the Library Committee, Pledge Secretary for many years, entering all data on computer almost weekly, Co-chair for ten years of our annual Book Sale, which involved finding and assigning volunteers to unpack and sort books by subject and serve during our sale hours.

In the late 1980s, volunteers staffed the church office on Sunday mornings, and I have served one Sunday a month since that time. I was one of the early presidents of our Women's Breakfast Group, and of Noonlighters. This latter monthly meeting was aimed at retirees, and we had many outside speakers. I was never at home with young children, except my own, so I never volunteered for the children's department; and of course never in the choir! Other volunteer tasks were undertaken without being the leader, such as the twice-yearly ground clean-up and yearly rummage sale.

I thoroughly enjoyed taking care of business for friends when they traveled for weeks and even months out of the country. Especially enjoyable was taking care of my good friend's mother-in-law several years and learning to know this delightful woman from Germany who lived until she was one hundred years old. To be included in the families' reunion and celebration of her last birthday was an honor.

When a new president was needed for the local Hemlock Society, I accepted. This Society has gone through several name changes as well as adding issues to their aims. I believed then, as I do now, that each mentally competent adult should have the right to choose death with dignity, when terminally ill or in an incurable and unacceptable condition to that person. Resorting to Derek Humphry's original principles and purposes, a new national group, Final Exit Network, was established. I join others who support all right-to-die with dignity groups. Polls show that legalization of an individual's right to death with dignity is wanted by the majority of physicians and ordinary citizens.

This above all,
To thine own self be true,
And it must follow as the night the day,
Thou canst not then be false to any man.
(Shakespeare, <u>Hamlet.</u>)

CHAPTER 21

CONCLUSION

These famous words have been my support and guidance for many years.

Since childhood experiences influence, and even establish, our later attitudes in many or all areas of life, it seems appropriate to explain the major factors that affected all of us, though not all in the same manner.

I firmly believe that Daddy's leg amputation, with his need to overcome the related limitations, was a major factor in his treatment of his children. Add to that the encouragement and demands that he must have received from his own family, physician, and friends to strive for a normal life after the amputation. These and his own energetic temperament had great effect on the demands he made of his children. The ensuing harsh treatment was due to his expectation that we had the physical abilities to succeed and were not burdened by the physical disability he had!

Beyond the physical issues, he wanted his children, perhaps especially since we were "minister's children," to be obedient as well as to strive for the highest achievement possible. This demand for achievement was particularly directed to his boys, but also to Barbara, who was very strong, outgoing and adventuresome. She was the only child who openly questioned or argued with him. His family background was German, a very authoritarian system, although I have no inkling of his siblings' treatment of their children. Mama later told us that he was known at Bethany as "being the person with so much good and so much bad in the same individual, " a statement she would occasionally repeat.

I think, too, that he wanted the very best for his children and was angry with himself for not being able to provide adequately for us. It was not envy but his long-hoped-for expectations that he – and pioneer experiences – would enable his children to be at the head of the line, with education, morals and talents, and reasonable living conditions. Sadly too, minister's children were supposed to be "perfect" and set examples for others.

While I definitely do not approve of his unreasonable punishment and demands on any of us, I balance his condition with the excellent teachings he endowed us with. I can appreciate also why Mama did not confront him and protect both herself and her children. She could not drive, and even if she had taken us all later when Edward and Barbara could drive, that would still mean eight bodies in one old Model T or Model A Ford, with no room for clothing or food. This thought comes to mind only because our neighbor woman left her husband and took her four boys back to the States. Today, of course, I think any Social Service Department would step in and remove us from these parents, but undoubtedly would return us to Mama's care. I am confident that Daddy would improve if he received counseling. It is regrettable that not all of his children saw all the "good" in him, and understood or accepted the whys and wherefores of the "bad."

Daddy's teachings caused me to examine my beliefs and my actions and to make changes in my church membership and my married life. While I still have respect for both relationships, I now have more respect for myself. I'd like to look at the overall picture and summarize the development and outcome of these pioneer-raised Beard children. Keep in mind how all this relates to the wider population, even though percentage data are not available.

Future of these eight Beard children:
    One child died very young. Of the other seven:
    One had mental problems, but was not mentally deficient.
    One in particular had many of the same strong, desirable characteristics as her dad, but conducted them in a most positive manner; a very rewarding life to all.
    One never married; six did.
    Four got divorced.
    Three remarried.
    Five had children, none more than three.
    One adopted children.
    One married a minister.
    One became a grade school teacher and married a school teacher.
    One or two became skilled in musical talents.
    Two remained farmers full-time.
    None was ever arrested or spent time in jail.
    None ever became a smoker or an alcoholic.
    Three received Bachelor's or Master's degrees.
    One earned a ministerial degree.
    All became more liberal; four became agnostics or atheists.
    All served their community in some manner or another.
    The three born in the States remained in Canada.
    Three of the four born in Canada moved to the States.
    Only one born in Canada remained in Canada.

Does this not all sound typical of our entire society?

And what about the influence we seven had on each other? In a <u>Time</u> magazine of July 10, 2006, an article on "The New Science of Siblings "by Jeffrey Kluger explains this current theory. According to Kluger, scientists now declare that, "From the time they are born, our brothers and sisters are our collaborators and co-conspirators, our role models and cautionary tales. They are our scolds, protectors, goads, tormentors, playmates, counselors, sources of envy, objects of pride. They teach us how to resolve conflicts and how not to; how to conduct friendships and when to walk away from them. Sisters teach brothers about the mysteries of girls; brothers teach sisters about the puzzle of boys."

He goes on to say that it is the older siblings who seem to be the strivers and the younger ones are rebellious; while those in the middle are "lost" souls. Just what he means by "lost souls," is questionable. Pertaining to my own family, I believe we all fall appropriately into these categories. Both Edward and Barbara were the strivers, though with very different temperaments, and Barbara could be classified as "rebellious." Elizabeth and Raymond had the "want to please" personality. Certainly Paul, Robert and I could claim to show rebellion in some manner. Paul would analyze all tangible items and did so with the intangible without the rest of us always knowing he was doing so. I was argumentative to some extent, occasionally pouting in childhood, and usually voiced just to mama, as I kept many feelings to myself and in this manner might be classified as "rebellious." Perhaps the illustration shown during my college days will support this view. I do not think of Robert as being rebellious as a youngster, but he certainly could have kept this attitude within. He tells me he refused to join a church, he backed out of a police career, and it took nearly eight years to settle his divorce, which of course involved others.

One major factor that I believe showed up in my relationships and type of personality is the emphasis Daddy stressed on the necessity and wisdom of examining, questioning, and analyzing all sides of every issue. So I often do so orally and thus it appears to others that I can't make up my mind, or that I am vacillating or perhaps intend to be argumentative.

And when it comes to the need for action, I hear my Mama say, "Ruth, if you don't do it, who will?" There were some years and some incidents when that remark was kept under wraps, but when an outspoken Asheville church friend, Augusta Young, died, this phrase renewed itself in my mind, and I thought, "Ruth, now if you don't do it, who will?" So I have become far more vocal than previously.

In any event, we seven Beards all became compatible with each other, although it might have taken longer between some of us than with others and also climaxed with differences in degrees of compatibility.

So why did it take me so long to write these memoirs? Well, frankly, my tendency to argue back and forth, whether with myself or others, forestalled my making a decision until I really faced my aging years. Probably my underlying feelings were that some of my siblings would openly disagree with my views. I need not face any objections from them now as Robert is the only one still living. He would not have undertaken this project himself, and I have indicated where he would disagree with me.

Web of Life

Envision a spider's web as the web of life. If I touch a strand in any one place, it will vibrate on other strands, generally commencing with the closest one. Apply that to my – or anyone's – life: will what I say or do not be heard and felt by others and thus affect them in some way?

Perhaps this would lead to no action by anyone, but also there is the possibility my action could affect other's opinions and beliefs one way or another, either to the detriment or benefit of society.

We are not alone in this world. The good that I do will live after me, as will the harm. It is my hope that any harm or wrong decisions I made in my lifetime have been forgiven, and that I did not seriously harm anyone, and that my right decisions, beliefs and actions have resulted in positive influence and actions by others. I believe that both my parents would feel blessed that their teachings truly benefited all their children and thus the wider world.

And though I have grown into an "old" woman of eighty-four, I still recall my childhood wish, reinforced by Daddy's calling out, "Go to it, old boy." And no matter where I move, or my aging years, the very first task to be undertaken is the nailing up of a pegboard followed by the unpacking of tools and making them readily accessible for this female who still has in her blood, "I wish I were a boy!" And who still hears her Mama say "After all, Ruth, "If you don't do it, who will?"

APPENDICES and WRITINGS

I have long given myself the fun of writing poems for many seasons and on special occasions, and they, along with other compositions, the earliest from 1946, might help readers – especially family members for whom this book was originally conceived – know me better. Therefore I am including special selections which reveal my development of interests and my changes in beliefs.

Also in these Appendices are several poems by my son Nelson, astounding in their depth and insight, all written when he was a young teen – or even earlier. Perhaps, had he lived to adulthood, he would have become the poet whose beginnings can be seen and sensed here. His poems are followed by an exchange of letters between a teacher of his and myself.

And I include some written materials from my sister Elizabeth that may, for some, complete the furnishing of this attic of memories.

APPENDIX A

CHRISTOPHEL/WENGER GENEALOGY

<u>Christian Wenger and Eve Grabiel -Arrived in Philadelphia, Sept. 30, 1727</u>

From Mama's genealogy volume, <u>The Wenger's Family History,</u> which I gave to my brother after the following information was obtained. Some facts are unclear, probably because not all entries were copied; however, they are included because this is the only Wenger history available.

MATERNAL GRANDFATHER'S SIDE.

1. CHRISTIAN WENGER. Married a German <u>Eve Grabiel</u>, had eleven children. Arrived in Philadelphia, Sept. 30, 1727, from Europe, Northwest province of France, now in Bavaria, Germany. He bought land in Earl Township, Lancaster County, Pennsylvania, May 19, 1759.

3. JOSEPH WENGER, born Aug. 8, 1747. Third child of Christian Wenger and brother to #2 Hans. (John Wenger married first wife, Barbara Hoover, born in 1747, died 1792, had 13 children. Married second wife, Anna Hachman, Oct. 1764, to Nov. 17, 1847, had 5 children.

9. CHRISTINA WENGER (11th child of above and lst wife) born June 15, 1785, near Edona, Virginia, died Dec. 22, 1850. Married William S. Reed, April 8, 1792 to May 18, 1874, had 5 children. Reed was born in Union Township, Elkhart County, Indiana. A Mennonite, who may have come from Ireland or England.

24. HARRIET REED, 4th child of above, born April 5, 1824. Married John M. Christophel on Jan. l, 1847, had 9 children. John was born in Bavaria, Germany, Feb. 2, 1819 and died May 31, 1886. He was a minister of the Mennonite church at Yellow Creek, Elkhart, Co, Indiana for 26 years, and bishop for 13 years.

229. ISAIAH CHRISTOPHEL, 4th child of above, born Feb. 24, 1852, died Aug. 28, 1912. Married Barbara Wenger, #228, Jan. 6, 1878 at Nippon, Elkhart Co., Indiana. They had our children, Susie, Martha (the author's mother), and twins Emma and Anna.

MATERNAL GRANDMOTHER'S SIDE

1. CHRISTIAN WENGER (see above)

2. HANS (JOHN) WENGER, son of Christian Wenger, born Nov. 9, 1731. Married Anna Shirk, had 12 children. Lived on a farm at Conestoga Creek, Earl Township, Lancaster Co., PA.

19. JOSEPH WENGER, son of Hans Wenger (#2), born Sept. 21, 1769. died 1825 of blood poisoning. Married, first name unknown Martin, had 1 child. Married 2nd wife, Elizabeth Zimmerman, Nov. 21, 1778, died Mar. 23, 1840. had 11 children. Upon Joseph's death, wife and 11 children continued with plans to move to Waterloo County., Canada West (now Ontario).

22 CHRISTIAN WENGER (twin) born to Joseph Wenger and 2nd wife, Dec. 20, 1802. Married 1st wife, Magdalena High (Hoch) died Feb. 4, 1858, had 4 children. Married 2nd wife, Elisabeth Good, Jan. 20, 1814 who died Nov. 15, 1875, had 10 children.

228. BARBARA WENGER, youngest child of #22 above and 2nd wife, Elisabeth Good, born Mar. 16, 1855 in Wayne Co., Ohio. Married Isaiah Christophel, #229 above, had 4 children. Susie W. Christophel, Jan. 2, 1879 who married Sylvester J. Miller. Martha Christophel, Dec. 15, 1883, died Feb. 1963, married David Ray Beard. Emma Christophel, twin, Aug. 27-1886, died Oct. 3, 1894, and twin Anna Christophel, Aug. 17, 1886, died of burns suffered when an oven exploded. Death probably between 1941-1949.

FURTHER INFORMATION FROM THE WENGER FAMILY HISTORY BOOK

#22. CHRISTIAN WENGER AND ELISABETH GOOD WENGER – in the year 1854, the above family moved from Lancaster Co., PA to Wayne Co., Ohio, where their youngest child, Barbara, (this author's grandmother) was born; from thence, in the year 1855, to Waterloo Co., Canada West (now known as Ontario); and from thence, in the spring of 1857, to Elkhart Co., IN. In Feb. 1858, when on a business trip to Canada, and while engaged in conversation with a friend on King Street, Berlin, Ontario, he dropped dead of paralysis. The remains were brought back to his home in Elkhart, Co., Ind. and there interred in the Mennonite Yellow Creek Cemetery. The members of the family were all Mennonites.

WENGER, Joseph b. Aug.8, 1747 d.? 1792
HOOVER, Barbara b. 1747, Wenger b. Jun 15, 1792
    d. Dec.22, 1890
m. William S. Reed, b. Apr.8, 1792
    d. May 18, 1874

c. Harriet Reed,   b.Apr. 5, 1824
    d. ?
m. John M. Christophel, b. Feb. 2, 1819
    d. May 31, 1886
c. Isaiah Christophel, b. Feb. 24, 1852
    d. Aug. 28, 1912

WENGER, Hans (John) b. Nov. 9, 1731
SHIRK, Anna Christina
Joseph Wenger b. Sep.21, 1769
    d. 1825
m. Elizabeth Zimmerman b. Nov. 21, 1778
    d. Mar. 23, 1840
c. Christian Wenger (twin) .20,1802
    d. ?
m. Elizabeth Good, b. Jan. 20, 1814
    d . Nov.15, 1875
c. Barbara Wenger, b. Mar. 16, 1855
    d. May 7, 1931

<u>Isaiah Christophel married Barbara Wenger. m. Jan. 6, 1878</u>

CHILDREN OF ISAIAH CHRISTOPHEL AND BARBARA WENGER
    Susie,   b. Jan.02, 1879   d. Feb. 1964
    Martha, b. Dec. 15, 1883, d. Feb. 20, 1963 (My mother)
    Emma, b. Aug. 27, 1886   d. date unknown, but young)
    Anna,   b. Aug. 27, 1886   d. probably between 1941 and 1949.

APPENDIX B

THE BEARD GENEALOGY, 1786-2006

Descendants of John Beard(1st)
1 John Beard(1st) 1786–1859
.. +Mary Magdalene Schwartz 1789–1842
.... Prepared by Cora Beard and Cousin Paul Beard
.... 2 Lydia Beard 1812–1881
.... +Philip Henry Miller 1825–1906
.... 3 Sarah Jane Miller 1852–1928
.... +George Washington Kemp 1851–1938
.... 4 Harry E Kemp
.... 4 Lulu E Kemp
.... +Chester Martin
.... 4 Earl W Kemp
.... 4 Carl H Kemp
.... 2 Sarah Beard 1814–1877
.... +John Lohr 1797–1875
.... 2 Mary Magdalena Beard 1816–1906
.... +Benjamin Yingling 1812–1858
.... 3 John H D Yingling 1840 -
.... +Catherine 1839 -
.... 4 Frank Yingling 1874 -
.... 4 Maggie Yingling 1877 -
.... 3 Noah B Yingling 1849–1924
.... +Rebecca 1846–1935
.... 4 Maud Yingling 1875 -
.... 4 Grace Yingling 1877 -
.... 4 George A Yingling 1877 -
.... 3 Alpha Yingling 1852 -
.... +Melinda 1855 -
.... 4 Idy Yingling 1876 -
.... 4 Edna Yingling 1879 -

.... 4 Walter A Yingling 1884–1885
.... 2 John Beard(2nd) 1818–1886
.... +Elizabeth Galle 1818–1899
.... 3 Sarah Jane Beard 1840–1842
.... 3 John Thomas Beard 1843–1914
.... +Mary C. Crossman 1849–1928
.... 4 Paul Barnetts 1883–1885
.... 3 Susan Beard 1845–1916
.... +William H. Myerly 1848–1894
.... 4 Florence Myerly
.... 4 Clarence Myerly
.... 4 Minnie D. Myerly 1875–1954
.... +William Frank Romspert 1871–1949
.... 5 John William Romspert
.... +Elinor Fox
.... 5 Ralph Myerly Romspert
.... +Sara Zoll
.... 6 Ralph Romspert
.... +Elizabeth Freemeyer
.... 6 William Thomas Romspert
.... 5 George Romspert 1905–1966
.... +Anna Marie McDonald
.... 6 George Charles Romspert 1936 -
.... 6 Anna Marie Romspert 1938 -
.... 6 Raymond Joseph Romspert 1943 -
.... 5 Willis C Romspert 1909–1983
.... +Mary Hagney
.... 6 William Arthur Romspert
.... 6 John Hagney Romspert
.... 6 Robert H Romspert
.... 6 Mary Agnes Romspert
.... +Fiddler
.... 6 Sarah Minerva Romspert
.... +Moore
.... 4 Laura Elsie Myerly 1879–1952
.... +John Thomas Fritz 1876–1941
.... 5 Susan Evelyn Fritz
.... +Harry Edward Reese 1899 -
.... 5 Charles Wesley Fritz
.... +Lena Fisher 1895–1988
.... 6 Glenda Fritz
.... 5 William Myerly Fritz
.... +Margaret Smith
.... 6 John Fritz
.... 5 Paul Thomas Fritz 1899–1967

.... +Marie Ecker 1897 – 1993
.... 6 Evelyn Fritz
.... +Vincent Yox
.... 7 Susan Yox
.... 7 Vickie Yox
.... 6 Francis Paul Fritz 1919 -
.... +Paulina Crowl 1920 -
.... 7 Ronald Eugene Fritz
.... 8 David Fritz
.... 8 Randolph Fritz
.... 7 Thomas William Fritz
.... 8 Thomas William Fritz Jr
.... 8 Joan Elizabeth
.... 5 Marian Rebecca Fritz 1901 – 1984
.... +William Elgen Lippy 1898 – 1936
.... 6 June E Lippy 1921 -
.... 6 Marian Jean Lippy 1930 -
.... +Norman Cook
.... 7 Scott Cook
.... 7 Bonita Cook
.... 3 Mary Elizabeth Beard 1847 – 1848
.... 3 Edward Henry Beard 1849 – 1930
.... +Ida Catherine Caylor 1854 – 1946
.... 4 Matie Irene Beard 1877 – 1965
.... 4 Harvey Edward Beard 1878 – 1968
.... +Fannie Rebecca Young 1881 – 1977
.... 5 Helen Elizabeth Beard 1909 – 1998
.... +Henry Paul Horne 1908 – 1989
.... 6 Sylvia Elizabeth Horne 1940 -
.... +Gabriel Joseph Argilla 1938 -
.... 7 Micheal Argilla M.D. 1964 -
.... 7 David Brian Argilla 1966 -
.... +Laura Williams
.... 8 Django Argilla 2003 -
.... 8 Ansel Argilla 2006 -
.... 7 Lara Lynn Argilla 1971 -
.... +Mark Mitchell
.... 8 Jennifer Mitchell 1991 -
.... 6 Lowell Paul Horne 1943 – 2005
.... +Sara Deubner 1947 -
.... 7 Jon Nicholas Horne 1976 -
.... 7 Jesse Dustin Horne 1978 -
.... 6 Barbara Jane Horne 1946 -
.... +Robert Cole 1943 -
.... 7 Kelly Ann Cole 1972 -

.... +David Robinder
.... 8 Michael Alexander Robinder 1992 -
.... 8 Magen Elizabeth Robinder 1995 -
.... 8 Joshua David Robinder 1996 -
.... 7 Karen Ann Cole 1973 -
.... 5 Earl David Beard 1912–2002
.... +Miriam Susan Luckenbaugh 1910–2003
.... 6 Edward Milton Beard 1938 -
.... +Bette Jane Norman 1941–2004
.... 7 Sandra Leigh Beard 1962 -
.... +Gary Victor Raim 1954 -
.... 8 Ruth Isabel Raim 1994 -
.... 8 Sophie Eliza Raim 1996 -
.... 7 Roy Dwayne Beard 1964 -
.... +Cindy Elizabeth Reed
.... 8 Miriam Nicole Beard 1985 -
.... +Brad Haltinger
.... 9 Lillanna J Haltinger 2004–2006
.... 8 Samuel David Beard 1988 -
.... *2nd Wife of Roy Dwayne Beard:
.... +Lynn Marie Fleming 1962 -
.... 8 Nathan Cooper Beard 1998 -
.... 7 David Norman Beard 1972 -
.... +Denice Yehnert 1970 -
.... 5 Clarence Edward Beard 1915 -
.... +LaVaughn Clara Shirley Hansen 1920 -2006
.... 6 Christine Anna Beard 1949 -
.... 6 Ernest Ross Beard 1950 -
.... +Anna Burns
.... *2nd Wife of Ernest Ross Beard:
.... +Marlyn Raibino
.... 7 Rosslyn Kamille Beard 1990 -
.... 6 Hollis Rebecca Beard 1953 -
.... +Brian Foster
.... 7 Sarah Melissa Foster 1979 -
.... 7 Daniel Foster 1985 -
.... 6 Daryl Harvey Beard 1954 -
.... 5 Alice Katherine 1918 -
.... +Raymond Kale Kordisch 1915 -
.... 6 Cheryl Diane Kordisch 1945 -
.... +Ronald Ogborn 1943 -
.... 7 Brent Ogborn 1969 -
.... +Tracie Brandburg
.... 8 Dustin Tyler Ogborn 1996 -
.... 8 Makayla Paige Ogborn 2001 -

.... 6 Larry Wesley Kordisch 1947 -
.... +Janice Kathleen Graue 1948 -
.... 7 Lane Katherine Kordisch 1971 -
.... +Matthew Crockett Roberts 1970 -
.... 8 Jackson Kordisch Roberts 1996 -
.... 8 Bradt Crockett Roberts 1996 -
.... 8 Luke Roberts 2001 -
.... 7 Lindsey Ann Kordisch 1974 -
.... 5 Carroll Milton Beard 1920 – 1991
.... +Doris LaVal Frock 1921 – 1969
.... 6 Charles Milton Beard 1948 -
.... +Deborah Lee March 1952 -
.... 7 Joel Paul Keller 1977 -
.... 7 Andrew Charles Beard 1982 -
.... *2nd Wife of Carroll Milton Beard:
.... +Pauline Elizabeth Hartley
.... 5 Irene Rebecca 1922 – 1964
.... +Benjamin John Hansen 1922 – 1998
.... 6 Clara LaVaughn Hansen 1952 -
.... +Robert Fix
.... 4 David Ray Beard 1881 – 1942
.... +Martha Christophel 1883 – 1963
.... 5 John Edward Beard 1915 – 1986
.... 5 Barbara Catherine Beard 1916 – 2001
.... +Edward John Olsen 1913 – 2000
.... 6 Carrie Gael Olsen 1937 -
.... +Gordon Dale Edmonson 1935 -
.... 7 Greg Allen Edmonson 1960 -
.... 7 Garry Brian Edmonson 1962 -
.... +Lisa Marie Blackwell 1970 -
.... 8 Alexander Sabastian Edmonson 1992 -
.... 8 Claire Noelle Edmonson 2000 -
.... 8 Ethan Alexander Edmonson 2003 -
.... 6 Liane Cora Olsen 1940 -
.... +Daniel Raymond Nolan 1940 – 1978
.... 7 Jennifer Anne Nolan 1971 -
.... +David John Neill 1969 -
,,8 Madeline Neill 2002
,,8 Matthew Neill 2005
.... 7 Emily Louise Nolan 1973 -
.... *2nd Husband of Barbara Catherine Beard:
.... +Douglas Pemberton Howell
.... 5 Anna Elizabeth Beard 1918 – 2002
.... +Byron Ernest Detrick 1913 – 2001
.... 6 Ralph LeRoy Detrick 1941 -

.... +Mary Elaine Cline 1940 -
.... 7 David Scott Cline Detrick 1973 -
.... *2nd Wife of Ralph LeRoy Detrick:
.... +Joyce Ann Stoltzfus 1953 -
.... 7 Sara Beth Detrick Stoltzfus 1987 -
.... 6 John Ernest Detrick 1944 -
.... +Whe-Lan Wu 1946 -
.... 7 Alex Alvin Detrick 1972 -
.... +Yuliya Bakhar 1984 -
.... 7 Athena Ann Detrick 1973 -
.... +Allan Shepard 1966 -
.... 8 Kai Robert Shepard 2006 -
.... 6 Joe Abraham Detrick 1945 -
.... +Venona Bomberger 1951 -
.... 7 Matthew Joel Detrick 1980 -
.... 7 Christian Bomberger Detrick 1983 -
.... 7 Benjamin Ernest Detrick 1986 -
.... 5 Margaret Irene Beard 1919 – 1920
.... 5 David Raymond Beard 1920 – 1984
.... +Lorraine Martha Campbell 1930 -
.... 6 Valerie Ruth Beard 1951 -
.... +Roger Tudor 1947 -
.... 7 Darin Gavin Tudor 1974 -
.... 7 Darcy Alan Tudor 1976 -
.... 7 Jamie Lee Ann Tudor 1980 -
.... *2nd Husband of Valerie Ruth Beard:
.... +Dale Morris
.... 6 Dwight Ryan Beard 1953 -
.... +Kathleen Elizabeth McDonald 1953 -
.... 7 Denise Lynn Beard 1977 -
.... 6 Cameron Edwin Beard 1955 -
.... +Karen Olineck 1961 -
.... 7 Austin Edward Beard 2002 -
.... 5 Paul Webster Beard 1922 – 2005
.... +Mary Glover 1927 -
.... 6 Kim Allen Beard 1956 -
.... +Linda Suzanne Curtis 1961 -
.... 7 Robert Andrew Beard 1985 -
.... 6 Keith Roger Beard 1958 -
.... +Kristin Irene Phelps 1958 -
.... *2nd Wife of Keith Roger Beard:
.... +Elisabeth Billingsley 1966 -
.... 7 Mariah Trinity 2002 -
.... 7 Haysten Trinity 2003 -
.... *2nd Wife of Paul Webster Beard:

.... +Marcia Joan Benton Coombs 1939 -
.... 5 Ruth Caroline Beard 1923 -
.... +Joseph Wolf Shatto 1929 -
.... 6 Carol Liane Shatto 1951 -
.... +Wil Dodson 1952 -
.... *2nd Husband of Carol Liane Shatto:
.... +Allen Tyndall 1950 -
.... 6 Nelson Lee Shatto 1955 – 1971
.... 5 Robert Kipling Beard 1924 -
.... +Eileen Boyd 1926 -
.... 6 Bligh Wilton Beard 1957 -
.... 6 Bruce Kipling Beard 1959 -
.... +Sheila Helen Fulton 1958 -
.... 7 Christine Elizabeth Beard 1982 -
.... 7 Ashley Robin Beard 1985 -
.... 6 Patricia Ann Beard 1961 -
,,+ Richard McCulloch
,,,7 Michael James McCulloch 1993
,,,7 Megan Lynn McCulloch   1995
.... *2nd Wife of Robert Kipling Beard:
.... +Luella Gay Wyman 1941 -
.... 4 Cora Elizabeth Beard 1883 – 1968
.... 4 Anna Olivia Beard 1886 – 1978
.... +John Arthur Smith 1887 – 1981
.... 5 Catherine Olivia Smith 1912 -
.... +Thomas Edward Bramble 1912 -
.... 6 Barbara Kay Bramble 1940 -
.... +Edward Emutis
.... 6 John Arthur Bramble 1943 -
.... 6 Margaret Lynn Bramble 1946 -
.... +Robert Robinson 1947 -
.... 7 Jessica Elane Robinson 1970 -
.... 7 Nathaniel Robinson 1975 -
.... 5 Thelma Elizabeth Smith 1917 -
.... +Charles Edward P Scott 1907 – 1976
.... 4 Edith May Beard 1889 – 1936
.... 4 Mary Alice Beard 1892 – 1892
.... 4 Ida Belle Beard 1893 – 1993
.... +Basil George Hunter 1890 – 1969
.... 5 George Richard Hunter 1931 -
.... +Patricia Ann Brennan 1935 -
.... 6 Jean Marie Hunter 1957 -
.... 4 John Paul William Beard 1897 – 1986
.... +Anna Marie Engler 1895 – 1990
.... 5 Hazel Irene Beard 1920 -

.... +Carl Albert Guyer 1926 -
.... 6 Carl Stephen Guyer 1953 -
.... +Beverly Ann Byer 1951 -
.... *2nd Wife of Carl Stephen Guyer:
.... +Lydia Mitchele Sweatman 1961 -
.... 7 Christopher Stephen Guyer 1987 -
.... 7 Stephanie Ann Guyer 1987 -
.... *3rd Wife of Carl Stephen Guyer:
.... +Kristine Rene Viers 1967 -
.... 7 Lauren Marie Guyer 1994 -
.... *4th Wife of Carl Stephen Guyer:
.... +Tracy Lynette Boykin 1959 -
.... 6 Paul Laurence Guyer 1956 -
.... +Donna Sue Wilson Lambert 1956 -
.... 7 Mark Wilson Guyer 1982 -
.... +Susan Elizabeth Hull
.... 7 Elyse Catherine Guyer 1985 -
.... 5 Harold Engler Beard 1922 – 2001
.... +Mildred Pearl Eicher 1917 -
.... 5 Paul William Beard 1926 -
.... +Bernice Belle Talbott 1927 -
.... 6 Jeffery Paul Beard 1953 -
.... +Nancy Jean Donelson 1955 -
.... 5 Elsie Marie Beard 1930 -
.... +Robert Elwood Lowry 1928 – 1998
.... 6 Susan Marie Lowry 1953 -
.... +Joseph Austin Hare Jr 1948 -
.... 7 John Kania Hare 1975 -
.... +Jennifer Jean Standish 1976 -
.... 8 Alora Elaine Hare 1995 -
.... 8 Brandon Joseph Hare 1999 -
.... 7 Kathryn Tanya Hare 1981 -
.... 7 Jennifer Marie Hare 1982 -
.... 7 Nichole Daniellie Hare 1984 -
.... 6 Sharon Kay Lowry 1955 -
.... +Terrence Patrick Lally 1955 -
.... 7 David Scott Lally 1985 -
.... 7 Micheal Sean Lally 1989 -
.... 6 Cameron Lee Lowry 1963 -
.... 3 Alice Rebecca Beard 1851 – 1916
.... +Henry Troutfelter 1849 – 1917
.... 4 Fannie May Troutfelter 1877 – 1924
.... +John Michael 1870 – 1921
.... 5 Bernard Hayden Michael 1898 -
.... +Lona Bankard 1886 -

.... 6 Bernard Hayden Michael Jr 1920 -
.... 3 Henry Beard 1820–1861
.... +[4] Ellen Fisher 1823–1889
.... 2 Henry Beard 1820–1861
.... +[4] Ellen Fisher 1823–1889
.... 2 Lewis Beard 1823–1876
.... +Leonora G. Driver–1880
.... 3 Jerome Lewis Beard 1861 -
.... +Nellie L Alchin
.... 2 David Beard 1825–1891
.... +Maria Bres–1912
.... 3 David Luis Beard Bres 1875–1947
.... +Luz Bittencourt Urquiza–1936
.... 4 David Edison Beard Bittencourt 1902–1981
.... +Marta Repfennig 1912 -
.... 5 David Gerardo Beard Repfennig 1933 -
.... +Maria Angelica Ben-Azul 1938 -
.... 6 Katherine Beard Repfennig 1970 -
.... +Paul Leonard Garrett 1970 -
.... 7 Oliver Garrett Beard 2001 -
.... 6 Marjorie Beard Repfennig 1972 -
.... 5 Rosita Jacqueline Beard Repfennig 1935 -
.... +Victor Manuel Alavardo
.... 6 [5] Alejando David Blanco Beard 1957 -
.... 6 [6] Maria Carolina Blanco Beard 1958 -
.... +[7] Paticio Peralta Z 1955 -
.... 7 [8] Paloma Peralta Blanco Z 1981 -
.... *2nd Husband of [6] Maria Carolina Blanco Beard:
.... +[9] Victor Manuel Alvarado
.... 7 [10] Dianna Alvarado Beard 1978 -
.... *2nd Husband of Rosita Jacqueline Beard Repfennig:
.... +Pedro Blanco 1930 -
.... 6 [5] Alejando David Blanco Beard 1957 -
.... 6 [6] Maria Carolina Blanco Beard 1958 -
.... +[7] Paticio Peralta Z 1955 -
.... 7 [8] Paloma Peralta Blanco Z 1981 -
.... *2nd Husband of [6] Maria Carolina Blanco Beard:
.... +[9] Victor Manuel Alvarado
.... 7 [10] Dianna Alvarado Beard 1978 -
.... 5 Daisy Lillian Marta Beard Repfennig 1940 -
.... +Patticio L Garcia Figueroa–1995
.... 6 Isabel Margarita Garcia 1962 -
.... +Marcial Eduardo Mege
.... 7 Nicole Marie Mege 1989 -
.... 7 Michelle Marie Mege 1991 -

.... 6 Claudio Eugenio Garcia 1964 -
.... +Anna Veronica Poblete
.... 7 Camilo Andres Garcia 1987 -
.... 7 Diego Alonso Garcia 1992 -
.... 6 Patricia Beatriz Garcia 1972 -
.... +Marcelo Patricio Mella
.... 7 Bautista Ernesto Mella 1993 -
.... 7 Valentina Belen Mella 1998 -
.... 5 Christian Emillio Beard Repfennig 1947 -
.... +Diana Duhalde 1948 -
.... 6 David Sebastian Beard 1972 -
.... *2nd Wife of Christian Emillio Beard Repfennig:
.... +Alicia Borquez Ebner 1952 -
.... 6 Camila Beard Borquez 1978 -
.... 6 Simon Beard Borquez 1980 -
.... 5
.... 4 Juan Washington Carlos Beard Bittencourt 1903 -
.... +Gabriela Tapia Moreno 1913–2002
.... 5 Juan Jose Beard Tapia 1944 -
.... +Maria Elena Moreira 1945 -
.... 6 Juan Beard Moreira 1972 -
.... 6 Andrea Carolina Beard Moreira 1976 -
.... 5 Carmen Paulina Beard Tapia 1946 -
.... +Sergio Anibal Fuentes Nunez 1949 -
.... 6 Pablo Andres Fuentes Beard 1971 -
.... +Elizabeth Abrana Lausic Rivera 1971 -
.... 7 Pablo Andres Fuentes Neftal 1992 -
.... *2nd Wife of Pablo Andres Fuentes Beard:
.... +Constanza Carolina Gallardo Nunez 1972 -
.... 7 Gabriela Fuentes Gallardo 2003 -
.... 6 Cristian Sergio Fuentes Beard 1972 -
.... 6 Paulina Paz Fuentes Beard 1986 -
.... 5 Inez Jacqueline Beard Tapia 1951 -
.... +Pascal Herpin 1946 -
.... 6 Sebastian Herpin Beard 1974 -
.... 7 Pablo Herpin Beard 2005 -
.... *2nd Husband of Inez Jacqueline Beard Tapia:
.... +Jean Marie Morlon 1950 -
.... 6 Heloise Morlon Beard 1987 -
.... 6 Raphael Morlon Beard 1989 -
.... 4 Fermin Enrique F Beard Bittencourt 1904–1972
.... +Esther Zamora Carvajal 1903–1981
.... 5 Edwin Fermin Beard Zamora 1934 -
.... +Marta Margery Serrano 1942 -
.... 6 Rose Marie Beard Margery 1962 -

.... +Arnoldo Saaveda Faundes 1964 -
.... 7 Javier Andres Saavedra Beard 1993 -
.... *2nd Wife of Edwin Fermin Beard Zamora:
.... +Maria Luisa Hevia 1936 -
.... 6 Victoria Carolina Beard Hevia Zamora 1972 -
.... 6 Edwin Luis Beard Hevia 1973 -
.... 4 Luz Maria Inez Beard Bittencourt 1911 – 1993
.... +Hector Infante Correa 1900 – 1984
.... 5 Luz Marie Infante Beard 1935 -
.... +Luis Berrios Navarro 1930 -
.... 6 Maria Luisa Berrios Navarro 1952 -
.... +Herman Llarra Verdego
.... 7 Luz Inez Llarra Berrios
.... 7 Alyandra Fabiala Berrios
.... 7 Patricia Llarra Berrios
.... *2nd Husband of Maria Luisa Berrios Navarro:
.... +Simon Halle
.... 7 Rachel Berrios Halle
.... *2nd Husband of Luz Marie Infante Beard:
.... +Hernan Nunez Medina 1925 -
.... 6 Luz Patricia Nunez Infante 1957 – 1984
.... +Alyandro Herrera Soto
.... 7 Francisco Herrera Nunez
.... 7 Karino Herrera Nunez
.... 7 Barbara Herrera Nunez
.... 6 Ximena Jacqueline Nunez Infante 1959 -
.... +Patricio Olivares
.... 7 Ximena Andrea Olivares Nunez
.... +Mauritio Cavrallo
.... 8 Camilo Cavrallo Olivares
.... *2nd Husband of Ximena Jacqueline Nunez Infante:
.... +Gazzy Jacob
.... 7 Soraya Gazzy Jacob Nunez
.... 7 Gazzy Jacob Nunez
.... 5 Ximena H Infante Beard 1937 -
.... +Hernan Capellaro Diaz 1933 -
.... 6 Ximena Capellaro Infante 1968 -
.... +Mauricio Balbi
.... 7 Sebastian Balbi Capellaro
.... 7 Crisobal Balbi Capellaro
.... 6 Pablo Capellaro Infante 1969 -
.... 5 Elena Maria Infante Beard 1939 – 1941
.... 5 Hector Sergio Infante Beard 1941 -
.... +Vania Benavides Manzoni 1941 -
.... 6 Hector Javier Benavides Manzoni 1971 -

.... +Alyandra Medina
.... 6 Paula Infante Benavides Manzoni 1973 -
.... 5 Octavio Raul Tadeo Infante Beard 1944 -
.... +Consuelo Flores Leon 1949 -
.... 6 Monica Infante Flores 1975 -
.... +Francisco Javier Feraandez Zabala 1973 -
.... 7 Gabriel Infante 2002 -
.... 5 Patricio Infante Beard 1945 -
.... +Elsia Giro 1945 -
.... 6 Patricica Infante Giro 1970 -
.... 6 Enrique Infante Giro 1972 -
.... 6 Jorge Infante Giro 1979 -
.... *2nd Wife of Patricio Infante Beard:
.... +Mari Pierre 1961 -
.... 6 Pierre Eduard Infante Lagrave 1989 -
.... 5 Juan Carlos Infante Beard 1949 -
.... +Ivonne Hidalgo 1953 -
.... 6 Juan Carlos Infante Hidalgo 1975 -
.... 6 Guillermo Infante Hidalgo 1975 -
.... 6 Cecilia Maria Infante Hidalgo 1977 -
.... 5 Maria Angelica Infante Beard 1949 -
.... +Juan Pablo Iturriaga Gonzalez 1948 -
.... 6 Juan Pablo Iturriaga Infante 1976 -
.... 6 Maria Franciisca Iturriaga Infante 1979 -
.... 5 Hector Javier Infante Beard 1971 -
.... +Alyandra Medina
.... 4 Julio Eduardo Beard Bittencourt 1912 – 1976
.... +Olga Gutierrez 1912 – 2002
.... 5 Maria Inez Beard Gutierrez 1938 -
.... +Pedro Saaverdra Avila 1948 -
.... *2nd Husband of Maria Inez Beard Gutierrez:
.... +Pedro Guzman Nunez 1934 -
.... 6 Maritza Guzman Beard Nunez 1958 -
.... +Juan Elgueta Videla 1954 -
.... 7 Maritza Elgueta Guzman Videla 1978 -
.... 7 Claudia Elgueta Guzman Videla 1982 -
.... 7 Constanza Elgueta Guzman Videla 1988 -
.... *2nd Husband of Maritza Guzman Beard Nunez:
.... +Pedro Saavedra Avila 1948 -
.... 5 Julia Beard Gutierrez 1942 -
.... +Edmundo Yanez 1940 -
.... 6 Edmundo Yanez Beard 1963 -
.... +Marica Peralta Jimenez 1965 -
.... 7 Constanza Yanez Peralta 1993 -
.... 7 Edmundo Yanez Peralta 1998 -

.... 6 Pamela Yanez Beard 1964 -
.... +Elisco Weinzierl
.... 5 Washington Julio Beard Gutierrez 1945 -
.... +Nora Eliana Pla Acevedo 1932 -
.... 6 Cllaudia Beard Pla 1969 -
.... *2nd Wife of Washington Julio Beard Gutierrez:
.... +Olga Gody 1943 -
.... 6 Rodrigo Beard Godoy 1979 -
.... *3rd Wife of Washington Julio Beard Gutierrez:
.... +Angelica Qrtiz 1946 -
.... 4 Francisco Miguel Beard Bittencourt 1913 – 1980
.... +Marta Llabaca 1910 -
.... 5 Luz Clara Beard Llabaca 1939 -
.... +Waldo Nunez Suarez – 1963
.... 6 Yamily Nunez Beard 1959 -
.... +Eduardo Collao 1959 -
.... 7 Guernica Collao Nunez 1981 -
.... 7 Nicolas Collao Nunez 1986 -
.... 7 Itam Collao Nunez 1991 -
.... 6 Waldo Nunez Beard 1962 -
.... +Ingrid Riffo 1962 -
.... 7 Waldo Nunez Riffo 1986 -
.... 7 Mario Nunez Riffo 1991 -
.... *2nd Wife of Waldo Nunez Beard:
.... +Monica Arriagada
.... 7 Mario Nunez Arriagada 1991 -
.... 5 Francisco Patricio Beard Llabaca 1945 -
.... +Laura Valenzuela 1944 -
.... 6 Jesscia P Beard Valenzuela 1978 -
.... *2nd Wife of Francisco Patricio Beard Llabaca:
.... +Guadalupe Bravo 1950 -
.... 6 Claudio Beard Bravo 1967 -
.... 6 Paola Beard Bravo 1970 -
.... 5 David Miguel Beard Llabaca 1949 -
.... +Maria Quiroz Castillo 1948 – 1997
.... 6 Cristina Beard Quiroz 1971 -
.... +Joan Manuel Boltes P 1973 -
.... 7 Maria Jesus Boltes Beard 1995 -
.... 7 Roser Marie Boltes Beard 1997 -
.... 6 Carolia Beard Quiroz 1972 -
.... 2 Catherine Beard 1831 – 1910
.... +Elias G Fuhrman 1830 – 1896
.... 3 Sarah Jane Fuhrman 1852 – 1925
.... +Peter S Resh 1851 – 1933
.... 4 Elias J Resh

.... 4 Mary C Resh
.... 4 Lillie Resh Wildasin
.... 4 Michael Resh
.... 4 Mrs John Strausbaugh Resh
.... 4 Howard C Resh
.... 4 Mrs Ralph Feeser Resh
.... 4 Mrs Charles Colehouse Resh
.... 3 Joshua Eli Fuhrman 1861–1863
.... 3 Amelia Catherine Fuhrman 1864–1935
.... +Daniel H Wertz 1854–1940
.... 4 Howard Hoff Wertz
.... 4 Cleatus A Wertz 1904–1969
.... 3 Ida Alice Fuhrman 1868–1953
.... +David H Leppo 1854–1895
.... 4 Elmer Elias Leppo 1891 -
.... 4 Claton Loy Leppo 1893 -
.... 4 Charles Herbert Leppo 1895 -
.... 3 Elverta Fuhrman 1870–1940
.... +Horatio S Garrett 1875–1960
*2nd Wife of John Beard(1st):
.. +Margaret Baker 1805–1897
.... 2 Susan Beard 1843–1906
.... +Mason Ellsworth Brown 1843–1925
.... 2 Issac Beard 1847–1893
.... +Mary E Branner
.... 2 Ruth Beard 1849–1854

APPENDIX C

INDENTURE – HENRY HARVEY, DAVID BEARD and CPR AGREEMENT

"**This Indenture,** made in duplicate this 2nd day of November in the year of our Lord one thousand nine hundred and eleven, between HENRY MILTON HARVEY of Irricana, in the Province of Alberta, Farmer, hereinafter called the party of the first part, and DAVID RAY BEARD, of Irricana, in the Province of Alberta, Farmer, hereinafter called the party of the second part, and The Canadian Pacific Railway Company, hereinafter called the party of the third part,

WHEREAS the party of the first part by agreement dated the 2nd day of May, one thousand nine hundred and ten, agreed to purchase the land hereinafter mentioned, from the party of the third part, and in and by such agreement covenanted with the party of the third part to pay the purchase money mentioned in the said agreement…..NOW THIS INDENTURE WITNESSETH that in consideration of the premises, and of the sum of Six Hundred and Twelve ($612.00) Dollars, now paid by the party of the second part to the party of the first part, the party of the first part hath granted, bargained, sold, assigned, transferred and set over unto the party of the second part, his heirs   …that parcel or tract of land and premises situate, lying and being in the Province of Alberta and being composed of the South East quarter of Section Six

(6) in Township Twenty-eight (28) Range Twenty Seven (27) West of the Fourth Meridian in the Province of Alberta aforesaid."

The Canadian Pacific Railway Company, hereinafter called the party of the third part,

WHEREAS the party of the first part by agreement dated the 2nd day of May, one thousand nine hundred and ten, agreed to purchase the land hereinafter mentioned, from the party of the third part, and in and by such agreement covenanted with the party of the third part to pay the purchase money mentioned in the said agreement.....NOW THIS INDENTURE WITNESSETH that in consideration of the premises, and of the sum of Six Hundred and Twelve ($612.00) Dollars, now paid by the party of the second part to the party of the first part, the party of the first part hath granted, bargained, sold, assigned, transferred and set over unto the party of the second part, his heirs ...that parcel or tract of land and premises situate, lying and being in the Province of Alberta and being composed of the South East quarter of Section Six (6) in Township Twenty-eight (28) Range Twenty Seven (27) West of the Fourth Meridian in the Province of Alberta aforesaid."

It appears that this agreement was for Daddy to purchase a parcel of land with or from Henry Harvey, which land was noted as 160 acres between Irricana and Airdrie. We are under the impression that Daddy was the cook for Harvey's farm crew and this would have given him first chance to take over from Harvey. Since Daddy's amputated leg gave him no strength for heavy farming chores, he remained at the tent location and did the cooking, and probably any other necessary chores as well. A photograph shows the crew's large tent and shed, which were their accommodations, but there is no indication of any dairy cattle or poultry.

While we do not know the exact dates, or details, we did learn that initially the Canadian Pacific Railway Company (CPR) was offering land at a good price, even at that time, on the basis of homesteading. This was later revealed to require the landowner to take up Canadian citizenship, and void the previous American status. Like many of his future neighbors, Daddy was not willing to give up his citizenship, and thus refused the homesteading offer. Later, on April 22, 1925, a document was signed between our Daddy and the CPR that did not require giving up his American citizenship, the land undoubtedly cost more, even though it was still a far cry from later value. . Many of his neighbors were also in the same fix of citizenship status.

APPENDIX D

Several sources help provide information about the church, the CPR, and our family's story. While not all are in agreement, or factually accurate, they all add to the picture of the past.

CHURCH HISTORY

From a publication by The Brethren Press, Elgin, Illinois, entitled "The BRETHREN Along the SNAKE RIVER," by Roger E. Sappington, we learn of the fluctuations of various congregations, and I quote "The oldest offspring of the Nampa congregation at Boise Valley was also having its up[s] and downs…However, by 1914 the council was quite definitely considering the possibility of securing a full-time pastor; by the end of the year, funds were being solicited, although the goal had been reduced to having a part-time pastor. This solicitation continued throughout 1915, and in 1916, the congregation employed D. R. Beard as its first salaried pastor. Although the pastor and his wife were quickly integrated into the life of the congregation by their utilization on committees and in the Sunday school, the change was not an easy one, and at the end of 1916 the council decided by a large majority not to reemploy Beard."

Daddy then offered his services to Fruitland, Idaho, in February 1917, and was accepted, but since funds were not forthcoming, the agreement ended in August of 1917.

To indicate the lack of documents in our possession throughout our farm life, the information given me by Robert varies from that on the two indentures I received from Paul. However, Robert does state that the initial property in 1910 was about seven miles northwest of the First Irricana Church, rather than adjacent to the church as it was when the folks returned in 1917.

Both the 1911 and 1925 indentures specify the same location. Thus it would appear that Robert's note of 2005 stating that Daddy was originally on the Beeghly CPR land seven miles northwest, was within this 160 acres of SE quarter of Section Six, Township Twenty-eight, Range Twenty-seven West of the Fourth Meridian. This new home was located just south of the road which ran between Irricana and Airdrie, although I do not know if either town existed at that time. Our land was about thirty miles northeast of Calgary.

From a 2006 letter, the following was obtained:

> "History of the Church" after the interview of 1986. Irricana Church of the Brethren comprising: Arrowwood, Irricana Town Church and Irricana West Church joined the United Church in 1968. There was no money transferred. It was felt by the Board of these three congregations that they needed an oversight denomination, because they were not guaranteed to be able to get another minister from the States. A unique merger was arranged where by Arrowwood and Irricana were allowed to continue to hold title on their properties. So these churches are under the oversight of Foothills Presbytery, Alberta and Northwest Conference and the United Church of Canada, but remain the owners of their properties.
>
> George Butler was instrumental in applying for and receiving money for the Heritage Site which is now Irricana United Church. The Irricana United West Church became an historical site on April 19, 1985, and since then monies have been given to us to help with maintenance projects around the church. Recently last summer the Government of Alberta

helped us pay to replace windows, a coal shoot and to paint the exterior of the church.

One bathroom was installed a couple of years ago on the opposite side of the old kitchen. A new compact kitchen was also installed next to the bathroom. This year the floors in the basement were all painted too. We are working on installing a lift sometime this summer.

Three families of the starting families are still active in our congregation: The Culps, The Wrays, and the Longs."
(Arrowood is misspent. The correct spelling is "Arrowwood." R.B.)

PAUL'S LETTER

In 1988, Paul wrote me the following, which may add insight to the foregoing, the documents he mentions are the ones quoted above. His additional comments are relative to his life, and therefore are included.

"I have strong memory of Daddy talking about coming to Alberta in 1910 with a partner in a buckboard. The partner was a Mr. Harvey. I didn't know his first name until I came upon the enclosed documents. (Paul's original note.) These also confirm that Daddy and Mr. Harvey first bought from CPR in 1910 and then Daddy bought from Harvey in 1911. Later Daddy signed agreement with T.C.. Beeghly in 1925. for this same property." This parcel was _not_ the place where we all grew up but close by, as indicated by Robert's note.

Paul continues, "Going back to Mr. Harvey, did you know that I met his son, Mel, about 1954 in Modesto, CA? Actually several years went by before I thought to ask Mel if his Daddy had ever lived in Canada. It was then that he and I decided that our Daddy's had been partners long ago. If the first names (in the documents) are correct, that would verify quite certainly that Henry and David were partners for about a year.

"Mel was the electrician who wired the spec house that Paul Sesser and I built in Modesto. He now lives in BC, along the coast north of Vancouver, but I saw him just a year ago last October. Mel is also a pacifist; and was arrested for protesting the nuclear bomb building project in Arizona or New Mexico, many years ago. What a coincidence!" (Note: My brother Paul was also a pacifist, and served as a guinea pig at Bethesda Hospital, Bethesda, Maryland. His time spent as a conscientious objector is what caused him to fall a college year behind me when actually he enrolled at La Verne three years before I did.)

INTERVIEW WITH ESTHER CRAWFORD, By Bernice Beard, 1986

On June 29, 1986, Bernice Beard, the author's cousin by marriage, interviewed Esther Long Crawford, in Airdrie, Canada. Excerpts from the interview add the color and texture of personal memory – sometimes factually flawed – to the history of the Beards in Canada. Mrs. Crawford, who knew Martha and David Beard, reminisced in the sanctuary of the Church that adjoined the Beard homestead.

ESTHER: My father [George Long] was the one that supervised the building of this church. And he and Mr. (Eldon) Wray and, as I said, Gumps -- everybody joined in then, but at that time when they built, why Davie (David Beard) was living across here, too, just across the fence like from the church.
BERNICE: Would you talk about Martha, David's wife?

ESTHER: Oh, she was a very quiet woman, and very courageous, I think you'd say. She raised six [seven. Author's note.] children, and without any of the comforts of life, carrying water and having to heat it on stoves, and just none of the conveniences that we have nowadays. I don't know how she managed, but those kids were here to church, and she was, usually every Sunday. And, course Davie had his handicap, too, but he preached here -- took his turn with the preaching.

He was a good singer, and he led the singing quite often, between him and my mother and a couple others.

BERNICE: That runs in the Beard family.

ESTHER: Yes, he was, was -- they had had some training, you see, at Bethany [College] or someplace. I think that's where my father met them. In fact, my father came up with Davie in the early days and in '10, I think it was. And it was with Davie that my father came up the first time or so.

[Mr. Beard's artificial leg] was quite a joke, you know, around among the men. He raised pigs and when he was at home, well, he had an artificial limb that didn't have the foot on because it was easier to get around, you know, on that than it was with the foot because of the leverage and things. And so these pigs, if the sows didn't behave themselves, he'd just give them a swat with his wooden leg. I guess he didn't need a club along with him.

BERNICE: Did Martha have a garden? What kind of work did she do?

ESTHER: I don't know just how much gardening [Martha] did, but everybody in those days, you depended for your potatoes and your vegetables on gardens. Your access to stores and things even was -- they were stranded here, you see, it was 9 miles to Irricana and more than that to Airdrie, and Kathyrn had nothing practically -- [grain] elevators but not stores.

BERNICE: Was Martha from back East?

ESTHER: Yes, she was I think from Indiana. When she came up... she had two children. I think they stayed with Michael's until they got a shack. They took and built and used what was the old church. They moved it from here. They (the church) had built an A frame church, you see, that they used here until 1918. And then they moved that across here and they used that. But I think they had had a shack or something before that. But then that was quite an improvement when they got this bigger building. Then he built onto it years later -- an upstairs kind of so they had more rooms when the children got bigger.

BERNICE: Would you tell me about the beginning of this church? I heard a man telling Paul something about two families starting from two different directions.

ESTHER: No, there were more than that. They decided to have service one Sunday in the summer, and they came. There were some living 4 or 5 miles southeast of here and then the Gumps lived 4 miles northwest of here. And then there were a couple of others. The Millers lived down here close. But they all set a time and they left home and they said now whenever they would meet, there they would maybe see about a location for a church. And so this was where they met, right close here I think, across the road maybe but near enough. And the man then down here, Miller, that was across the road and where those building are down there, he donated the land, I understood. And in a week they built a church.

BERNICE: How many were there? Goodness!

ESTHER: There were about 4 or 5 families or more. I don't know if the Wrays were here then. But they decided that this -- they put up a tent and had meeting that day. And they decided to build a church and they went and got lumber the next day and then that week -- and had service the next Sunday in that church.

BERNICE: And that was the A frame church?

ESTHER: Yes, like the old meeting houses back then -- that type of house.

BERNICE: Not the Swiss chalet A frame?

ESTHER: Oh no, no, no. Like your old meeting houses like the Brethren had back East. And they put that up in that length of time and had service in it. And that served until 1918 when I think this church was built. Then [the Beards] moved the A frame and had that for their house.

BERNICE: Tell me about this church.

ESTHER: This is the original pulpit and everything that way. That's why it's an historic site, you see.

BERNICE: So you have to keep it the same because it is a provincial historic site?

ESTHER: Yes, because they have given us money then to help restore it. The tower was in bad shape. It used to leak down through here and now they have repaired that just this summer, you see. . . . It never had a real steeple. . . . They are still working on the tower. They have those things to put up yet (wooden cornices).

BERNICE: They'll keep it painted white?

ESTHER: Oh yes, I think it will have to stay that way. We've had a new roof put on, of course. . . . Oh yes, the balcony's the same. Everything that way is the same. That's why when they could come in and wanted it for historicity, that's what impressed them. And you can open all these classrooms. We had a funeral here and they gave out 300 programs, and he said they ran out. So it'll seat 300 because these rooms all open and you put chairs back in them. That was how my father designed it. I had the blueprint for it a long time, and it got away, I guess.

BERNICE: Is that a quilting room back there?

ESTHER: No, we've never done anything that way. No, that's a Sunday School classroom. Oh yes, these are all classrooms you see, 1, 2, 3 there, and that was supposed to be the mothers room there in the corner where my daughter just came out and . . . upstairs you see, all along there, that's a big room up there. And that's usually the Bible class or something. . . .

We were Church of the Brethren here until '67 or '68, then we united with the United Church because it was so difficult to get ministers across the line and literature and everything; and so many of the people that came into this country in the early days, the Brethren that came in, they didn't come in really to make homes here, I think they thought it was a place to get rich quick. And they tried it out and some of them stayed and some of them didn't. But in the early days I've got a picture of 6 or 7 elders sitting over there . . . . There were members in Kindersley, Saskatchewan; in Vidora, Saskatchewan, there was a church; and at Arrowwood (Alberta), there was a church, and at Redcliff (Alberta) there was a church. And they were all small churches. But then gradually they faded out. The ministers were older and they disappeared or something and they united with other churches and that's the way they united here, because you found out that you couldn't get along with a half-dozen in a church. But if you put 2 or 3 churches together, then you had a body.

But we had a good, thriving church at one time. In fact, we had another church in Irricana where we had attendance of around 50, but then people move away and things change. But this church has always been steady because it was farmers here. . . . And then the community itself, we used to have Sunday School down there. In fact, they ran Sunday Schools in the afternoons at some of these outplaces. But then cars came in and people -- it's a whole new thing. And your schools, where you had little schoolhouses all over the country, now its busing and you've got one big school at Kathryn and one big school at Beiseker and no school in Irricana even because they're bused, you see. And it was the same with churches and things. Things then changed and so we united then with the United Church in Irricana.

BERNICE: The United Church of the Brethren?

ESTHER: No, no, just The United Church of Canada, which was three congregations that went together because of all these problems -- the Presbyterians, Congregationalists, and the Methodists went together in '25 to form The United Church of Canada. That's their crest there, you see. And then in '67--that was in '25 that was the big union all over Canada--   and then the Church of the Brethren united with them. We went in with them and we still hold our Love Feast in Irricana and if anybody wants baptism, there's a baptismal font under there.

BERNICE: Do you have feet washing?

ESTHER: Yes, and we have the regular Love Feast in Irricana, I don't know how long (it will continue). We're getting a new minister. This (present) minister went along with it and so did the others that we had.

BERNICE: Back to Martha again. She was courageous and so forth, did she have a sense of humor? What kind of personality did she have?

ESTHER: Not particular, I wouldn't say, not an effervescent person that way, no, she was very quiet, but she had a very hard life.

BERNICE: Did she have a lot of friends?

ESTHER: Oh, yes, in the church, I would say. You know, we were all friends in those days. (Chuckle) But she didn't have time for anything too much in a social line or anything that way.

BERNICE: And I guess she sewed for the children and did all of that?

ESTHER: Oh, yes, I think she had to. I don't just remember but her health was never very good.

BERNICE: Well, now I see what is meant by life on the prairie. I couldn't quite picture it before.

ESTHER: Well, there were no trees. Now you see trees everywhere. But when my folks came here there wasn't a tree between here and Calgary, you might say, except a little brush down here at Airdrie, straight west of here. There were no trees. They planted trees then and there was an irrigation system in and then that way there was water. And then as people came in, they planted around their houses and things. No, these spruce trees around even weren't planted until about 12-15 years ago. So, it was a bald prairie, and I mean bald. Part of the reason that there weren't trees was because in the early days there would be prairie fires. Indians in the early days, maybe, around, but their time had passed when the settlers moved in.

BERNICE: It was really difficult if there was a dry season, for instance. Were there many droughts?

ESTHER: We didn't seem to know about that then. I guess it came and went, but the prairie grass was good; that's why these fires got going . . . . And the prairie wool as they call it is very nutritious have a pasture yet where it grows. And it's very nutritious grass. And there were big herds of cattle in the country in the early days; but when my father came and Davie, there were only a few houses between here and Calgary. And there was Halfway house down here, a fellow that had a big herd of cattle. Everybody would settle in a place where there was water. You had to have a spring or something that way, 'cause water is a (problem) until you'd get wells drilled, you see.

BERNICE: Why was it necessary to have irrigation? Wasn't there enough rainfall?

ESTHER: It was an experiment. It didn't work out in the long run. But the CPR (Canadian Pacific Railroad), you know, they put the railroads through, had this idea of bringing water and making it a utopia in here. And they put ditches in all across the country. And the land, of course, cost more because it was irrigated and it was supposed to work. But when they tried irrigating on the surface it brought up the alkali and things, and it wasn't suitable. Suitable maybe in small places or for a pasture or something where it could run, but it didn't prove out for wheat farming.

The CPR owned the land here. You bought your land from the CPR. It was a money-making project for the CPR.

BERNICE: So actually irrigation is no longer used.

ESTHER: No, in fact my father got permission then to plow the ditches shut on his land and a lot of others did. But some places it still is running. Down here at Keoma and Kathryn there's still an irrigation canal that goes through and I think some people still have access to it for in their pastures. And now, they have these sprinkler systems, you see, and anyone has access to it there, well that works. That's OK, where you can sprinkle from the top. But in ditches and things, it works all right down at Brooks, somewhere south of here, sandy land and for vegetable gardens and corn or something that way but not for wheat. It didn't work for oats or barley.

BERNICE: That certainly must have been a disappointment to a lot of people.

ESTHER: Well, it was. You had bought this land and paid so much more an acre for it and then you were to pay every year I think, too, when you were making use of the irrigation. So that's why some of them got cut off of their land, they didn't have to pay that anymore.

Bernice Beard also spoke with Eldon Wray, one of the members of the Church and an early settler with his wife Ruth. He spoke about

Raymond [Beard], whose uniquely artistic marker is in the small cemetery behind the church

ELDON WRAY: Afterwards, after Raymond's funeral, it came out that he had been here three weeks before to the service and visited with a few of us, and he had told some of them that he wanted to be buried here when he died. . . . He was inquiring about the lot and he had said that he wanted to be buried here, and it was only three weeks later that this happened. The plots here were about 14 feet wide by 22 feet wide and the Beard baby that was buried here many years ago, there's no stone or anything and so we don't know exactly where in this plot that the baby was buried except that it was in this plot.

When they dug the grave for Raymond, they didn't hit it.

…This was part of the land that the CPR was given for putting the railway across Canada. And so they sold it. You see, they went down to the States at different times, even to Annual Conferences and advertised land here for sale, you see. . . .

END

Quoted by permission of Bernice Beard.

APPENDIX E

WRITINGS

My earliest writings, about eight years old. Pseudonym Fred Lovesdale. One was printed in the Gospel Messenger, a publication of the Church of the Brethren.

Alone With God

With God I love to be alone.
To him my deepest sorrows moan.
He hears no matter what I say.
He listens, while I softly pray.

Each night my prayers to Him I say.
He sends His light upon my way.
His own sweet will, I'll try to do,
To be to others kind and true.

"Be merciful to me, O God.
Show mercy on the steps I've trod.
O Father, forgiveness to me give.
That I a righteous life may live."

The Ugly Duckling
(1946, College Sociology Term Paper)

Those of you who have known me these past some fifty years may have no idea that this Ugly Duckling was my opinion of myself when I was in my early twenties. Dr. Lowell Weiss, our La Verne College Sociology teacher, responded in a manner to my 1946 sophomore term paper which gave me more confidence in myself and helped me greatly to leave that 'ugly duckling' behind. Excerpts from my paper are herein given, and Weiss' comments will be quoted at the end.

Revealing my childhood feelings now may help others today, especially adults and parents, to realize what effect their actions have on youngsters and also alert them as to their responsibility and opportunity to change or control the situation for any child in their midst. Here are the basic notes from my term paper.

The Ugly Duckling January 1946

Temperament: My disposition is to worry and I can find no better phrase that describes my temperament than "a pessimistic chronic worrier." I have always worried about financial matters and about security.

Attitudes: To start my life off on the wrong foot, I was the odd one in the family – not odd in mental capacity – but odd in number; there being two older sisters and four brothers, and I being the odd girl amidst three boys. The three younger boys were close enough together in age to find companionship with each other, as were my two older sisters. But I was left without a close female sibling.

During my pre-school days then I either had to play by myself or with boys, and the majority of this time I played with boys. I seldom ever played with dolls. Soon I had to find some pastime that could be done alone. Until I learned to read, I cannot remember any form of play except to be pushed around by others.

When I reached nine years of age, I was informed that I needed glasses. Oh woe betide, that that should ever happen to me. At first I thought I would be the envy of the school kids and at home since I was the only one in both places to wear them. But it was not long until phrases like, "Oh be careful, you'll break her glasses," or "you'd better not play ball until you get used to them," rang around me, and I became more and more sensitive of my handicap, for now it had become a real handicap.

Many nights I sat on the porch with one eye on the book I held, but never read, and the other eye on the children playing ball, while tears rolled down from both eyes because I wasn't 'one of them.'

Due to my inferiority complex and resentment at being shown 'how' in front of others, I developed a fear more than a dislike of sports. This dislike was a defense reaction to hide my real feelings. I can't blame others for resenting having me on their side in ball games, but I wonder if they realize how I felt when they start to throw the ball and then see that I am the one to catch it, so they turn and throw it to someone else. If I don't get ready to catch the toss then the teacher thinks I'm not co-operating and so I get a C grade.

When I was ten years old, both sisters left home and went to Calgary to High School. Due to Mama's ill health, I had to resume much more of the work. It was like pulling teeth to get any of my brothers to help me, but Paul was the unlucky one most of the time. He and I never got along and we always disagreed no matter how absurd or trivial it was – neither of us would give in. Both of us always wanted to be proven right.

I developed a dislike for cooking because complaints came from my brothers. This complexity was not limited to cooking. Every time I began to play the organ or sing, slams and insults would start flying. Probably they were not as insulting as I imagined but rather typical sibling jealousy and childish reactions.

Finally I quit trying to develop any ability. I felt that "because I am afraid of some specific activity, I dare not attempt it. Because I dare not attempt it, I become ever less capable of performing it. Because I become less and less capable, I have less and less courage to attempt it."

Because of this inferiority complex and the lack of companionship, I drew more and more into myself. I confided in no one. I can clearly remember suppressing many questions and doubts when I should have expressed them and had them satisfied. I even resented any one suggesting or questioning me about anything.

I used to try writing poetry and my first poem was published in our denominational church paper. When my parents complimented me on it and encouraged me to keep on, I immediately burst into tears and declared I would never show them any more. I resented being left out and I resented being helped so that my parents were often at their wits end to know whether to ignore or encourage me. It is not exactly their fault then that I did not develop any talents.

Daydreaming became my relief from a world without a close friend and with closed doors to consolation. I had two phrases with carried me under, not over, every barrier: "I can't help it," and "I don't care," which I know caused a great deal of ill feelings and sadness..

My first attitude toward school was not positive, as I had been influenced by my older siblings who complained about homework and the cruelty of the teacher. Before that first day of school, I declared that I would jump out of the buggy and hide in the coulee until it was time to come home. Most certainly I would never go beyond the last compulsory grade. How attitudes do change! Some fifteen years later I was literally begging the Canadian Government to let me return to school. After Grade l, I had very good teachers, and my attitude and conduct became one of the highest of the students.

(Years later, my sister Barbara informed me that she was instructed by my parents to sit beside me in the buggy and put her arms around me holding me so that I could not jump out.)

During Grade 2 through Grade 7-1/2, I was alone in my grade, and total enrollment of the eight grades was usually less than nine. I had no one to compete with, and this only encouraged my lack of open rivalry with my siblings. My parents tried to give me inspiration to improve my grades by competing with myself. This I did secretly but I never let on to them that I was interested in my grades.

I believe this lack of competition during the formative part of my school years is partly responsible for my lack of a competitive spirit today. I compete, but only if I am on the top or run a close tie; otherwise I give up trying. Having very little perseverance does not correct the matter either.

Being alone in my grade, I had to argue points with the teacher. I can't say I developed the art of argumentation, but it did increase the like and habit for it. However, one improvement that did grow out of this situation is that it is much easier for me now to say, "you are right, I'm wrong." My independent nature was also increased because I had no one to work along with.

It was not until Grade 9 that I became acquainted with a girl in my class and who became my very good friend. Prior to this time the only available playmates were boys so is it any wonder that I always seriously wanted to be a boy? I even used to call myself "Daddy's boy" when I was little, and Daddy would encourage any of my feeble attempts by telling me "You can do it, old boy."

Races, Classes and Handicapped: One of the most valuable teachings at home was the stressing of equality of all races and classes of people. We children thoroughly disliked and feared my first grade Herbert Spencer teacher because of his threatening attitude and cruel disciplinary methods.

But we were taught not to disrespect him because he was a Jew. We were also taught that 'nigger' and 'chinky' were never to be used. There were many Chinese families in Calgary, and they operated many of the stalls at the Farmer's Market where we took farm products for sale.

In the case of handicapped people, I never thought of considering them queer nor inferior to myself. Rather I always felt sorry for them and often spent my time trying to amuse them. This attitude was probably due to the fact that Daddy was physically handicapped, having had one leg amputated when young and now always wearing a wooden leg.

Learning by Imitations and Suggestions: After I became self-conscious, I refused any conscious teachings if I felt that I could not do it, and especially if any sibling was learning at the same time I was.

Paul and I, being of such close age, were often together in this phase of life. He was always more alert and ambitious than I and learned easier and faster. I so resented this that I gave up trying to accomplish anything the minute I saw he was getting ahead, or even when he began to show interest. His interest, thank goodness, never turned to collecting poems, nor composing them. That field was clear from family members.

My independent attitude comes not only from the foregoing reasons, but also from my mother's repeated statement of "Well, what would you do if I weren't here?" or "what would you do if you could not say 'Mama?"

I always liked reading. My parents, having had college education's, always upheld the better literature and encouraged attendance at educational programs, as well as listening to good music.

My Ego Structure: Even though I had such an inferiority complex, I have never been satisfied with being a follower; however, if I sense too much competition or higher qualifications from others to do the job, I pull out.

I have become a lot more moody and have periods of melancholy and despair practically all the time. The worst part of this is that I don't particularly care whether I control my moods or not. I haven't accomplished anything in life and the only goal I have left looks very discouraging. My moods would swing about every three months. I would say to myself, "There's no place for you to go now but down," and three months later, I would convince myself, "You've reached the bottom, now it's time to go back up." If I knew now that I would be an old maid all my life, I would just as soon someone would eliminate me, since I haven't the courage to do it myself. However, every time I think about that I decide, and worry, that I had better settle some of my skeptic beliefs.

Most of my ideals, values, and virtues have been knocked down by people who profess to be Christians, and the majority of them are inconsistent and hypocritical of the beliefs they process. How can I then keep my ideals and goals when the very people around me who advocate these ideals are continually going against all that they say they stand for?

Conclusions: After I hand this in I know I will worry if I expressed myself the way I meant to, whether I said too much, or whether I didn't say enough to make my point clear. All in all, I am very disgusted with the whole paper, but then look at the boring subject about which I wrote!

Dr. Weiss's Evaluation: "You were very frank. In common with most introverted people (I am one too) you have a great deal of insight into yourself. The paper is well-done. Your opinion of yourself, however, is much —- much too low. That is apt to be the introvert's trouble too." He graded Content as "–A," and the Organization and Technique as "A."

Our church offers members an opportunity to note our personal credos from time to time. I did so on Sept. 19, 1993.

This I Believe

(The italics are side remarks made either when presented at the Unitarian Universalist Church of Asheville, or added later when copy was sent to my siblings.)

It was very disturbing (*yea, totally unacceptable*) to learn that to date only MALES had volunteered to state their credo. (*I heard my mother from her 30-year old grave say, "Ruth, if you don't do it, who will?" That I could ignore, since I fully expected other UU women would do so in time.*) But when I heard my Dad, from his 50-year old grave, rise up and say to me, "Go to it – old boy!" I knew I had to take a turn. Well, Dad, since you were a minister in the Church of the Brethren who commanded your children never to question the Bible, I suggest you lie back down and close your ears, because you're not going to like some of what I say.

As a young child, I questioned the existence of God. I could not then, nor in the years that followed, nor can I now, envision any "maker" controlling all that exists, nor answering all the prayers, nor rendering punishment. I suppose I was about 8 when I first asked God to prove to me that he existed by laying a marble, a gold one, at my feet. I even promised I wouldn't touch it, and I knew I could never take it home or show to anyone. But he never did. I went from "prove to me, help me believe, let me believe," to finally "make me believe," until by end of college, I knew I DID NOT believe, at least not in a controlling God.)

So how about an impersonal God – a Creator but not a Controller? I don't know the source of the world's beginnings any more than anyone who believes in a God can explain "her" beginning. Any scientific theory proposed has more validity for me than believing in a spirit who, or which, created the world. Our entire universe – our physical science laws, natural laws, spiritual laws – I call "Universal Truth," and one or more of these powerful forces are what I envision when the word "God" is used. Nor do I find it essential to believe in any traditional God in order to live a worthy and moral life. My skeptical nature has served me well, I think, while still allowing me to keep an open mind and to accept what once I may have rejected.

I believe that each individual holds power and responsibility within oneself, so I am a humanist. Reason, Logic, and Objectivity are my gods. Whether I am a secular humanist or a humanistic atheist, it matters little. What is important is to make these terms acceptable and respectable in our society. *(This summer, 1993, at our UU camp [the first one I've attended], I took "Teaching Atheism" from Tom Kunesh, a UU Taoist atheist, and not only enjoyed it, but was convinced that the term "agnostic" was now a past cop-out, and that "atheism" needed to be given its proper due and respectability, since neither Deism nor Theism is essential in order to lead a moral and ethical life, though most religions have good features.)*

My spiritual being, or oversoul, tempers the impersonal so that reason and logic are complemented with feelings. This animating spiritual force connects us with each other. And this connection is the source of strength available to us through our relationships, meditation, prayer, and other channels. For me "prayer" is a sincere feeling expressed not to any divine power but directed through my mental and spiritual being to that of others. *(As Dr. Sydney Freeman, one of our previous speakers, said, "Spirituality is the most difficult of terms to explain, and the one encompassing the most fraud or misconceptions. The multiple interpretations most often incorrectly given to the words "spiritual, spirituality, etc.," leave individuals wide open to giving and accepting fraud. Our spiritual nature is also the one of which we presently know the least and therefore in our seeking will present or accept unscientific theories or findings.)*

A universal belief of major religions is the belief that one should treat others as one wishes to be treated. The fact that Jesus was not the first to teach that had much to do with my awakening that it was immaterial whether "Christ" taught that or not (AMEN). This "Golden Rule" underlies my belief of the best moral behavior regardless of "who taught what when," and regardless of any mystical being or supernatural act. Furthermore, to "Know thyself," and "To thine own self be true," are constant axioms in my life. *(Good ol' Plato and Shakespeare.)*

I believe moral behavior should be taught from the best teachings and parables from all major religions, and from proven ethical behavior. Such morality can be taught without a belief in a superior being or in an afterlife, and thus can be taught in schools. Some of the same critical standards that we use for scientific works should be applied to the field of religion, but we need now to start with the children and encourage them to question religious dogma. Such teachings and questionings would lead to more unity and a more authentic and solid foundation for one's beliefs.

I believe two major evils of our country are (1) exorbitant salaries and perks, while others have difficulty in just existing, and (2) the way our justice system works. I believe a humanistic democracy can and must replace our capitalistic system. My father often said, "Man's laws are made for the lowest common denominator. Live as far above the laws as you possibly can." This to me again leads back to the Golden Rule, and this belief also puts responsibility upon the receiver.

With reverence for life, I believe population control is seriously needed and long overdue, and hopefully will be voluntary. On one occasion, I lit a candle for my aunt's death after her 100th birthday, remarking that *"memories now had to come from cousins and siblets."* Come on, folks, when there are eight, live, single births in your family in nine years and three months, isn't the term "siblets" appropriate? We have "piglets," don't we? I believe our moral compass is out of kilter when more importance is given to animals than to people's legitimate needs – and I stress "legitimate" – or to the unborn than to the living. And out of kilter when terminal and suffering lives are prolonged.

I believe our Sunday services are a time for "reverence for life" – for intellectual and spiritual pursuits. Since "worship" implies revering a deity or sacred object, this term does not seem appropriate for UU churches. I believe taxation of all church property should be considered and that UUism is the appropriate denomination to lead the way.

We are all sojourners in this planet, one time around, and its caretakers. When I am overcome with the horrors of this universe and find I can do little or nothing to help, I get comfort from the poet's words "Our little systems have their day; they have their day and cease to be." And I gain some hope that positive changes will occur.

I'll close with the words of my mother, who was raised as a Mennonite, joined the Church of the Brethren, and became a closet UU long before I realized it. She said, "Start where you are and make that corner of the world a better place for your having lived in it." I may not always succeed in my endeavors, but these are the principles by which I strive to live. Thank you.

I paraphrased Shakepeare for the program given by the End-of-Life Choices group, of which I was the president. This program was presented at our Unitarian Universalist Church of Asheville, November 2006.

TO BE OR NOT TO BE -
OUR END-OF-LIFE CHOICE

To be or not to be:
That is the question:
Whether 'tis nobler in the mind to suffer
The loss of freedom caused by outrageous laws
Or to unite against a sea of opponents
And by opposing, stop them.
To die: as we each choose,
And by our freedom to say we end
The heartache and the thousand natural shocks
That flesh is heir to, 'tis a consummation
Devoutly to be wish'd.

To die, to sleep,
When death is imminent and life has nil to gain.
Why should we die as now the law commands
Thus causing further grief and loss of dignity?
No, NO, let us choose how death should come,
And let assistance be there when we ask for help.
Give us our right to choose our death with dignity.
Death with dignity. To die: to sleep, forevermore.

MERRY CHRISTMAS & HAPPY NEW YEAR (2004)

'Twas the night before Christmas and all through the house
My computer wasn't stirring, not even the mouse.
My printer was turned off and so was the scanner
And my mind was operating in similar manner.

Then all of a sudden the keyboard was humming,
And then in a moment my mind began strumming.
'Tis time to get busy and write friends and lovers
Especially the first, since I have no such others.

Relatives are included in these thoughts of mine
As I drum up past doings and what's coming in time.
Just a year ago after extreme hustle and bustle,
I moved to an apartment to lessen work muscle

But my volunteer duties and computer fiascoes
Still keeps me hopping on hands and my toes's.
Hemlock Society has become End-of-Life Choices
And my work has expanded to include more voices.

Still leader of local and now Veep for the State
Keeps me at my computer and staying up late.
"Although we are many, we speak with one voice,
The message is simple, it's all about choice."

Should we not be treated as kindly as animals
And peacefully go as we match with our morals?
I've passed on the church's archival collections
But warn my successor of needed protections.
My once-a-month duty in church office continues
And I've joined our "Singles plus 50." No dues!
This summer I took a long-dreamed of home trip
To visit with family so to Calgary did zip,

My niece and her children and grandchildren too
All but niece Gael were unknown, so new.
I saw parents' graves and that of my brother,
Though general areas only of two sisters' other.

And behold, from Beiseker comes niece Valerie.
Also Phyllis, my first roommate came visiting me.
Calgary was beautiful – more trees did abound
Population a million, a number so round.

Saw Rocky Mountains, Banff and Lake Louise
Where mountain-bred chipmunks crept up to my knees.
Made Elderhostel class worth all the green cost
To see my relatives and early memories, half lost

Though I came home with joy and sadness combined.
I'd love to go back next year; the cost never mind.
So great to have relatives to Asheville come visit.
I welcome visits from others, with this I'm explicit!

Friends needn't wait either for invitation direct
But surprise me! If I'm not here, what the heck!
So back to remembering it's the landlord's place
And I'm only the tenant; must accept this new pace.

I've requested a new roommate which he says is okay,
And a four-legged young kitty is coming to stay.
What's the best advice to give at end of the year
Just study the candidates, and open your ear
Look at both sides and see all parties' roles
Who really gets benefits and what's hidden by polls.
Remember eventually that death comes to us all.
Should each or should Ashcroft decide on that call?
If you believe that individuals should have final choice
Then to Ashcroft and legislators, express loudly your voice.

Each day makes a difference. Try to enjoy far more
By fully living and relaxing in two thousand and four.

When I was working for the AgeLink Program at Western Carolina University, I was very much involved in finding volunteers and in acknowledging their services not only for AgeLink but also for other agencies. My administrator asked me to honor the current volunteers as well as recruit others for many local organizations. After this event, I was asked if I would preserve my talk for use by other recruiters. I entitled it "The Risks of Volunteering" with the subtitle, "The Good feelings will get you if you don't watch out."

The Risks Of Volunteering

Has anyone ever told you of the risks involved in playing the good guy? Or do you think volunteering is going to be "giving" and "giving" and "giving" without any thanks from anyone? Do you think you can keep your feelings under control? Beware of volunteering unless you're ready to accept the risks involved.

When the fearful child you've been working with for months still clings to you in tears, but one day she jumps from your arms and says, "I got to find Susie, she's my new playmate," will you be able to let your own tears of joy flow with happiness?

You've visited a lonely woman in a nursing home for many months. She has shown no recognition or awareness of your efforts to help her. Are you prepared for the day she suddenly smiles and clasps your hand and doesn't want to let go? Can you accept her teary smile and let your tears join hers when she finally makes an effort to speak? You're taking a risk, you know, whenever you give "unto others."

Suppose the elderly gentleman takes forever to come to the door as you deliver his Meals on Wheels dinners, and then he begs you to sit awhile. You know you should be hurrying on to the next recipient and then on home to your own spouse. Can you afford the risk of feeling good about chatting with him for more minutes than usual, and more importantly, just listening? Can you really afford to let that satisfied feeling engulf your heart while your head says, "Hurry on?"

You're stuffing envelopes for mailings from the YWCA, or answering the phone for Hospitality House, or sorting donations for Habitat for Humanity. Can you accept their thanks, so profusely given you? Or will you discount their gratitude because you're the one who needs companionship today? Can you exchange your guilt feelings for acceptance of their honest thanks? It's a risk, you know, to be on the receiving end, especially if you view volunteering as only an activity of "giving." Remember, someone said "it is in giving that we receive."

When you say "No" to a request for your volunteer services, do you feel guilty? Can you still your troublesome thoughts when you think you haven't done enough? Do you wish you'd said "Yes" to that request instead of, "Sorry, I can't do anymore." Yet you know all the while it's a much-needed relaxation time that you need. You take the risk of making the right decision for yourself at a particular time, and that risk means feeling good about yourself when you've said "No."

The greatest risk of volunteering is not the negative feelings that erupt, nor the tiredness or boredom that creeps in, nor the lack of appreciation from those you serve. Such feelings are temporary and quite easily forgotten. The greatest danger of volunteering is to have your heart overflow with joy for the spoken and unspoken happiness that others have gained from your presence – for your efforts. It is the tears you've shared, the laughter you've exchanged, the contagious smiles, and the changing of every life you've touched, that will live forever in your mind and your heart. Forever is a long time.

If you can accept that these good feelings are going to "get you," you'll be a great volunteer, my friend!

Poems By Nelson Lee Shatto

SAND CHILD

Sand Childs for Sale
Come all Barren Couples,
Who want to fill their debt,
To Society.

Buy a Sand Child.

Yes, be the first on your block
To own a Sand Child.

Youngsters born of one neuter test tube,
Given the best genes and chromosomes
That Money can buy.

Raised to the age of two,
Studied through clear "sand" cages
Then sold to you!
Think of how proud you will be
Owning a Perfect Child!

This great privilege can be yours
For only $29.99!
($35.99 for single persons.)
You won't find a better bargain
Any where.

Think of what it would be like
To own something you could mold,

Be you single or sterile.

Here is Feldspar.
Second to be made.
She has been given only the highest quality genes
For the same low price of $29.99,
You can own her.

Here is Turquoise,
Blue eyes, blue hair, blue skin.
He could be your possession
For $29.99.
Are they not both quality pieces of Merchandise?
Buy my Sand Children.

(Signed) Me.

SMALL BOY

Small boy,
Large, dark forest
Mysterious, yet beautiful
And overflowing with feelings.
Birds of Death he sees.
High flying.
Sadly beautiful.
Roots tangled, housing small things.
Things working out their lives unknowing.
And then he feels a force,
Mixed up, but pounding relentlessly, Driving him before it.

Out into a clearing.
No, a meadow.
And oh the grass!
Grass to run in, roll in,
To feel with your toes.
Smelling of summer and calm sleep.
Mist all around,
Making soft the hard edges
And dancers.

Birds chirping the tune.
He feels as if at a masquerade,
Everyone looks happy, but is dark around the edges.
It frightens him.
Growing larger and larger.
Grass fades.
Forest fades.
Dancers disappear.
Only the mist, the Force, the birds
And he are left.

And he can't fight them all
So he runs
Runs through the nothing.
The Force follows him.
The birds scream,
The mist seems to beckon him
With a thousand different shadows.
He can't stop running.

The Force catches him.
Grips him.
But turns kind.
The boy is wary but must succumb.
He does.
The Force turns black.
He screams and runs,
Hides in a cavern.
Here at last is real safety.

The cave wraps him in majesty.
Rocks, streams, waterfalls,
The music of the underground
Pushes him.
Through cathedrals, passages,
Rooms.
It grows louder.
Too much at one time.
His safety kills him.
But the Force is turned.

————The End————

Writings by Nelson's teacher, Mr. Bickford, and the author's response.

Richard Bickford's writing, given to my son, brings solace to my soul. Mr. Bickford was his favorite teacher at the Harrisburg Academy, and he and Nelson exchanged their writings.

December – 1970
In life's cycle of joys and griefs
each must bear his own lonelihood
in crowds, in field and hill,
four walls, and long nights,
faded dreams and good-byes. . .

bringing a final acceptance
as when the Inner Voice speaks
to the Self by opening doors
to the expanding, new Now,

for to recognize is to share
import of discovering the You
in the low but long echoes
of memory's range. . . as each
bears his own lonelihood.

Bickford signed it "Always my best to my faithful friend!"

Mr. Bickford's letter to me upon the death of my son, Nelson, who was one of his students at the Harrisburg Academy, 1970.

Dear Mrs. Shatto,
    No letter is harder to write than this, and I had hoped to be able to come down for a few minutes – and attend the services

for our beloved one. It has been impossible, but not because so many moments in the past few days, that my thoughts have not been of you and Nelson – and others who loved him, as well.

Too, the acceptance of why – would be his question, I'm sure. So much we cannot know, understand or interpret. Life and death has to be this way in the plan, and we can question why forever, and never know.

Nelson was the one in thousands of my pupils over forty years, who had so much, of talent and curiosity – so much of challenge – so much of true genius. I am glad to have shared with him the friendship and teaching, the unity of brotherhood, and the joys and sorrows of growing up.

I find words always inadequate at times such as this in which you, who were so close to his life knew him so well. Perhaps the unexpressed is partially the why, who can say?

Sometimes when time and mood concurs you could write me the details of the tragedy, and of the services. I shall be grateful, and only when you can feel to write.

Nelson has left us a wonderful memory in this incident of tragedy, and his personality still ever with us. I was glad I saw him at Christmas. This I have to remember, too.

My sincere sympathy and my prayers as I write this Saturday afternoon in the moments of his memorial.

Richard Bickford. 2:35PM 6/26/1971.

This was my response and though it is not word for word, it is representative of the reply I write to Mr. Bickford. It reveals the anguish, regrets, turmoil, and memories that I experienced. Unfortunately, any adult faced with unexpected death of a child, or even an adult loved one, endures these same or similar feelings. With all sincerity I trust that I have your respect and understanding of a mother's feelings, and that sorrowful rapport is honored by all of us.

"Mr. Bickford, I have not forgotten your earlier request for details of Nelson's death. Indeed I have tried to set my mind to it, but have found it impossible to complete when depressed, and when begun in the lighter side of the cycle of joys and sorrows, this mood quickly disappears. I wonder how open to be with my thoughts, and beliefs, where to begin or how to say in writing what I feel so intensely. Your poetry, your direct expressions of compassion, give me assurance you understand and I am most grateful.

The basic facts are what others know — his grabbing a sub to eat as the group hiked to the quarry for a swim — the quarry instead of one of the three pools because they did not want to conform to rules and wear suits, nor hair nets over long hair. Food, deep cold water and no lifeguards. The two girls, I'm told, had had first aid training and did all they could once they found him. I do not know how long it was before they missed him. It had rained hard on Sunday eve, or was it Monday, and the water could not have been very clear.

But the whys and ifs — may I be free to share — I have no answers. What to tell you first — a combination of factors — It was a surprise to Nelson to find himself a leader — he not knowing it was inevitable. I, not preparing him for it but wanting and believing he could handle it, and normally he surely could have.

How does one know what really caused him to ignore these water safety factors — his growing rebellion against our culture, his urge to join peers without regard to objectivity or his desire for life's experiences. A combination of these and more —

But my dream—why my dream and why did I not, or was it planned that I <u>could</u> not—listen with the third ear and be aware of influence, or change the eventual ending? I seldom remember dreams, and seldom have recurring ones—but interpretation could have followed.

I was not going to be caught unaware again, but the spirit was evidently weak. For several months, I dreamt I was called to the hospital (not the same one that actually was involved) because Nelson's friend was badly hurt. Whether his parents could not be located or I could get there quicker was never clear—nor who called me. But I left a note for Nelson telling him where I was, who was hurt, and asking him to come as quickly as he could. On a few occasions I dreamt that he had left me the note—am not clear whether he asked or expected me to follow. Nor did we always see each other there, though I do remember at times, his arriving and knew he had hiked across the mountain rather than by cab. The outcome or whether the friend's parents arrived never was finalized. But he and I felt a mutual concern for the boy and rapport for each other in being there.

At one time I almost told Nelson of this dream but decided he would insist on knowing who the friend was, and would perhaps want to tell this friend, so without too much deliberation I decided not to tell him yet.

No, I do not profess to have ESP. There are too many times when thoughts have not materialized, but many major events in my life have been cloaked in dreams or imaginings.

And when the chaplain called me, I thought, "Has he fallen off the porch while painting? Has he had a concussion—surely it can't be more than a broken leg—I can't think about it or I'll never make it to the hospital." When I saw the chaplain and officer, I instinctively wanted to turn and run—and run—and run. I knew then my dream was about

Nelson, though I could only sense the outcome because of the chaplain waiting at the hospital entrance for me.

What if I had told Nelson my dream? Could I not have listened closer and lessened the outcome? Or would that have made it worse? Or just postponed it?

A month before his death, I was driving the older girl and Nelson home from Hagerstown and in the rain, skidded, spun around over the embankment, though no one was hurt, it could have resulted in a serious accident. Was this a coincidence? A purposeful accident so the girl would feel less guilt in her part of suggesting they go to the quarry?

The previous Friday afternoon Nelson and I visited the music store where he appraised and played pianos and organs; thrilled to show his knowledge; excited to think one would soon be his; torn between a new piano or a used organ; postponing his final decision!

Saturday we drove to Swallow Falls stopping at a lookout along the way. A beautiful mountain valley – hushed, beckoning – a few farms, one church spire, roads converging into one which lead through the gap, now to be seen and now gone. After a few quiet moments, he said "How could anyone live in New York when they could have this?" And I wanted to scream at him to consider how he could consider the life style of the rock musician he wanted to be with this dream of quiet living. But I knew I must wait for him to discover this himself – and most surely he would have – and eventually, though too long for me, he would come to realize he had far more to give to the world, and as important, more to get. The "one" who could choose almost any career – so much harder to make a choice than one with less ability and intelligence because the choices are not available to him. I passively nodded agreement.

Could I not have given him strong support; he listening but pretending not to hear? He said, "Don't you wonder where that road would take us? If only one could float across the valley. Could we follow that road?"

We decided we could not do both that day and went on to the Falls, knowing full well without either saying it that we would come back the first chance possible to take 'the road not yet traveled.' He also knowing that he was free to follow it without me if the opportunity presented itself, and both of us knowing that I would probably not do so without him though he would want me to feel free to do so. And if he had traveled it, he would tell me about its peculiarities, the views, the termination, and strongly suggest that I should take it sometime. And I did so later.

With all my grief, but disbelief in afterlife, there was such a strong feeling of his spirit hovering over that valley, beckoning me to join him, pleading with me to float across the lowlands to him, but never letting me reach him until I was far enough from this side so no one could pull me back, I hear them calling. I cannot tell you how much I wanted to join him. If there is "life after," I would be with him, not to stifle nor engulf, but to continue sharing. And if this were finality, well then, my pain would be ended too. But remembering I still had a daughter now pulled me in the opposite directions from him.

But we went on to the Falls — our first trip there — berating each other for not bringing a picnic lunch, promising ourselves another time — straying away from each other and back again.

And then he started hinting at going in the river like some other young people did, and I resisted answering; his eyes tempting me but never nagging nor complaining till finally I said it was his decision. His shoes were in my hands before I finished and he yelled some joyous sound and was gone.

What if I had said "No, not in your clothes—not in cold, river water—not in unknown areas?" Would it have influenced him on that Tuesday.

Sunday evening we had a heavy thunder and lightning shower and he said he was going out for a 15 minute walk in the rain; something he loved to do. "Never forget what it is to be young!" And off he went.

It was an hour and a half before he returned so I had grown frantic because of the close lightning. He sneaked back to his room and finally I went up to him. When I broke down and cried, he realized I was worried for him—not angry because his clothes and shoes were sopping wet. He assured me he understood that I still expected him to have independence and freedom.

Monday he resisted friends' urging him to go swimming but still objecting to my buying swim trunks for him. He did not get to the work of painting the porch. I could not be too angry that first day out of school but he was to start picking fruit on Wednesday, and he was so glad to be earning some money as he had with his paper route in New Jersey. He felt disgusted with his friends that felt such labor was beneath them.

On Tuesday morning I put some rolls in the oven for his breakfast and since he did not have to be up yet, I went into his room, put my arms around him to waken him, and he sleepily, and as in childhood put his arm around me. He would have to get up, I said, when the alarm went off and get his breakfast out of the oven before it burned. Then he should get to the painting job. I kissed him goodbye and left for work.

What if I hadn't gone in his room? Would he have thought I was more serious and he'd better listen to me? I thought of calling him at noon but decided not to "bug" him about the job. He was already blue because we could not get tickets to J.C. Superstar for that night.

What if I had called him before he left the house? Did he hope to rush—eat and run, swim and still get back to get some painting done — to please me?

Coincidences? Predestination?" There are other thoughts. My agnosticism and the possibility that he would be alienated from me. There were going to be some hard times ahead for both of us, but surely he would have come around as most young people do. So I go through the cycles of depression, resentment towards others, and Nelson, feeling guilt that I betrayed him by not following him, determination to shape up, confident that I will stay "on top," only to start the cycle again. The cycle of joys and sorrows.

The joy of having him rush home to watch ghost stories, expecting me to watch with him, he setting the atmosphere with all his candles; his quick response of "sure" when asked if he would grind nuts, or roll pastry—those simple but infrequent jobs as pleased to do as if offered a new musical record. His insistence to read compliments from his statements. "Some of my friends argue and fight so much with their parents, you and I don't have that trouble," or "how can kids think they're so wonderful and their parents so awful—how do they think they could be so wonderful without wonderful parents." Or "we had sorta an encounter group at YP tonight and I was told I must have an excellent teacher from the questions and answers I gave." And I asked, "Oh, and who is your teacher?" And he unabashedly and coolly looked directly at me" You know good and well who is my best teacher." Was there ever such a boy! Such a son!

Mr. Bickford, if I have burdened you with my grief and torment, I cannot say I am sorry for to do so would negate my belief that you understand; would reduce the relief that comes through purification.

But if I have offended your beliefs, or alienated your love for my boy by one iota—I would regret it—and the latter I could not believe.

If you have questions and do not feel free to ask, I would be hurt. What – and if – I can answer is up to me. I have no answers – only these inner thoughts. More than questions, I would wish for answers. Knowing you through Nelson, and your written words, has made it easier to write my inner thoughts.

The overwhelming number of sympathy letters and cards I received from individuals and groups far supercedes the number most families receive for a child with anticipated or unexpected death. My feelings, and writings about this event, are included with the expressed desire that readers will realize how greatly talented and intellectual was this young adopted boy.

I could only endure my loss by constantly repeating to myself that Nelson would want me to enjoy this, or enjoy that, or take a ride, or see a movie that we both would have enjoyed together. So I drove around the mountains, envisioned him beside me and commented on the remarks I was sure he would make. At the same time, I knew Christmas would be extremely difficult to bear. I must plan something special after Christmas in order to survive this so-called happy season. So I planned my first and only cruise, and went to the Caribbean Islands. Had I not taken this option, I might not have survived because of this heartbreaking loss of my son.

Today, going through my stored papers, I came across letters from SAVE THE CHILDREN FEDERATION. I had completely forgotten that I began supporting a young nine-year old boy and his family in Seoul in 1972. I not only have translations of this child's letters to me but some of his original words in Korean, which of course I cannot read.

A SIMPLIFIED VERSION OF WHAT I BELIEVE – Elizabeth Detrick, circa 1994 (Condensed further by Ruth Beard)

Here is the Doctrine of God that I embrace, and my husband, Ernest, does also.

1. God is Creator and is still creating. God is Love, a living Presence, a Spirit.
2. We leave God; God never leaves us. God is Holy, the source of all life.
3. God gives us freedom. We have a choice. God is <u>not</u> all powerful. God does <u>not</u> "have the whole world in His hand." If God did, we wouldn't be in this mess of greed and power.
4. God is without beginning and ending.
5. God <u>cares about us.</u> God does not take care of us.. It is not "God's Will" when we suffer.
6. God has no Gender.

JESUS

1. Showed us what God is like, by his life, teaching and example. We need the Old Testament (Old Covenant) to understand the New Testament (New Covenant).
2. I used to pray to Jesus because I couldn't understand about God. Now, I learned that Jesus doesn't want us to pray to him, but to God. During youth, especially High School days, Jesus was the best and reliable friend that I had. Calgary days were lonely, frustrating, and knowing Jesus helped me through life.
3. It's proven that our thinking can affect our 'endorphins,' re Norman Cousins, and all our health..

HEAVEN AND HELL

1. I believe that the Bible says "The Kingdom of Heaven is <u>within you</u> now or can be. No one knows what really happens after death. Certainly no streets of gold, nor sitting around doing nothing. Our duty is to do the best we can here. No one knows if we will know people in the next life.
2. Theory of Hell for bad people is a cooked up story by Roman Catholics, 300AD, who were not getting enough members, so they started preaching hell, fire and damnation to scare people into the church – and lots of churches are still doing it.

I do not take the Bible literally. The Hebrews wrote in poetic form, not meant to be taken literally, any more than our sayings today like "Hit the nail on the head," or "chip off the old block." Forgiving others is essential. Leave this world a better place for others. Avoid being judgmental. Live by the Golden Rule regardless of who made that statement.

A letter from Elizabeth to the author in 1988 reveals her thoughts, confirms many of my memories stated earlier. (Condensed, with some explanations added for readers)

July 29, 1988.

Dear Ruth,

Our big 50th wedding album is before me and turned to your wonderful pages of writings. We certainly do thank you for all that you wrote, and the pictures. I remember the day the picture of us with the dolls was taken. (see photo in 'Our Alberta Prairie Life.')

Yes, many a time our <u>little</u> bedroom window was opened and let down and then fastened up when needed with a nail. What a place to put a little sister under the eaves. I remember also the trunks and boxes under those eaves and of being careful not to let them fall off the ledge down the stairs; and the dirt that collected up there after a dust storm.

One time or so, Barbara and I slept in a wagon that had wheat in it. I remember the rain on the roof of our barn, and the sunrises and hunting eggs in the cow mangers. I remember Daddy letting me drive you all to Kathyrn at least once – and I could change a tire. (This would have been one of our Model T Fords.)

I remember the trip with you back home for our Beard reunion (in 1960), and Paul later wrote me and mentioned how lonesome and empty things seemed when Barbara and I left home. Cousin Paul and his wife, Bernice, interviewed Esther Long Crawford and she got a few things incorrect. Our folks raised seven children, not six. Edward, Barbara and I went to Herbert Spencer for 6 or 7 years even though Esther did not remember that. She also failed to mention that our daddy had a hand in designing our home church too as well as her father.

Then just between us, Esther often referred to David Beard as "Davie," and how he hated that name. No wonder he forbade any of us, or anyone else, from using any nicknames. How I got by with 'Betsie,' I'll never know. Well, I remember how upset he got when neighbors called Edward "Ed," or Robert, "Bob," and no "Ruthie" was allowed either.

Yes, now we'll head for our 60th. Life is a lot easier and more pleasant than years ago. It was a good move to come here (———) The first good move was when I went to Bethany. I found real friends and support. My most lonesome years were the ones in Calgary. I missed out on growing up with the rest of you.

APPENDIX F

CAREER HISTORY of RUTH BEARD

LIBRARY EXPERIENCE: **(Paraprofessional and Professional).**
Dickinson College library, Carlisle, PA. Order Librarian. 1952-56.
PSU, Middletown Campus. Harrisburg, PA. Library Assistant. 1965-67.
W.Deptford Jr.Sr.H.S., Thorofare, NJ. 1967-68.
Haddonfield Public Library. Haddonfield, NJ. Cataloger. 1968-70.
Frostburg State College. Frostburg, MD. Head, Reference Dept. 1970-75.
PSU, York Campus, York, PA. Head Librarian. 1975-79.
Lancaster Public Library, Lancaster, PA. Head, Adult Dept.1979-1983.
Warren Wilson College, Swannanoa, NC. Acquisition Lbn. 1984-86.
Southern Highland Craft Guild. Asheville, NC 1994.

ACCOMPLISHMENTS:
Prepared first public Serials Holdings catalog.
Developed first Student Library Orientation Handbook.
Held bibliographic orientation for faculty.
Supervised general library orientation for students.

Co-authored Library Student Work Book.

Wrote successful LSCA grant of $181,600 for retrospective conversion, reviewed bids, hired vendors, project and regular staff for 15-member Adult Dept.

Established Rental Book Collection with Friends of Library, and Grants Resource Center with Junior League.

Planned Adult & Young Adult Programs with Reference staff.

Wrote Library Column and edited staff's articles for local newspaper.

Improved office, acquisition & book processing procedures, financial record keeping and reporting methods.

Temporary position: updated records and inventory when operated by non-professionals for years.

OTHER EXPERIENCE:

Social Research Assistant at Western Carolina University's Center for Improving Mountain Living, AgeLink Project. Conducted 500 surveys of children, parents, and senior volunteers and coded and entered results in SPSS-X.

Recruited and trained volunteers, presented programs to sponsors and clubs.

Edited, re-coded members, and typed genealogical project undertaken by research scholar who died before all work was done. Genealogy covered nearly 400 years, 212 descendants, and 232 endnotes/bibliography. Wrote instructions for code identification, conformed endnotes with Chicago Manual of Style, and responsible for choosing publisher, binding, and copyright application. Saw book through to publication

About the Author

Ruth Beard was born on a farm in Alberta, Canada, in 1923. She earned her Bachelor's from LaVerne College, LaVerne, California, and her Master's in Library Science from Drexel University in Philadelphia, Pennsylvania. She served in public, private, and university libraries in New Jersey, Pennsylvania, Maryland, and North Carolina, where she retired in the mid-1990s.

From childhood on Beard bristled at the words "can't" and "impossible." She married and amicably divorced, adopted two Asian children in the 1950s, and left her conservative faith for a humanistic atheism and started volunteer work with the Final Exit Network. In sharing the hardship and poverty of her family's pioneer existence, she details her own fascinating life path and those of her six siblings.

Printed in the United States
108657LV00005B/43/A